The Soul of a Writer

Intimate Interviews With Successful Songwriters

Susan Tucker

with
Linda Lee Strother

Journey Publishing Company
Nashville, Tennessee

The Soul of a Writer

Intimate Interviews With Successful Songwriters

By Susan Tucker

With Linda Lee Strother

Published by:

Journey Publishing Company
Post Office Box 92411
Nashville, TN 37209 U.S.A.

Every effort has been made to verify the spelling of names used in this book. We apologize if there are errors.

Copyright © 1996 by Susan Tucker and Linda Lee Strother
First Printing 1996
Printed in the United States of America

Library of Congress Catalog Card Number: 96-76088

ISBN 0-9651705-2-7 2195

Creativity is letting go.
It's play and it's fun.
It's letting your heart speak.
It's finding your own voice.
Creativity is exciting and sometimes it's painful.
It is being forgiving of yourself.
It's listening to yourself.
But, ultimately, it's a way of getting to know yourself
and the world in which you live.

This book is dedicated to all who strive to succeed in a creative
endeavor.
It is meant to be a source of energy, a creative fire.

This book could not have happened without the contributions of so many people.

I wish to express my deep gratitude to all of the wonderful writers who let us look into their creative lives. I enjoyed so much having the opportunity to sit and talk with you. It's been an experience I'll never forget. Come for coffee sometime.

A special thanks to Kent Blazy, Jill Colucci, Jess Leary, Jim McBride, and Kim Williams for allowing me to use your original lyric sheets for the cover shot. You guys are so cool!

Thanks also to Rae Levine, Dr. Scott and Mary Murkin, and Pat Rolfe for your valuable gifts of time to proofread.

All of my love and appreciation to my Grandmother, Sylva Walkup, and to my beautiful daughter, Tracy, for their support and encouragement, and to Kim; your faith and support made it happen. You always helped me keep my vision in focus. I love you.

And, finally, to Linda. You helped me take my idea and give it form and make it a reality. Thank you so much.

Susan

Any journey starts at the beginning and this one began more than two years ago. It wasn't until one day last year, when I typed a mock cover for the book, that I realized the book could be a reality, and so it is.

I would like to thank Susan Tucker for including me in her dream and allowing me to realize one of mine. Also, thanks to my daughter for her tolerance. Final thanks to the songwriters who made this book possible, because it is their words that sing the music of our souls.

Linda

Introduction

*I first came up with the idea for this book when I was frustrated with a
song that I was working on. I started wondering what songwriting was
like for other writers. To satisfy my own curiosity, I composed a list of
questions, asked my friend, Linda Lee Strother, to help, and we set out to
find writers who would share their insights with us. We knew we wanted
to interview at least twenty-five writers and that they should be diverse in
their experience, style, and approach. We had absolutely no trouble finding writers to talk with us.*

*They were all very open and willing to speak candidly about their
fears, their methods, and the roller coaster ride of songwriting. During
the hour or two I spent with each writer, they shared some wonderful stories on how some of their hits were born. They talked about low points in
their careers and who their influences and inspirations have been.*

*I suppose the most important thing I learned through writing this
book is that there really is no difference between me and the writers with
songs on the charts. We all struggle. They have no magical secret to success and seem just as mystified by the process as we all are. Some of the
other things I learned are: (1) keep it fun; (2) give your writing the priority it deserves; (3) those who persevere will succeed; and (4) being creative means being open to life.*

*I've kept all of the answers in the writers' own words, so that you
can feel like they are talking directly to you. I hope that, as you read this
book, you will highlight lines, dog-ear pages, and make notes in the margins. It is meant to be used. And when you're feeling particularly frustrated in your writing, I hope that you will pull it off the shelf and reread
the parts which you found to be inspiring. May everyone who reads this
book find comfort in knowing that we're all traveling this road together.*

Creatively yours,

Susan Tucker

TABLE OF CONTENTS

CHAPTER ONE
INSPIRATION, INFLUENCES, AND ENCOURAGEMENT

CHAPTER TWO
CREATIVITY—THE FLOW

CHAPTER THREE
THE PROCESS

CHAPTER FOUR
THE SONG

CHAPTER FIVE
CO-WRITING

CHAPTER SIX
LOUDSPEAKERS IN YOUR MIND

CHAPTER SEVEN
WRITER PROFILES

CHAPTER EIGHT
GENERAL ADVICE

WRITER BIOGRAPHIES

The Soul of a Writer

Intimate Interviews With Successful Songwriters

CHAPTER ONE
INSPIRATION, INFLUENCES, and ENCOURAGEMENT

Mary Ann Kennedy - I'm just a big old conglomerate of a whole bunch of different influences. I guess the only thing original about me is how I've put the influences together.

Kim Carnes - My passion for the music, what I feel inside, is the complete motivation, one hundred percent.

John Jarrard - I really think that creativity tends to follow fun.

Kim Copeland - I don't work at keeping myself inspired to do it. It's just something I can't not do.

1. Are there specific places or things that inspire you?

Tony Arata - I kidded with somebody the other day when they asked, "Where do you get your inspiration to write?" I said, "my house note, school tuition," and stuff like that. Ultimately it comes down to really bare bones. You're trying to make a living. That's what you're trying to do.

I write a lot in my car. I put down just a guitar rough or something like that, and I ride around and listen. I've never been one who can sit down and write. There are people who do it, day in and day out, and do it great. Their success is borne out by the fact that they do it very well. But I've never been one who really could sit down in a room and come up with something. I'm always working on something, a line or a melody or something like that, but I don't have any really special room or special place or special time.

I think for some people, that's the way it works, but I don't think anyone who wants to do something has to believe that you can't do anything else. I just never ascribed to the "suffering artist" mentality where you've got to have a special place or you can't be bothered or whatever. I think you can write doing the dishes if you really want to write songs. Of the great authors that you read about, a lot of them have had many jobs apart from writing books, and you're talking about a much bigger thing to me. When you start talking about writing a book, you're talking about a whole other level. And if those guys can do it working at foundries or electrical plants or newspapers, then anybody can do it. I've always tried to practice that. There again, that's *my* philosophy. The only secret I've ever found is that I have no secret at all. It's more just a matter of trying to stay true to writing the song, however that's done. I've just always believed that if you want to write songs, you'll write them. You don't have to be cloistered in a room somewhere.

Pam Belford - The shower is great for me and also drying my hair.

Kent Blazy - I can probably be inspired anywhere. Radnor Lake is an inspirational place to me. There is something out there that just makes me want to write songs. It gives me a different perspective on things. Walking the dog is great for me too. If I get stuck on a song, I've got two Labs and I'll put a leash on one of them and take him walking for sometimes maybe an hour. Just work on it in your head while you're in a different setting.

Steve Bogard - I like my little office. My inspiration is that I enjoy the games, getting cuts, getting singles, having hits. It's really a business where you have to make things happen. No matter how good your publisher is, you have to keep them stirring the froth.

Rory Bourke - I find my inspiration in the person I'm with.

Gary Burr - Not really. Not for inspiration. Well, let me put it this way. After all these years, I feel like I'm pretty well versed in the craft of songwriting. I think you could lock me in a closet and I could come out with a song if I had to. But being the proper little Pisces that I am, there is something about the ocean, that I can't go more than six months without getting to it. I have to head to L.A. or Florida or somewhere where there's an ocean to look at. Basically, when I need inspiration, I just turn off the radio. A little silence will do me a long way.

(WOULDN'T IT BE NICE IF NASHVILLE WERE NEAR THE OCEAN?) I've heard this from a lot of people, especially all of the new refugees from Southern California. It's really the only thing missing. That and a good fat-free muffin shop. If we could have an ocean with an ocean-side, fat-free muffin shop, we'd be covered.

Kim Carnes - The car is a great place to come up with the second verse you couldn't think of, or maybe the bridge. I think because the windows are up, and there are no telephones ringing, no distractions. For me that's the biggest fight as far as writing, between kids around the house and other things that take you away from writing. You need to find that place where nobody's going to interrupt you.

Debi Cochran - Nashville is that place for me. I moved here in October 1993, so I spent three years driving up from Alabama, once or twice a week, to be here. And just the idea of knowing that I have a much-coveted staff writing job in Nashville is inspiration enough for me. I like writing in this little office, it's like a little nest. But also, especially when I was driving, it's a two-hour drive to get here from where I used to live, and I did a lot of writing on the road.

Jill Colucci - (DO YOU FIND THE WOODS INSPIRATIONAL?) Absolutely. In L.A., I had ten feet in between my neighbors and now I've got 3.2 acres and I can't even see any neighbors. This is incredible to me. I find it inspirational. In fact, I'm putting a studio in downstairs, but because of this view and the fireplace, in the winter I found myself coming upstairs. I didn't want to do that. I want this to be a home up here, so I don't have my guitar and papers out. I keep it separate, but I keep gravitating up here with my guitar. And I've been doing some writing alone this year, which I've really been enjoying. I've done a lot of it in the daytime with this view and in the evening with the fireplace.

In February I felt like I needed to be at the beach, so I went and got a condo at the beach and I wrote. My front yard was the ocean. It was so successful that I am going to do it more often. I've decided that at least one month out of the year I'm going to spend at the ocean. I find that extremely inspiring. The negative ions ... the calmness and looking out ... something about the vastness of the ocean. There being no end, and the sky. It's so vast that somehow it can enhance the state that I need to get into.

Kim Copeland - Driving the car. I think that's probably true for everybody. Typical places that free your mind. The car, the shower. Water and nature are inspirational to me too. I used to go camping a lot, and when I first got into songwriting, the place that I was always most inspired and came up with the most ideas was camping, sitting by a river. Any place where it's quiet enough that you have no outside interference and can hear your inner voice.

Gary Earl - Hiking in the Rockies and Sierras. Hearing great songs. And of course, there's nothing better than being in love.

Robin Earl - I get inspired by listening to music. I get lots of ideas after I've been singing for a while. I like to sing when I'm driving. I get ideas when I'm kind of in an emotional state, really happy or sad. I also like to get a lot of exercise. Exercising outdoors or while listening to music inspires me, gives me energy.

Kye Fleming - You know how you've always got this perfect place in the back of your head? I think in this last year, I got the perfect place. But wherever I was before, it was the perfect place if the inspiration was there.

I'm sitting in the middle of a couple hundred acres now, and I think that I've always been leading up to that place. When I write there I can be stuck on a line or something and I just walk outside and feed the ducks or feed the chickens. I just wander around and that's a continuation of the creative process. Not being interrupted by somebody or the telephone. Life and songwriting can just kind of interweave a little easier because of those surroundings, and I think that was always what I was looking forward to.

Lindy Gravelle - The outdoors. Nature. Being from Oregon, all I have to do is think about those images.

John Jarrard - I don't seem to write as well at home. There are so many distractions. I do better when I come to the office.

Mary Ann Kennedy - I know a lot of my peers don't like to listen to their competition. Boy, I do. I need it. I'm just a big, old conglomerate of a whole bunch of different influences. I guess the only thing original about me is how I've put the influences together. I guess some ways of being inspired to me are to go out to the Bluebird, or to put on a CD of Bonnie Raitt or Mark Cohn. And as far as physically, probably my number one place to be is on a horse. Out in the woods or loping through a field. That just gives me that whole bliss of life thing. What I contribute to the songs is born out of rhythm. And I think a lot of that and a whole lot of songs have been born on the back of a horse for me. Those hoof beats.

Sandy Knox - Well, I love baths. Anytime I want to escape or shut down you can find me in the bathtub. I've been known to take three or four a day, just to go away. If I leave Nashville, I would probably live on the beach somewhere on the East Coast. I have a big attraction for that. As far as getting away, I don't go on vacations very much. I don't travel that much. I guess my hobby is bathing. I'm a professional bather. I've made it an art in my house. Salts and goo and all that stuff.

I think a lot of people get creative ideas and flows going when they're doing mindless things like taking a shower, bathing, driving, walking through the grocery store. To me, grocery shopping is automatic. I don't have a list and coupons and a map. It's not an organized situation for me. I walk in and pick stuff up off of the shelves, whatever moves me. When you're doing something like that, that's so easy, your brain is free to follow other things. I was walking in this store in Green Hills one time and this little old lady came around the corner. She had to be seventy-five or eighty years old. She was little and had on her Sunday finest. All dressed up just to go to the grocery store. With our generation, that got kind of lost. She looked at me and said, "Is cat food on this aisle?" I said, "No, I think that's on the next aisle." And she said, "Right church, wrong pew." Then she walked away. I went, right church, wrong pew, what a great idea. I didn't have to write it down. I've never forgotten it. For me, if I don't forget it, it's going to get written. If I forget it, it's not worth writing. I wrote it. But it was a real difficult idea to get across. Things like that happen all the time. Normally when I sit down and say I'm going to write today, nothing gets written. I write when I feel it or when it moves me.

Kostas - I live between Nashville and Montana, and wherever else. I don't just live here in Montana. So much of my life was spent here, and it's a neat place. The great thing about growing up here in Montana was that I was never under the pressure of the industry. I was never even aware of the industry. I just did what I did because that's what I thought I was supposed to do. I wasn't writing songs for anybody but myself. I was performing because that's what I used to do for a living. It's kind of independent the way people think up here. (DO YOU HAVE A BIG WINDOW AT YOUR HOUSE TO LOOK OUT OF?) The biggest window I have ever had is the one in my mind.

Jess Leary - Anything that has to do with nature inspires me. You know, it's a wonder I'm not like John Denver reincarnated or something. By the way, I listened to him a lot too. It's all his fault. Anytime I can go outside and be in nature is good. Going for a walk in the woods or at Radnor Lake is a good one for me. My own backyard. I have a little fish pond that I made. It's just a little yard, but it's very beautiful and it's peaceful.

Jim McBride - My wife says I'm a mole. I used to write by candlelight a lot. Music is enhanced, to me, in darkness. You're not distracted as much. But there are places. Older buildings. I hate to see all the older buildings be gone off of the Row, because there's something about them. There's a different energy in them. I've been in the glass and the chrome, and that won't do it for me. I love going to the beach. I can get inspired there. There are just some places where there's a vibe that I can feel. One of them is back down in Alabama, a place called Mentone. For years, a lot of artists and writers have settled there. Apparently they feel the same. There's a creative vibe that I could feel the first time I went there. New Orleans is the same way.

Wayland Patton - I used to have an office when I was at Polygram. I didn't necessarily write there all the time, but it's nice to have a place to go to, that when you walk in the door, you know that's why you're there. It's more of a psychological thing I think. A discipline thing. You're there to write songs. When you go in, something clicks. I don't have a place now. I'm at MCA music and they have rooms available anytime you want to go in and write. There is something about growing up and working so long in straight jobs, where you get up every morning and you shower and you go into work, there's something about that in me. I like that. I like to get up and get ready and go to work . I don't necessarily have to go to an office anymore. I've got a place at home. I've got a room and a computer. I write on my computer. And I've written songs driving down the road. I'm always writing. I do try to make it a point to be disciplined and each day to set aside some time to work on something. Just to keep the wheels well oiled and thinking in terms of writing and being creative. It's like a parable in the New Testament, the parable of the talents, where each person was given a certain amount of money. One guy went out and made a bunch of other money, and the other made a little bit. And the other, knowing that his master was really shrewd, just went out and buried his so he wouldn't lose it. It was taken away from him because he didn't use it. So I like to use it. I like to work and try to be disciplined every day.

Pam Rose - I'm always inspired by the ocean. I get up there and there's something that feels like home about the ocean. Lately I've gotten into a thing where I almost feel like I need or want to go away to write. I've never done that before, I just started this last year. There's no telephone and no fax machine and no list of ten thousand things to do. So, I've gone to the beach. The two places that I enjoy the most are the ocean, and I have a friend who has a house in Arizona out on the desert that's incredible. One of the things I like about the two places I've mentioned is that you can see forever. There's no end to what you can see. There's a vastness and I am really inspired by that vastness. Mountains, I think, would do the same thing.

Joyce Rouse - Actually, the driving is what's real inspirational for me. I get a lot of great ideas cooking and driving. As far as a workplace, I finally have a marvelous, marvelous piano in a room that is painted the right color, and there are just very few other distractions. It's pretty much just the piano, a chair, and a sofa. No books, no work or paperwork or any of those things.

Wayne Tester - No. Just the beauty of music. It's getting back to that basic, "enjoying the music." You get in this business and the business end can take over, and you feel like the music gets lost. You have to find that place of childlike approach. Wow, this is music. If you can remember that, you're okay through it all. If you don't, it will drive you nuts. It's got to be there. It's like the criticism. You've got to take the good business and the bad business, you've got to try to wade through that.

Trisha Walker - In trying to look back on what I have written and what I hope to write, I'm really influenced by the South as a region. Small towns in particular. I'm always amazed when I go home at how different it is, and yet how nothing has changed. So, as a region, the South. And as a culture, I was thinking the other day how the world is getting so small now. We're so homogenized. I think it is important for people to cultivate their culture. And for me the South has a culture all its own.

Marijohn Wilkin - I don't think so. Not any more.

Kim Williams - The Devil's Nose. It's a real high peak in east Tennessee, where I'm from. It seems to put everything back into perspective. High places to me are inspirational. Waterfalls.

2. Is there a particular type of music that can inspire you?

Pam Belford - I guess I really like the kind of sixties pop feel, but I think that's because that's one of the first things I was writing. I listen mostly to country on the radio, but occasionally the button moves. I do like other things. I don't like really hard rock. I like soft rock, pop, big band music, and even contemporary Christian, for a nice Jewish girl.

Kent Blazy - I guess the person that inspires me the most just by putting him on is Van Morrison. There's just something about his music that fires me up, no matter what mood I'm in. His music is almost timeless to me.

Steve Bogard - I think we (in the business) should listen to country radio, we should learn to love country radio, and even with its faults, learn to understand what it's doing, what it wants to sound like, what it wants to be like, and try to make our songs work within that if we can. I have two teenagers, so I get a lot of their music, I get a lot of alternative stuff.

Rory Bourke - My collection of music is totally eclectic. I listen to a lot of classical music, blues, some folk, rock, and country. I think to be a writer, you have to listen to everything.

Gary Burr - I like anything that's good. I still go back to the Beatles albums. Whenever I get dry lyrically, I usually turn to Paul Simon or Randy Newman or Leonard Cohen or some of those people that really do it well. They're a big help when I'm thinking that I've rhymed my last rhyme. I put it on and I realize that I've got a long way to go. As far as listening to music, I have pretty random taste. Whatever's on the radio, I listen to pretty much. I do listen to the radio a lot. It's fun. There's certainly a wide variety of things to listen to. I like string quartets and symphonies and stuff like that. Anything if it's done well. The right song on the radio and I pull over in tears.

Debi Cochran - I like singer/songwriters like James Taylor. I sort of go in phases. I bought a Nancy Griffith tape and then I had to buy everything she had. And so I can almost guarantee myself to get a song if I listen to a Nancy Griffith tape. Mary Chapin Carpenter. I love listening to her stuff, because she's so intelligent and it works on radio. I think it's great. Rosanne Cash. And I remember the first time I heard Lyle Lovett when he was still trying to get his songs cut somewhere. He had just gotten to town, and a friend of mine had a copy of his songs, and popped them in. *This Old House* came on. "This old porch is like a steaming greasy plate of enchiladas." And we said whoa, who is this guy? And the next song on the tape was *God Will, But I Won't*. "God will forgive you for running around, but I won't." I said, man this guy is a genius.

Jill Colucci - It's funny, I used to listen to radio a lot when I was in the car. I used to listen to music a lot more than I do right now. I'm kind of in a new phase. It may be temporary, it may be permanent, I don't know. I'm not listening as much to what's going on. Of course, I need to be in touch somewhat, so I'll put on CMT and catch the videos and catch some of the current product, but I think that's healthy for me right now not to listen to as much as I used to.

I never did write for radio. You can't. If you try to write something that's working on the radio right now, till it's cut and it gets released, that's one to two years down the road. It will be old news by then. It wouldn't even be current. As writers, we need to set the pace, not follow the pace.

Sometimes I'll throw on a Bonnie Raitt CD or Wynonna, or Pam Tillis, or a variety of my favorite artists.

Kim Copeland - Anything with killer lyrics and a great melody. I like a lot of different styles, but I don't keep up with trends in music. I tend to stick to classics and I still tend to gravitate towards writers who perform their own music. I still put on old James Taylor records and Carole King and I like Carly's new stuff too. Melissa Ethridge. I can get caught up in the groove or the overall feel of songs, but for me to be inspired the lyrics have to be there.

Kye Fleming - Four or five years ago, when Shawn Colvin came out with her first album—major inspiration. It's like, "yes, that turns me on." I don't sit here and try to rewrite any of it. It's great. The next year was Mark Cohn's *True Companion*. That song just wiped me out. It feels like every year or so there's another somebody who comes on the scene who just feels totally fresh, and I guess it's always a little more left of center than I write, which inspires me. It's not that I want to write that far left of center. It takes me listening to that to get inspired to take the next step with what I do.

John Jarrard - I really think that creativity tends to follow fun. When I get blocked up, most of the time it's when I forget how much fun this is and just what a blessing it is. And sometimes in those cases, it's good for me to go back and listen to my record albums. Go back and listen to the stuff that I listened to when I would have given anything to do this for a living. That helps me to remember how much fun it is and puts all this in perspective.

Al Kasha - The two kinds of music I love are gospel/country and theater music, because it's very honest. Black churches inspired me because of the diminished chords musically and a lot of reaching out to Jesus. The other influence was the craft, lyrically, that a lot of theater writers write. In my career I wrote *Pete's Dragon* and *All Dogs Go to Heaven*, and the Broadway show, *Seven Brides for Seven Brothers*, so I've had a lot of influence in writing what I call story songs. The difference between a pop writer and a theater writer or a person who writes musicals or a person who writes country songs basically is that with country songs or theater songs you have to be a storyteller. You have to get into the character rather than just saying, "I love you and you love me." Most pop songs deal with emotions and most theater songs deal with emotions, too, but they tell a whole story, beginning, middle, and end. So, I would say Al Kasha is a combination of gospel music with a little bit of theater put in and musical comedy, because I lived out my fantasies there as well as being a storyteller.

Mary Ann Kennedy - I love the kind of stuff that Pam [Kennedy-Rose] and I did, as artists. Shawn Colvin, that first *Steady On* album, just doesn't get old. I love Bonnie Raitt's work and I'm an old fan of Fleetwood Mac. Joni Mitchell. And just hearing well-written, emotional, moving country songs. I guess the first one that comes to mind is *I Want To Be Loved Like That*. That kind of a moving, well-crafted, country ballad. It's hard to beat one like that. (DO YOU LISTEN TO THE RADIO?) I do. I love to listen to what's happening out there. I'm part of it. I respect what's going on and I want to be respected within it.

And I love Native American music. The Native American flutes. That's kind of like my meditation and soul-searching music.

Sandy Knox - Really varied. A lot of time, especially this last year, I haven't wanted to listen to anything with lyrics. Classical or instrumental, because if I hear lyrics, then I start working. You and I are talking here right now, and if there's a song going, this ear's listening to that song and that lyric and I'm going, why did they use that word and blah, blah, blah.

I like a lot of Manhattan Transfer. I love blues and R&B. Billie Holiday. I like classical. I love the Beatles, Elvis. The radio, I don't listen to country. I find myself getting mad listening to the stuff that's out there. There's a lot of it that I think is good, but there's a lot of stuff that I think is *not* good. If you ask any writer, they will tell you that the ditty they have on the radio, that went number one, is not a work of art. Then they can open up their catalog and show you five or six other songs that will knock your breath out. The lines are poetic and deep, but those aren't going to get cut. I don't really care for a lot of the songs on country radio. pop, I like pop. Adult contemporary music. It's broader. It's got more variety lyrically. I hate to say this, but lyrically it's more intelligent than country.

Jess Leary - I put on, almost consistently, Loreena McKennitt, who is a Canadian artist. She plays harps and Irish-based instruments with a real neat percussive kind of background. It's very artsy music. It has nothing to do with country music, but it just opens my soul up somehow. It's totally beautiful and inspiring and relaxing and emotional. Enya. I listen to her when I'm painting. When I'm cleaning the house even. Sometimes my head needs a rest, and I just need it to float in some beautiful music. Beautiful, inspiring sounds and different instruments. Because in country music you've got your five instruments. You've got your steel and your bass and your electric and your fiddle and keyboards. Pretty much that's it. There is a sound for country music. And so, sometimes I just need to hear something else. Being from an Irish heritage, I do tend to lean towards those types of instruments. I've always been very turned on by Irish music and Irish folk music.

Jim McBride - I listen to the oldies a lot. I can listen to those old songs from the fifties and early sixties and they make me feel good. They are very peaceful. The world will probably never be like that again. And I don't think I'm fooling myself. It was a better place to live back then. I think it *was* the good old days. I've got a tape of classical music, and sometimes I slip that in. I have to be careful though, or I'll go to sleep driving. I like a little bit of all kinds of music. Basically what I do to get away from this is to not listen at all or listen to that old rock and roll.

Wayne Tester - For me, every music style is inspirational. I remember in grade school listening to KISS and AC/DC. I loved it. And then in high school the Cameo, *Alligator Woman* record came along. That was the black funk and that did something to me. It was weird, but it brought out this different way of looking at music somehow. And I remember hearing Sister Sledge, *We Are Family,* in a disco, and it did something to me. Then I got into Amy Grant in college, more of the acoustic mellow stuff. I grew up with bluegrass and country from my Mom and Dad listening to it. Jim Reeves and Floyd Cramer. So, it's all wrapped together for me.(DO YOU LISTEN TO THE RADIO?) All the time. I'm a channel flipper. I have two country stations, a soft, mellow station, rock and roll and old rock and roll and, an R&B. So, I have a variety.

Trisha Walker - R&B was a big influence. And of course growing up in the South and the culture of the South. I grew up in church, so gospel music. I've had a rekindling of interest in the old hymns of the church. At the same time, because the area I grew up in had a high population in the black community, I heard a lot of black gospel music, which just thrills my soul every time I hear it. Music that was more groove oriented as opposed to country, which was more lyric oriented. I guess I began to love country music just about the time I was getting out of college, and I could appreciate the simplicity of it and yet realize lyrically that was a it real challenge to be able to write something so stripped down and yet so meaningful as country. If I get bummed out about music, I usually go to something else besides music. I've always been a big sports fan. I'll go to a ballpark and watch a baseball game, or get outside and get away from it.

Kate Wallace - I don't listen to country music. I can't stand it. I loved Hank Williams and Patsy Cline and Merle Haggard and the days when it was really legitimate. I loved the Eagles era of country rock. And Linda Ronstadt was instrumental in that too. Loved all that stuff. Just about everything else—you can pull the cord and flush the entire thing. These days, as they sign Ken and Barbie and they do these really mediocre songs, I find it almost impossible to listen to the radio. I like the folk-rock, country-pop end of things, which means everything from Emmylou Harris to Sting. I love Sting, I think he's just brilliant. I like a melody and/or groove that's sort of infectious and a lyric that's not too artsy-fartsy. There is nobody like Bob Dylan. If you're going to get way out there with the lyrics, don't even bother. The master is Bob Dylan. I hate corny stuff. I think we have a responsibility as writers to make the population feel good, but also to instruct and educate emotionally.

Marijohn Wilkin - Well, no. I don't listen to a lot of music. I get inspired if I hear a writer who I think has great potential. I love to write. Love to work with writers. I love to develop a writer.

3. What or who have been your biggest influences?

Tony Arata - Probably it started in eleventh grade for me. Not as a songwriter, but really becoming fascinated with the written word. I had a great teacher who turned me on to a lot of books and forced everyone into writing creatively, kind of grammar be damned. Just write from the heart and then we'll worry about the grammar as we go. Her name was Sally Scott, and that was the first time that it ever really dawned on me how potent the written word was. I had been playing the guitar a little bit, so I just figured, well, what the heck, we'll start trying to write some songs. So, I really started writing songs in about the eleventh or twelfth grade. Of course, none of those have ever seen the light of day, thank God.

I also come from a family of teachers, so I've been exposed to books. I had an older sister, so I was exposed to a large span of music. It was quite diverse. The big band stuff to the Beatles to Wayne Newton. When I went to college I played in bands. The only prerequisite to playing in a college band at that time was that you owned an instrument. Early on, I started trying to incorporate some of those original songs into whatever performances we were doing. Some went over and some didn't.

Also I was very aware of another gentleman who really is the shining star to come out of my hometown of Savanna, Georgia, and that was Johnny Mercer. I was probably a sophomore in college when it really dawned on me that this guy was from my hometown.

I don't know that there was a time when I went out and said that this is what I'm going to do. It was kind of an evolution of some sort. I really started getting serious about writing songs later on in college and knew that I wanted, in some way, to pursue that.

Pam Belford - The first person I remember being influenced by was Janis Ian. *Society's Child.* I started trying to write that way, which of course was crazy because I was no where near anything controversial in my own life. But I sure took a shot at it. Then of course I went to college in the early seventies, that was the whole protest thing. I was writing those kinds of songs. Like Joni Mitchell, Judy Collins, Carole King. All those people were my influences.

Kent Blazy - The Beatles and Dylan. There were so many different influences. There was the people who were in the rock side of it, and then you get into the Merle Haggard and Buck Owens and Kris Kristofferson. I grew up in that era when there were so many different things on the radio. You could listen to Top 40 and hear the Beatles and the Rolling Stones, The Four Tops, Roger Miller, Frank Sinatra. I grew up loving everything. I always loved radio songs, the hit songs, songs you could hear once or twice and sing.

(WHAT ABOUT THE SINGER/SONGWRITERS?) I had a lot of those I liked too. Joni Mitchell, Jackson Browne.

Steve Bogard - Ray Charles, black music, soul music. In Nashville, Rory Bourke and Charlie Black. They showed me the two sides of country music. There's the rock and roll side of country music and there's the Disney World side. We're the guys who keep our families happy, coach little league after work, and come in everyday and write songs like a job. Then there's the side that rocks and stays up all night and goes on three-day benders to find creativity. Early on, I established my way. I'm an office guy; I like to be home for my family when I'm home, and when I'm at the office, I like to be at the office. I think that people have the misconception that those of us who do that, come in and hammer away at songs, that it makes them kind of mechanical or factoryish, and I just don't agree. I think you can avoid that. There's a danger of that. If a guy wants to be a staff writer, I think you need those one hundred songs. I think you need to co-write a hundred songs and eighty will be bad or at best medio-cre. First of all, you're polishing your craft. Co-writing and being with people that you mesh with, just having a conversation, you get titles, you get ideas.

Rory Bourke - Gene Kelly and Fred Astaire. I love movie musi-cals. I was brought up in an area where my first friend was a girl and her dad was manager of the MGM Theater. So I was in the theater at an early age. I grew up with that music on the screen. I think those people just seemed like happy people. I have a cousin named Gilbert Corrigan who's a pathologist down in Louisiana. He had a very strong influence on me when I was twelve or thirteen years old. He loved country music and he used to go down on 105th Street in Cleveland and go to these country shows. He really encouraged me to go forward with this.

Gary Burr - The Beatles were the first people that I was really into. I would go home from high school and go over to a friend's house, and we would dissect Beatles albums and learn harmony parts. That was back in the days when, if you turned the speakers all the way to the left or to the right, there would be nothing but the background vocals. So, that's how we learned how to sing background harmony. It was great. It was a mistake, but it was great.

My mom was into country, so when I would go around with her, I would listen to Eddie Arnold, and later Glen Campbell and people like that. Marty Robbins. For me, it was the Beatles, Poco, Pure Prairie League. The Eagles. The Eagles were really later, but the Beatles were my biggest thing. Paul McCartney was it for me.

Kim Carnes - I've never liked just a certain type of music. I've always been eclectic in taste. In the early days, I loved Dylan, listened to him constantly. The Rolling Stones, and big time Smokey Robinson. Van

Morrison. When I want to put on albums that are timeless, I put on Van Morrison.

Greg [Barnhill] and I are doing club dates together. He wrote *Walk Away Joe* and it's killer. I've done so much work and recording here over the years, but when I was going back and forth on whether I should move here, and I heard that song, that made the difference. I heard *Walk Away Joe,* and went, "Whoever wrote that, that's where I need to be, because that's the best song I ever heard." And Trisha's record of it is, for me, what's impeccable music. Trisha and Wynonna I think are so good. If somebody asked me which song I wish I had written, definitely it would be *Walk Away Joe*.

Debi Cochran - My biggest influence probably is the music of the Southeast. Muscle Shoals and also Johnny Sandlin and the Allman Brothers. Growing up in Fort Payne and loving music the way I did, and dating musicians and hanging out with them all the time, I remember when we all became aware from the backs of the albums, these songs were being cut in Muscle Shoals. Aretha Franklin and Rod Stewart and Paul Simon. Linda Ronstadt was there when the Eagles were still her backup band. The list goes on forever. And just knowing that music was being made in this small town, just inches away on the map from where I lived, was very inspiring and made me realize that it could be done. A couple of people could go into a radio station and in between the songs, use the equipment to record a single that would then be released nationally, which is actually how the first records were made in Muscle Shoals. You literally had the three minutes that the song was on the air for the vocalist to sing his deal, and then the D.J. had to get back on the air. So, listening to Percy Sledge and Wilson Pickett and all those things that were coming out of Muscle Shoals at that time, I learned to read the backs of album covers. I learned earlier than I guess the average teenage music listener to read the names of the producers, to read the names of the songwriters.

Jill Colucci - I've spent the last twenty-five years in L.A., but I was born and raised in Ohio. From a very early age I had support to follow my dream. I didn't know it was a dream then. I was too little. It later became my dream. So my parents were very influential in my career. They drove me sixty miles each way, one hundred and twenty miles round trip, twice a week, to do this TV show. Once for the rehearsal, once to tape the show, and that was through snow and the hard winters of Ohio. They were really very inspiring and so they come first. But my musical influences are just what I enjoy listening to.

I loved pop music in the seventies. I was a big Eagles fan and still am. I like the more organic things in pop music. I've been a Bonnie Raitt fan since before she was ever as big as she is today. I followed her career for years. I love Bonnie. I love Don Henley from the Eagles. Bruce Hornsby, Melissa Ethridge. The more acoustic, organic music from pop is what I love, which is what's so great about country music. Country music has that to offer. It's very influenced by the Eagles.

It's interesting. For years I really struggled because the things I wrote were in the cracks, so to speak. I'd play my stuff for the publishers and producers out in L.A. and they'd go, "This stuff is great. You've got to play this in Nashville. This is country." And I'd play it for people here and they'd go, "Man, this is killer, but this is too pop for here. You've got to go to L.A. with this stuff." I felt like a Ping-Pong. I was wondering, what's between Nashville and L.A.? And I realized, the rest of the country is, so how do I get my music to them?

I guess in 1988/89, country music changed so much that it began to embrace what I've always written. That was very fortunate for me. Travis Tritt recorded *I'm Going To Be Somebody.* That was my first number one. People like Travis came along who were a little more contemporary and had some rock and roll and R&B influence. Wynonna did *No One Else On Earth.* You know, there aren't many people that would've recorded that song when she did. Now they all say, "Why didn't you give me that song?" At that time it was very courageous, and it was very fortunate for me because a lot of people wouldn't have chosen to do that song.

Kim Copeland - When I was young, I remember listening to my parents' albums. They had everything from Hank Williams to The Mills Brothers and The Platters; Sam Cooke and Nat King Cole. I loved the harmonies and rich vocals on those old albums. As far back as I can remember, I've loved music. At the age of two or three, I can remember dancing, singing and making up songs. Later, I loved the Beatles and James Taylor, Carly Simon, Carole King, that whole group. And I was a big John Denver fan when I was first learning to play guitar. I was also really into Simon and Garfunkel. I loved their great lyrics and harmonies. During that time, I also discovered Don McLean. I saw him in person in about 1971. It was just him and his guitar on stage. I was just blown away and that's probably when I really got tuned into the writing side of it. Before that, I don't think I realized that I was always drawn to those artists who happen to also write the songs they sang. I started playing guitar when I was about twelve and writing was just a natural extension of that to me, because I always wanted to sing what I was feeling. I wasn't a very natural guitar player, so it was probably easier for me to make up my own songs than to learn to play the ones off the radio.

Gary Earl - My tastes are eclectic. Until I was about eight years old, the only music I spent much time with was a stack of old used juke-box seventy-eight rpm records: Merle Travis' *I Like My Chicken Fryin' Size* Hank Snow's, *Abba Dabba Honeymoon*, Hank Thompson's *I Got a Humpty Dumpty Heart*, and Johnny Cash's *Get Rhythm*. But later on, I got a transistor radio and listened to R&B out of Chicago and rock out of Oklahoma City. After studying classical music in college, I went to Nevada and played in casinos where I might spend six months playing in a country showband, then six months playing in a Top 40 dance band, then three months playing jazz fusion, then maybe a cabaret piano bar. Then going to L.A., it was film and TV music. One week the music supervisor might say, I need R&B rock like Prince, and then the next week another company might want 1940s Big Band songs, or even a middle eastern score. So I've learned to appreciate about anything and everything. But in particular I love good clever lyrics that aren't afraid to use humor, like the writing of Bob DiPiero, Mark Sanders, Karen Staley and Kostas, just to name a few. And my favorite stuff musically is still that old roots honky-tonk hillbilly sound I grew up on. The Tractors remind me of Merle Travis and Hank Thompson in that way. One of the high points of my music career was spending a couple of days playing with Merle Travis during the filming of Clint Eastwood's *Honky Tonk Man* movie.

Robin Earl - The Beatles were a big influence. In eighth grade, I got a guitar and a friend and I learned a lot of the Beatles songs. I sang all Paul's parts. I also loved singing Linda Ronstadt songs, Nicolette Larsen, Bonnie Raitt. I sang all the time. I love all the old Motown songs. My first country influence was probably Kathy Mattea, and then Trisha Yearwood and Martina McBride.

Kye Fleming - I started playing with words early on. The first time I really, really focused was maybe junior high school. It could have been partly the "only child syndrome" and my dad being in the Navy. We moved every two years, so I had myself to talk to, and I think that that really did kind of turn my thoughts inward. I've kind of been in my head all my life anyway. So it was just bound to come out somehow. And then my aunt gave me a guitar when I was in the ninth grade. I wrote my first song and I thought, aha, this goes together.

That was a long time ago, so my influences back then were folk. Some Dylan. I tended even then, without thinking too much about it, to lean toward the females. Joni Mitchell was like a major, major, major influence because of her love of words. She's an absolute poet. If she never put any of that to music, if she didn't even have music as a vehicle, she would be one of the best poets of our time. Incredible. She was the biggest influence and then maybe more lyrically than musically, James Taylor, Simon and Garfunkel, that whole era. And, of course, I grew up with country in the background somewhere. My uncle was a Chet Atkins freak so he played that kind of guitar and everybody sang at the family reunions. Hank Williams, Hank Thompson, Merle Haggard, Patsy Cline, all those were just kind of in there somewhere.

But when I sat down to really getting inspired about what I wanted to say, it was more Joni Mitchell.

Lindy Gravelle - Hank Williams, Patsy Cline, Willie Nelson. First writer I really studied was Gordon Lightfoot. Harlan Howard. I listen to all kinds of music, a lot of pop too. Carly Simon comes to mind.

Janis Ian - When I was a kid, just folk music and jazz. Dylan and the Beatles. Nashville is a huge influence for me

John Jarrard - Kristofferson, Waylon Jennings, Willie Nelson, Otis Redding.

Al Kasha - My early influences, being born in New York, were many of course, but I would say Sammy Cahn and, as a young boy, Rogers and Hammerstein. When I was seven years old, I was in *Annie Get Your Gun* on Broadway, and Irving Berlin wrote that score. To me, to this day, he's still the number one writer at ASCAP and still probably the greatest songwriter that ever lived, because of his sincerity as well as his craft. I've also been influenced by the Beatles, Elton John, and Bob Dylan.

Mary Ann Kennedy - I guess that would be everybody from Rodney Crowell to the Beatles. It's evident in my music because, I think, that's always been my mission: to combine the old with the new, the different influences.

Sandy Knox - I was an Elvis freak when I was a child. I was just a freak. I heard his first record, *Don't Be Cruel,* when I was about four or five. Roger Miller was a huge influence. We were moving overseas and we were living in New Jersey. My parents were figuring out which albums they were going to take to Madrid. I was probably six and in kindergarten. They took two of Roger Miller's and one Trini Lopez. This Roger Miller record had *Dang Me, Chug-A-Lug, Do-Wac-A-Do*, and *King of the Road*, all of his big stuff. I wore those out. I remember I knew all the words.

Our house was very musical. Nobody in my family played an instrument or sang, but my parents loved music and were always playing and buying records. They loved to dance and were pretty social, having people over and stuff like that.

Then my teachers found out I could sing when I was eleven and my parents put me into voice. All my teachers were very influential. Teachers are very, very important. I was in junior high and I wanted to play the drums in the orchestra or the marching band. I wanted to be on the big drum, but they told me the school system required a year of choir first. And so I had to take a year of choir. There was this teacher named Ms. Hinkle. You had to sing for her so she knew where to place you in the choir. I got up and sang for her, and her mouth just dropped. I didn't know if I was in trouble or what. I had never really sung for anybody before. I didn't think anything of opening my mouth, and so that afternoon she called my mother and said, "Are you aware that your daughter has a really great singing voice? You need to get her into some lessons." Now, if Ms. Hinkle had not taken the initiative to call my mother, where would I have gone? My writing spawned out of my singing as a child and being in musicals and performing. What if Ms. Hinkle had not called? I may have been a drummer. A professional marching band drummer.

Then the next teacher was Ms. Scandrett, who was the next choir teacher. I still talk to her. Very influential. The next one was Ms. Lafferty, my high school teacher who was really tough on me. By this time my head was pretty big, because I had this big voice and I could sing. I'd always sat first chair. Ms. Lafferty put me last chair which brought me down a lot, and was really tough on me my four years of high school. On my last day when I graduated, she pulled me into her office. She was a very somber woman, not the fun choir teacher that I was used to. She was a very tough cookie. She brought me into her office and said, "You know, I've always been very hard on you." And I said, "Yeah!" And she said (I tear up when I think about it), "You are the most talented child I've ever taught. You have the potential and ability to make it if you really want it." But, she said, "You're going to have to get disciplined." She was really tough. She said, "That's why I sat you last chair." Those were some of my influences.

Rupert Holmes, Roger Miller, Elvis and the Beatles, of course. Johnny Mercer for the lyrics. One of the greatest teachers I think writers have is just listening to what's gone before them and has proven, year after year, to be classic.

Jess Leary - My early influences were actually folk musicians, being Joni Mitchell and Melanie. I was also into bluegrass at a pretty early age in life as far as just musical influences. I ended up having a banjo when I was about thirteen. I know I was the only person in my whole state with one, especially at thirteen. But I saw one in the store and I had already been playing guitar since I was ten, and I just had to have it. I just knew it was going to sound really neat, and I actually found somebody in my hometown who taught banjo and mandolin. So I took up both of those instruments. That way I just kind of jumped in and started playing anything with strings on it. Then listening to some of the bluegrass records and going into the folk records and getting into the singer/songwriters like Melanie, Joni Mitchell. As time went on, into the Linda Ronstadt era and Emmylou Harris, through the sort of seventies rock thing and then into rock. Fleetwood Mac and Heart. All along still listening to the country/folk. Somehow I wound up in country. I don't know how I got here.

Wayland Patton - I believe that my mother is the main reason that I began writing. I think the reason I write lyrics is that my mother was an English teacher and also, part-time, sold the *World Book Encyclopedia*. With the *World Book*, we also had the Childcraft series. In the Childcraft series there was a book called *Poems and Stories of Early Childhood*. Instead of reading stories to me at night, I remember my mother reading poems. I think that made such a big impact on me, in terms of rhyme and meter.

Pam Rose - From listening to what I've done, or what I did with Kennedy-Rose, or anything that I'm doing now, I think one of the first adjectives that people would put with that is *eclectic*. I have truly been influenced by so many different things. I guess to start, the gene pool is in my favor, as far as music goes. Both my parents are musical. They both play the piano and sing. I grew up having a piano ever since I could remember and hearing my parents play and sing. I was raised Baptist, so a lot of the music I heard many times a week were hymns. I can't help but think that's rolling around in there somewhere. My mom did teach me piano, bless her heart. She tried. I wasn't a very good student because I was too impatient, and I wanted to play what I heard in my head and didn't want to do those stupid, little exercises. And then in junior high, I wanted to be in the band. I wanted to play the drums I remember, but that was pretty much like, "Oh no, she wants to play the drums." But my uncle was killed in World War II and he was a trumpet player, and so I kind of inherited his trumpet. That was the first instrument that I studied in school. I played the trumpet for a couple of years and then I discovered the guitar, through folk music.

(WERE YOU IN THE CHOIR?) Well, first I was just in the band because you had to chose one or the other, but I learned to play the guitar when I was twelve. My cousins turned me on to the guitar. We spent summers together learning every single note off of Peter, Paul and Mary records. I slowed their records down so I could pick out every note and that's how I learned to play. It was hard to sing and play the trumpet, so I gave up the trumpet and joined the choir. I was very, very influenced by my teacher. There I learned about choral music and continued learning about classical music. I actually studied composition and conducting and college level music theory in high school. I exempted several years of theory when I got to college. Then I went to Florida State and my classical training continued, because at that time if you were a music major, you studied classical or you studied nothing. And it was a very, very strict school at that time, so I was actually forbidden to sing in nightclubs. You were supposed to sing opera. You weren't supposed to drink or smoke or play in nightclubs or stay up late or any of that stuff, of course, all of which I did. Then I started really getting into the Beatles, the Grateful Dead and Rhinoceros and Zephyr and Pacific Gas and Electric and all those weird bands. Grand Funk Railroad and Jefferson Airplane. During that time, I really was very influenced by that. I didn't really fit in, so I kind of took three years right then and just really listened and absorbed and became a sponge. That was a real transition for me.

Then from that point on, Crosby, Stills and Nash. Incredibly powerful influence for me. Steven Stills. Lindsey Buckingham of Fleetwood Mac is all-round my favorite guitar player. Streisand, Julie Andrews, Jimmy Hendricks. Those you don't usually even use in the same paragraph with each other, but I feel like I was truly influenced by everything except rumbas and polkas.

Joyce Rouse - Generally a lot of women. Judy Collins, Linda Ronstadt, Emmylou Harris.

Wayne Tester - Dave Loggins, because he's the one that signed me to MCA Music Publishing, my first-ever publishing deal. He taught me about songwriting and the depth of it.

I started playing piano when I was five years old. I played in all the rock bands and a gospel quartet in high school. I was also in the jazz band and studied classical music. In college I started traveling with a comedian, and we tried to write songs so we could play some music as well. I guess that was the start of it, the infancy of it.

I always used to take David Foster records and play keyboards with those. So he was a big influence, and the inspiration behind wanting to do this for a profession.

Trisha Walker - In terms of learning music, my music teacher. Musical influences would have to be artists more in the R&B field. Aretha Franklin. A lot of Big Bands.

Kate Wallace - Gordon Lightfoot, Joni Mitchell, John Stewart, Joan Baez, Emmylou Harris, Bonnie Raitt, Jackson Browne, James Taylor. Joni Mitchell, James Taylor, and Gordon Lightfoot, to me, are three of the greatest songwriters ever. Gordon Lightfoot's got sixteen albums worth of songs, and there are probably five songs that I would never care if I ever heard again, there are probably two hundred that are simply great, and one hundred that are wonderful. He's a poet, and so is Joni Mitchell. I'm citing people that have had long, productive, extraordinary careers, and I admire them. That would be one side of what influences me. I also really love 1-4-5 rock and roll, like Chuck Berry, Jerry Lee Lewis, and the early Beatles stuff. There are two things that move me in terms of songwriting. One is just an amazingly poetic lyric, or the stuff that just gets you right here. That's so simple, or so groove oriented. Like *Achy Breaky Heart*. That's a song that everybody in this town would like to lift their leg on and pee all over. But if you listen to that record, it's not the lyric that's happening, it's the groove. The tracks literally jump off the turntable. Songs aren't just about melodies or just about lyrics, it's about how they meet.

Marijohn Wilkin - Music is a calling. As sure as a minister is called. As sure as a doctor feels he has to be a doctor. Some doctors are just doctors for the money, but most do a service. Music is a service. It can change the hearts and minds and moods of people. I was called to write. I was called to be in music, but took it me a long time to realize that.

When I was in college, I was offered a movie contract because I rode a horse and sang in the university band. I would have been like a Dale Evans. Tex Ritter's Monogram Studios. But I turned it down to get married. I could have gone into music then.

My husband was killed in World War II, and I had no idea of being a career woman. At that time you could either be a school teacher or Rosie the Riveter. There weren't any choices. Then, a few months after his death, I was offered a road job with a big dance band. I sang with big dance bands then, but I turned that one down.

Then there was one other way I could have come in. I was doing some USO shows during World War II. The man who was doing our arranging for these big shows had been the piano player for Lawrence Welk. He said, "I think you should go to Chicago and audition for Lawrence Welk." He said, "You could get that job." Well, there was my other offer into the music business.

As I look back, I either would have come in through Hollywood, through L.A., through Chicago, or Nashville. I couldn't see all that then, but I can see it as I look back. And I say, man, I didn't have a choice. These things are spiritually manipulated.

I was teaching school, and these pop songs were coming out. I was not giving my attention to my children, and the teaching was becoming a chore. And the pulling to write ... it was painful. I had to write so bad. And so, that was it. I was called. I can look around in Nashville and I can pick them out. Some can make it okay without the calling, but it's much easier for those of us who are called. It just is, because we're doing exactly what we're supposed to be doing. It opens the doors. When I see people just beating their brains, I think they need to go look for a different career.

I was already in my thirties when I moved here. I was no young chick. It gets much easier as you get older because you can see so much. You have such a panoramic view of where you've been.

4. How much of your encouragement comes from within?

Tony Arata - Well, I think ultimately, when you're talking about doing something, no matter what it is, first and foremost, you do it because that's what you enjoy doing. Sometimes you go into a profession with the given knowledge that if you earned the degree and are hired, you'll do very well. Still somewhere in there, there's got to be the belief that you really want to do this. Steinbeck had the best quote about it. He said that he could either be a writer or bet on horses. So he took the "less sure" of the professions and went into writing novels. But he knew that that's what he wanted to do. There's a certain amount of it that comes from other people saying "you're a songwriter." *The Dance* was probably the first really big song that came out, but before then I really felt like I was a songwriter because I was among songwriters, and I was standing in the ring, slugging it out with them. I had written some things that I was fairly proud of. As long as you come up with a few of those and are willing to play those in front of anybody, then in some way, you are a songwriter, regardless of whether or not your song is recorded.

I think too often songwriters are judged on cuts, units sold, awards won, and they are not judged on the true art of the craft. Some of my favorite writers here are not the guys you see on the charts all the time. That's not to say that there aren't some on the charts that I really enjoy, but I've met some songwriters here that I just stand in awe of. They've not won Grammys and they've not had number ones and they've not sold thousands and millions of albums, but they really have the essence of the craft and that's what you always are striving for. They know a lot of what they do is not going to be accepted by the masses, but that in no way, shape, or form makes them change what they're doing. That's an inspiration. It's also an inspiration to see the people who are at the top of the charts all the time and who, week in and week out, crank out the songs that you hear on the radio. That's hard to do. That's damned near impossible, so you have to admire that side of it as well. I think it's a little bit of both. The drive comes from trying to stay true to what it is you believe in your heart, and also, in all honesty, trying to make a living at this. I was working for a magazine the whole time *The Dance* was out. I never thought that made me any less of an artisan because I had a job. You can be a songwriter doing anything. It's quite interesting to see all the shapes that it can take.

Pam Belford - That's the harder one. By the grace of God, sometimes it's there and sometimes it's not. I've gone for a year or two at a time, where I've been writing because that's what I do, but there are times when I don't enjoy it. I just do it because I'm supposed to do it. Then suddenly something will happen and I'll snap back into it. Right now, I'm in a "snapped back into it" phase.

Steve Bogard - All of it. I'm one of those people that would be doing this whether I got money or not.

Rory Bourke - I came into the writing business in a different way from anybody else I know. I went to work for Mercury Records in 1966, then six years later I left and had built up a lot of friends here in town. I left a national promotion job to be a songwriter, so I never really had the same kinds of things as people going from publisher to publisher. I was fortunate. A friend of mine named Mac Allen, who was at WKDA here, introduced me to Don Gant at Acuff Rose music. Don took me under his wing and really wanted me to sign with Acuff Rose, but they weren't offering money at that time, so he called Henry Hurt at Chappell Music and told him, "He won't sign with us, but he's going to be a big writer. You need to sign him." I don't have the myth of getting off the bus and pounding the pavement. Everybody has to take that step of belief in their own way. When I left Mercury, I left a really good paying job to just say, this has got to work out. I didn't have any way back into the business. I had made it pretty clear that I didn't want to be a promotion man anymore. I was with Chappell Music for about fifteen years.

Gary Burr - I never knew that I wanted to be a songwriter, but I always knew that I wanted to do something in the music business. I still don't think of myself as a songwriter. I think of myself as somebody who's in the music business, and I do a lot of things in it. One of the things I do is I'm a songwriter. When I first got the bug to do this I was at Woodstock. Me and my best friend sat there in front of the stage, and we looked around and saw all of this magic going on around us, chemically induced and otherwise. We just decided that this was something that we had to do. I sang and he played the drums, and when we went home we put a band together. From that point on I just knew that I was never going to have a regular job. I was going to make it in this. There was really no other option. I just knew that this was what I was supposed to do.

Kim Carnes - Most of it. My passion for the music, what I feel inside, is the complete motivation, one hundred percent. That's always the reason. I can't imagine not doing this. And I think you have to have that to get through all the ups and downs. There are so many more down times than up. So many disappointments, that it has to be so strong inside you. Then you can just keep getting up off the mat. Otherwise, it'll ruin you.

Debi Cochran - I guess most of it has to be you. You have to have somebody who really believes in you who has the power to help you, like a publisher to give you a job. A producer who believes in your songs, co-writers who are maybe a little further up on the ladder than you, who will help you. But you also have to be very, very driven to do this, because it's very difficult and it's like pushing the camel through the eye of a needle to get a song on a record. And then to expect it to ever be a single. There's so much talent in this town. If you really stop to think about who you're competing with, you would just quit. I believe people are born with the drive to do the things they do, and I was born to do this. Whether I do it poorly or successfully, nonetheless I'm here.

Jill Colucci - I can't imagine doing anything else. I really can't imagine it. Again, because I have been singing professionally since I was five, I've been in this business all my life. It's very fortunate that I can do it because I don't know what else I would do. That's not to say that I never get discouraged, or that I don't get down. But I never think of doing anything else. I never think of stopping, so it's not something I really have to encourage myself about. It's just being aware of the fact that there are ups and there are downs. Just like in life, there are ups and downs in the business. You just have to wait it out through the slower times or make extra effort at that time to make things happen. Sometimes things just roll. It feels like you're not doing anything but writing and things are getting cut, and things are flying up the charts and it's a wonderful experience. If there are slow times, I'll do a few things to generate more activity. Maybe try to pitch a little harder or something like that, but I never, ever consider doing anything else.

Kim Copeland - I suppose a lot of it does, but not consciously. I think that writing is a part of you or it's not. I don't work at keeping myself inspired to do it, it's just something that I can't not do. I think if you have that drive within you, you'll do it. You can learn the craft, but the fire inside is there or it isn't.

Gary Earl - Well, it's an internal thing that I'm not sure I can verbalize. There was a point when I was in school that I used to think there must be a gazillion interesting things to do. But now I have a hard time imagining doing anything else. It's almost unfathomable. I've always had songs in me.

Robin Earl - I've always felt like I was supposed to be in music. I did a pretty good job of ignoring that for a long time, but the feeling remained. Everyone in my family loves music, but they're not involved in the music business, so I've had to pretty much make my own way in that area. There were times when I had to make myself keep going, when it seemed much more logical to choose another path. But I do try to follow my own instincts better than I used to, and things seem to go better when I do.

Kye Fleming - I was twenty-six when I moved here, so I had already had a lot of knocks. I was playing the coffee house circuits out of New York and playing colleges and stuff. I just couldn't be dampened.

Had somebody sat me down and told me the odds, I wouldn't have believed them anyway. It wouldn't have mattered. I thought I was above the odds or something. It was very strange. I remember in the ninth grade, my mom told me that I needed to go do my homework. I was playing a guitar and probably had been for hours, and she said, "You know, you've really got to go do your homework." And I said, "I will, but this is how I'm going to make my living." I've always remembered saying that almost like somebody else said it. I don't know if it's destiny, but something in there always kept me going. The times when it seemed and felt the hardest were all before Nashville. By the time I got to Nashville, it was like, this is it, and things took off quickly.

Lindy Gravelle - That kind of fluctuates between encouragement and desperation. I think I get hooked on when it feels good. I'm lucky in the fact that I play live, and I use my gigs as a testing ground for my material. When I get a good response, I'm encouraged to keep writing. You know you're on to something or you're challenged to make yourself a better writer. The general public is less discriminating to me than a room full of writers. Somewhere in the middle is best, if you can get a mixture of both. It's hard to listen to a song anymore without analyzing it and tearing it apart. You don't hear it with the same kind of ear as before.

Al Kasha - I came from a very poor home. My father was an extremely violent alcoholic. There was a lot of dysfunction in my home. That sometimes is the good part, because you see a lot of drama. And being into music and being a songwriter both in music and lyrics, my imagination opened up and I could live within that world of writing. Writing songs to give people inspiration and hope. That's what I always try to write about, inspiration and hope.

Mary Ann Kennedy - My buddy, Ray Kennedy (by the way, we're not related) was saying something to a young writer that I had just signed. The guy had just done a showcase for the label. We were going for a deal and it didn't pan out. He told him, "You've got to remember, you've chosen a business that is ninety-nine percent rejection. You've got to just keep believing in why you did this. You can't be affected by it. It's all opinion and it's a lot of rejection."

That was well said, and it's a great point. We've all been in the meetings when you have some of what you considered your best songs turned down. *Safe in the Arms of Love* was written twelve years ago and rejected many times for the lyric being too this or that. A little too edgy and country folks won't understand "strip your heart and it starts to snow."

That kind of imagery. The music as well. Everybody loved it, but it was awfully hip for the time. But that was a song that we did believe in, and here twelve years later, it's paid off big. Hopefully, you don't have to wait that long for them all, but that has happened. And I think, once you do receive some success along the way, that encourages you to keep going. So, I guess just that and the pure joy of doing it. If it still brings to you that joy, you've got to keep going. Don't get hung up on what you've done. Just go on. Push yourself. Dig in and be an open channel for the next project.

Sandy Knox - We do have to be pretty disciplined because it would be easy to play video games all day or go gift shopping or whatever. You do have to try to be disciplined, make a schedule and work, but there are times when I don't feel like writing. I have nothing to say. I don't want to write. I have learned to just let that be okay. It's okay if I want to spend days reading or watching movies or walking through parks or art galleries or going to Davis Kidd. Sometimes I go in there and go through books for hours and hours. I used to feel guilty about it. I don't anymore. I know that I will write again. I've been through this before. There was one period where I didn't really write much for about three years, but then, when I came back, I really was writing. I was never-ending for about the next four years. I've kind of hit one of those modes right now where I'm thinking of really good ideas and storing them, but I'm not ready to write them. I've written since I was eleven and I signed my first song when I was sixteen; so basically for twenty-one years, my mistress, my master, has been writing and the music business. Right now I'm defying my master a little bit and not interested in taking direction from it.

Jess Leary - I do talk to myself a lot. Don't tell anybody. What keeps me going musically? It's more like, music keeps me going otherwise. It's just there one way or another, whether I'm writing a song or whether I'm listening to something or whether I'm thinking about a song I like. It could be anything, but I basically wake up loving the fact that I'm in music, and I don't remember a time when I didn't feel that way. It's been since a very early age that I knew I would have a career in music and a life in music. I think it was one of those things that chose me. For some reason, musical instruments were easy for me to play. And singing harmony is easy for me. I definitely view it as a gift. A definite blessing. It's always been there for me, so it's not a forced thing.

Jim McBride - I would start writing about ten o'clock at night and sometimes write until one or two in the morning. This was just about every night. For a while we had a little studio in Huntsville, so that was a place to hang out and be around other people who wanted to do that. It scared me to death to come to Music Row. It was like never-never land. It scared me to death but I did it anyway.

Pam Rose - The main thing is, I don't know how to do anything else. There have only been maybe two or three times in my life where I've said, forget this. I am not doing this anymore. Just screw it. That's when I realize that I really am not trained to do anything else. I don't know how to do anything else.

And then, I guess, I have a very strong spiritual connection that has nothing to do with religion. I feel that in nurturing that connection down through time, I've learned a lot about self-esteem and where that comes from and where it's good for it to come from and where it's not so good for it to come from. I have learned time and time again, when you rely on it to come from the outside, you can fall on your face and just end up feeling like shit. So, down though the years, I've learned how to make a connection with my big self that nurtures that self-esteem and that inner voice and that inner compass, actually, and to really stay more in touch with that. That has helped me get past the basic element, which is fear of rejection. If you have that, you're screwed. You have to make peace with that. And just stamina and good common sense, which is always a weak link for me. I guess all of those things have been really important as far as what keeps me connected enough to go on.

Joyce Rouse - That's so central to all of it. To me, creativity and spirituality are so closely intertwined, sometimes they're indistinguishable. With me, in many ways, the music and the creativity have been so suppressed from exterior places in my life. Like, unintentionally, by my family, and by trying to be a music major at a school that was just not where I needed to be. At times the messages that I've gotten are, you're not good enough to do this, or this isn't the right thing for you to do. I have let that get me down for a period of time, but at some point there is always this wellspring. Now I can look back and see that I can't *not* do this. I cannot *not* create music. It's such an important part of my mental, my physical, my spiritual, and my emotional health.

Trisha Walker - Sometimes it's encouraging and sometimes the well is pretty dry. One of the most difficult things is in trying to pursue something creative and learning how to mesh the creative and the business worlds of it. I've been in Nashville about fourteen years now, and there are some days when the encouragement I came here with gets kind of beat up just from the business side of it. But that's what the playing and performing offers me. I can go out and play for somebody, and an audience member or a fan will come up and say how much they enjoyed it, and the encouragement is rekindled again.

Marijohn Wilkin - Years ago I used to tell writers that everything is on a giant tape machine somewhere. Everything that ever has been. Everything that ever will be. And if you plug into it, you'll receive it. You'll get it back. You'll get it in your head. So now, of course, I just tell them it's in that great computer. And we're either plugged in or we're not.

The interesting part to me, whether people are outwardly religious or not, they are still inwardly knowledgeable of the fact - at least I am - that I did not write this song. It's a constant accepting or rejecting. An idea comes into your head. Is this a good idea? If I think it's a good idea, I accept the idea. Accept or reject. Then that's when the lines come. When I'm really fortunate, I'll have an entire chorus come at one time, and that's melody and lyric. But, that is when I am really tuned in, plugged in.

Kim Williams - Part of the motivation was the fear of it not working. Now that it's working, it's working really well. I'm going through a stage that, financially, I'm getting real secure and things are working. Now what do I do, now that I can do all the things that I've wanted to do? Does my writing change? Do I keep doing the same thing? It's like there is a letup right now in the war. I need to be re-challenged.

5. Were you encouraged by family or friends in the early days of your writing career?

Tony Arata - My momma was probably the biggest supporter all along. When I was sitting on the edge of the bed in my bedroom at home, she would never bother me and never ask, "Why don't you go out and play baseball like all the other boys?" My family was always very supportive, even right down to when my wife and I were loading up the rental truck to come up to Nashville. My father came by and I think like any father, he was petrified of what we were going to do, but he knew that this was really what I wanted. I was very lucky. I have a very supportive wife. My wife, Jamie, was the one who got us up here. She's the one who really made it possible for us to move. So I was never told, that's ridiculous, or don't do that. And I was never told, you'll never make any money at that. I hope that as a father now, I'll learn from that and know that if your child really wants to do something and they really work at it and are trying, then they deserve support. I never got anything but support from my family.

Pam Belford - I was always encouraged. My family's been great. The night before I moved down to Nashville, I think my dad was concerned for me, because I really didn't know what I was doing. He said, "What are you going to do for money?" And all of the sudden it's like, oh! He did remind me about that old adage that for every light on Broadway, there's another broken heart. I had this picture in my head that when I came down here, there were going to be ten people with guitars hitchhiking in and ten people with guitars hitchhiking out. That really wasn't far from the truth except for the hitchhiking part. Over the years, my dad and mother and all their friends and all my friends have really been so encouraging.

Kent Blazy - My folks had lived in an artistic community, Woodstock, New York, long before it was known for its music. Since about the turn of the century, it was a town where artists and writers came and lived especially in the summertime. They had a playhouse and theater. It was a hotbed of creativity. I can remember my folks talking about all the people they knew. I think they had a better perspective on pursuing that type of career, so when I started playing guitar and doing this, they were very encouraging.

Steve Bogard - Absolutely. My parents supported me every way they could.

Rory Bourke - No. Really negative encouragement. We're Irish Catholics and we were to be priests, lawyers, or doctors, not songwriters.

Gary Burr - They were great. My mom and dad were both the level-headed New Englanders, and they basically said, you should stay in school, you should da, da, da, all these things. And when I told them I was going to leave college and go to California and play in a band, their reaction was, this is not a good thing to do. You should think of this. You should think of that. And then after they got all that out of their system, they basically put their arm around me and said, "Okay, now, if you're doing it anyway, how can we help?" They were great. They bought me amplifiers and shipped them out to California when my band didn't have any equipment. We were really smart. The only way the band could get to California was to sell all of our equipment for the money. Went to California as a band, but we had no equipment. So, it took us like two years to get our equipment all back.

My parents were very supportive. My first memory of performing was at a family thing when I was five. Some family party where they stuck me on the coffee table and had me sing *You Ain't Nothing But a Hound Dog*. That's my earliest memory. It was the last family gathering I went to, coincidentally.

Kim Carnes - No, they didn't discourage me, but they didn't encourage me. As far as a career, they didn't encourage me at all. My mom, in fact, was really against it. She didn't understand. It was so foreign to her. She thought, like a lot of other people, that rock and roll is a bad business. She has since come around and is really proud of what I'm doing. She realized that I'm following my heart. My dad used to say, "When are you going to get a real job?" So many people of that generation, what they don't understand, scares them.

Debi Cochran - Absolutely not. There is no musical or poetic talent that runs through my family. I have one sister. She loves it now. She thinks it's great that I have this career. But it's certainly not something that she would have said, "Yeah, I think this is a good idea, why don't you be a professional songwriter." My father always said, "You need to be a teacher or secretary, because you can always get a job." That was his view of how women could support themselves. And I guess it was apparent to him very early on, that I was not going to get married and settle down when I was young, so he wanted to be sure I had a responsible job so I could take care of myself.

Kim Copeland - Well, I don't come from a musical family. No one in my family plays or sings. They're very creative, each in their own way. But I don't come from a family that really encourages exploration of your creativity, so I don't think they've ever really understood the paths I've chosen. Some of my family members have gotten into my career and been very supportive and that's been great. I guess others have scratched their heads and wondered what I'm trying to do.

(DID THEY EVER TELL YOU TO GET A REAL JOB?) Yes! Directly and indirectly. I think deep down they probably support it, but don't understand the whole process.

Gary Earl - I got a lot of support to play and write music from a very early age. My father was a welder for a gas company and he had very hard work, digging ditches and welding pipe. I remember before I started school, he would talk about the big blonde piano-playing lady or the black guy who tap danced on Lawrence Welk. He would say, "Now, if you could do that for a living, that would be something. You don't want to do what I do." And Mom made sure that I had every opportunity to perform. She worked hard and sacrificed a lot to buy me a piano and guitar, and I spent most of my time banging away, doing my own songs, not necessarily what my lessons were. Then my aunt and uncle in Nevada (I call them my West-Coast parents) even gave me a place to stay with them when I moved west. So yeah, I've gotten a lot of support from family.

Robin Earl - When I was young, my older sister was always bringing home records. I listened all the time and learned everything on the radio, loved anything with harmony parts. I started writing songs with my friend Barbara at age six, and our teacher sent us around to perform them for the classes at our school.

My first music job was in Reno, and this was after I'd done several other types of work while pursuing music on the side.

At first my parents were not very happy about this, but I think after they realized I'd made a commitment to it, they became very supportive. They've really been great, very encouraging, and my older sister and her husband have been unusually supportive. The major influence in my writing success has been my husband Gary.

Kye Fleming - My mother and father just believed I could do anything. Absolutely anything. They were very proud of me and even in the beginning. When I was in high school, I played coffee houses and bars and stuff. We never even really talked about it that much, but I could feel the support.

John Jarrard - No. I wrote with friends. My family had no clue as to what this is all about.

Mary Ann Kennedy - Very much so. My mom's side of the family always performed. They had a little country band. I've got pictures of me from when I was a little-bitty kid, sitting on my uncle's lap while he was playing the steel guitar. My mom sang in the band, so I kind of took over the dream that she had. With her generation, it was more like you get married and you have your kids. I very much credit her and her side of the family for giving me this natural gift that I'm so blessed to have. There's a whole lot of work involved, of course, and I've been pretty disappointed sometimes, but I just feel like so much of it was just kind of given to me.

Kostas - On both sides of my family there's always been a lot of music. My dad was a frustrated rock and roll player from Greece, playing Greek rock and roll. That's something he enjoyed doing, and I just happened to be there too.

Jess Leary - My mother was a singer and played piano. The way she puts it, the day she got married, she stopped playing and singing. I don't know what that means. She always sang and we always had a piano in the house. I have four sisters and they all sing. We all sang a little bit with each other and always have, so I grew up singing. My dad says he's totally unmusical. He was more of an artist. He was into the art thing, so I got my painting stuff from him.

(HAVE YOU FOUND THAT YOUR ART FLOWS INTO YOUR MUSIC?) Absolutely. In fact, that's a way for me to kind of unwind, to start a painting or dig one out that I had started and just put on some good music and sit in front of the thing. Just pick some colors that turn me on, just anything beautiful. I've found, a lot of times, it's just that tuning out thing, when you almost become invisible and at the same time you become a sponge. You don't really know it, but you're absorbing maybe what you're listening to. Sometimes silence can open up so much room for creativity.

Jim McBride - No one in my family had done anything like that. Growing up, my mother's side of the family was kind of musical, and they sang mostly gospel songs. My uncle on the other side of the family was the one who taught me to play guitar. Nobody had ever come close to making a living out of music, so that's just something that wasn't discussed. I had no role model in my family. (DID THEY EVER TELL YOU TO GET A REAL JOB?) No, because I always had a real job. From the time I was twelve till I left the post office when I was thirty-three, I've worked all different kinds of jobs. I always had a job, and music was something I did on the side. When it came time to do this full-time, I'm sure they were a little concerned, but they were encouraging.

Wayland Patton - Mom and Dad were around when the first couple of songs were recorded. And of course Mom and Dad would come out to hear me perform. They heard me through the bedroom walls late at night. They were very supportive. I remember that after Mom died, I was a regular on the Louisiana Hayride for a couple of years. That was about two or three hours from where we lived, and I remember saying that my dad used to bang on the wall and tell me to quit, and now he's driving hundreds of miles just to see me perform.

Joyce Rouse - I guess the word *black sheep* isn't quite right. I'm a creative person in a family that is otherwise not really artistically or creatively inclined. And I think they would have encouraged me more had they known how, but they really didn't know what to do with my creativity. So, I can't say that I got a lot of encouragement. But I did have a piano teacher who encouraged it and other music teachers through the years who did.

Wayne Tester - No. My mom was instrumental in getting me started playing piano at the outset. As far as doing this as a profession, they didn't really understand it at first. And now that there's some success, they go, "Wow, yeah!" Especially with this Garth thing]*The Change]*. They understand it real well now.

Trisha Walker - My family was very encouraging.

Kate Wallace - I am so lucky. I've always been encouraged by everybody.

Marijohn Wilkin - They thought I was insane! But I was not writing country, so I wasn't quite as insane. I was writing big pop stuff because I didn't know anything about country.

Kim Williams - They looked at me like I'd just lost my mind. Although it was a dream for me, I knew all along that it was obtainable. My mother-in-law's way of getting to me was to ask, "Have you sold any songs yet?" Most of my friends wished me well, but feared I'd lost my mind too. It encouraged me that when I came to Nashville, I really started blending in and meeting people. I told my wife that for the first time in my life, I feel good about myself. Either I'm not crazy, or there's a hell of a lot of people just as crazy as I am.

CHAPTER TWO

CREATIVITY—THE FLOW

*Kim Williams - When you sit down and you **don't** make a bunch of rules about what you're going to write, that's creative.*

Al Kasha - I think a definition for creativity is seeing the truth and then communicating back to the audience the truth they already know.

Kye Fleming - What I'm after is that open channel, and that's also giving voice to the unconscious.

Rory Bourke - Every morning I go kicking and screaming into work. It's hard and there's a part of me that can feel the tension and resistance to having to put it on the line.

1. What is creativity?

Tony Arata - There's always so much to draw from, and creativity, I don't believe, is in making something up. A great deal has already been said, if not all of it. And certainly you're not going to invent especially many chords, and you're not going to invent many earth-shattering ideas. I think creativity is in taking those basic elements that already exist and making them into something. The hard part, as I see it, is in taking the themes that everyone is the most familiar with and putting some new twist on it. The creativity comes in inventing a way of expressing this time-honored theme, in a way that no one has ever really put it before. That's the hard part. It doesn't necessarily have to take a real complex fashion either. I think creativity isn't expressed only by being really outside with an idea or with a presentation. Sometimes the creativity comes from taking even the simplest themes and presenting them very simply, but in some way that sounds fresh.

Pam Belford - It's like a surge of energy that enables you to express everyday experiences in a form that you can share. It's making a mountain out of a molehill.

Kent Blazy - Creativity, to me, is seeing that blank piece of paper and then two or three hours later, you have a song. It's just living life. Everything that you do can inspire you, if you're open to it. Looking out the window, riding in the car, being with people who you care about, all that just opens you up to letting your feelings come out. It's one of those things that as much as feeling it from the heart, you have to develop it. You have to keep your mind open to thinking that way and being aware of what's going on around you, and do everything that you can to try to bring that creativity out.

Steve Bogard - I think creativity is love. I think creativity is feeling something in your heart and wanting someone else to feel it, wanting them to be better for it, that makes you better for it.

Rory Bourke - The ability to make something out of nothing. To take an idea and bring the abstract to some form of concrete. I believe that creativity in the arts is a blessing and a curse at the same time, because in order to be truly creative, your mind has to be completely open. It has to be open for everything to come in and be a potential idea. That's nice, but you also have to be open for the demons. I don't mean the weird demons. When your mind is open to everything, everything's going to come in. Sometimes everything that comes in is not always comfortable. So there's a price to pay for being highly creative. We've seen people become drug addicts and have all sorts of things they have to work through.

Gary Burr - Creativity is not being embarrassed to sound like an idiot. That's the big thing about being a collaborator. You've got to be comfortable enough with somebody to say whatever it is and play whatever it is that comes into your head and not worry that it's going to sound stupid. Almost a hundred percent of the time that a collaborator has said to me, "Now, don't laugh, this is going to sound really dumb," it's made me a fortune. Not a fortune, but every time my collaborator says that now, I hear bells go off, because generally, those are the lines that are different and make the song special. So every time I hear that, I think, there's a mortgage payment. Creativity is just no shame.

Kim Carnes - Being able to express yourself through your art form, whatever that may be. As a songwriter telling a story, put words together that affect people emotionally in some way, whether it's how they feel, or wanting to get up and dance to a great rock and roll song. I think the most creative people have the ability to touch other people with their art.

Debi Cochran - Creativity is a combination of preparation and luck. There are people who are very successful in this town because they're technical or because they're political. And there are other people who are just creative geniuses, and everything they write sounds like it's worthy of Joni Mitchell. So there are different levels of that. I tell people that talent is not the most important criteria for getting a record deal or a songwriting deal or an A&R job. Talent is not the thing. Persistence is the thing. You can be actually a mediocre talent and if you're driven enough, you can be very successful.

Jill Colucci - I guess creativity would be a development of something original. It's energy and it's inspiration. It's unique and from the heart and it's yours.

Kim Copeland - Creativity is the ability to look at any given situation without the interference of outside limitations. I think everybody is creative, but some people access it and nurture it and some don't. I would much rather have a creative plumber who comes into my house and looks at what I want and then says, "Okay, how can I make that happen? It's different, but what if we tried this?" than one who looks at it and scratches his head and says, "It's not in the manual. It can't be done."

Creative thinking can apply to every walk of life, and I make a conscious effort to surround myself with creative-thinking people.

Gary Earl - Finding alternative ways of expressing yourself. I've had some people say, "Oh, I wish I was as creative as you or as talented as you." My response to that is, "Hey, you're a teacher, or whatever, and what you do is every bit as creative as what I do; it's just a different form of expression. My brother is a great carpenter, and he's designed and built his own earth-sheltered solar home. Yet I've heard him say, "I wish I was as talented as you." He's as good with wood as I am with music but doesn't always realize how creative he really is. Everyone you meet is creative in some area of their life.

I've held people when they've died, and it's like there's that little sparkle in the eye - that's the only thing that leaves. Everything else looks the same. Just that little sparkle in the eye. That little thing you can't really put your finger on and you can't really express and science can't really put into a box. That's a real part of us and it brings in things that just seem to come from nowhere. I don't care if you call it gut feeling, intuition, creativity, or whatever. There are a zillion names you could put on it, but I feel that's where your creativity comes from. That deeper or higher part of you. It's something that we can't really explain, and maybe that's the whole beauty of it.

Robin Earl - I think that creativity is creating in any area of life, whether it's creating a song, creating a building, or creating an idea. Everything you think and do is creating.

Kye Fleming - It's got something to do with being that open channel. A child is totally creative because he hasn't learned to put up the walls and the blocks and the edits. He sees visions, his mind is totally open, and his heart is totally open. I think that's what true creativity is, and as adults we are constantly trying to get back to that innocence and openness.

Lindy Gravelle - It's a life force. When I really feel like I am alive, then I'm creating; or when I'm creating, I'm really alive. It's synonymous to life to be creative. I think that God or whatever it is that created this planet we're on—when we're creating, we're like it. And we're in tune with it. And hopefully it's creating something for the better of mankind or the world, not creating something evil. It's the expression of mind, soul, and feeling. It's making something out of nothing, or using material that we have that ends up being something else. It's changing matter. Music is such a trip. It's an oral art. It's pretty tough to tell somebody who hasn't written a song how it's done.

I have a theory. I think kids today have been desensitized so much by all the exposure to television, movies, videos, you name it. They have to be overpowered with stuff, including sound, to respond to it. Our folks could listen to things in lower volume and be just as touched. When you are willing as a listener to respond to that stimulus, to give of yourself, you're really appreciating it. You're giving it your focus and attention. Whereas kids, they've got so many distractions that they can't focus, and they just blow themselves away with the volume and these big bass speakers you hear. I think they're not really giving themselves to it, and they have to be overstimulated.

Janis Ian - The act of making something out of nothing.

John Jarrard - The degree to which we are creative is the degree to which we can open ourselves up and let it flow through us. "It" being the wisdom, joy and love, the spirit of which the universe is made. I don't think this is about us. I don't think this is about how smart we are and how much good stuff we can think up. I'm not smart enough to do that.

Al Kasha - That's a hard one because it's so personal, but I think a definition for creativity is seeing the truth and then communicating back to the audience the truth they already know. To me that's the definition of being an artist.

Mary Ann Kennedy - I guess it would be stepping aside and letting something flow through. Being the channel. Allowing the energy to come through and then knowing enough when to grab it and run with it.

Sandy Knox - I'd say freedom. People are creative in so many different ways. I mean, you can have a great accountant who can be really great at creating a math system or juggling the books for that matter. My mother and my father aren't musical in any sense, but my father is a silversmith and a goldsmith and a furniture maker, so he's creative with his hands. My mother can't sing but she can sew and paint and draw. I'm creative with words and music and my voice, but I couldn't draw a four dimensional box if I tried. So, creativity, I think, is just freedom.

Kostas - It's something that is all around us. We're just doing what comes naturally. It's a labor of love. I think that through your senses, through your being here as a human being, you absorb what's all around you, and it goes and touches your psyche. What goes in must come out. It comes out through everybody in a different way, because God has given everybody different abilities and different talents and different loves. For some, they become woodworkers, some become mechanics, some work with horses, some work with fields and raising crops, and some work with music. For those who work with music, they hear the music in their head, they see it all around them. Life itself is music. It goes through different stages. It may be a blue sky and a funny-shaped cloud, but when you use that blue sky and funny-shaped cloud in a song, or in a certain pattern of notes, then it becomes music. So it's like food: you eat it, but before you eat it, it's a different form; but then after you eat it, it becomes energy. The same thing is true with life. Your senses absorb all that is around you, and then it comes out in the form of music and words.

Jess Leary - Creativity is working and living your passions, whatever they may be.

Jim McBride - To me it's emotion. It starts inside and then it turns into something that you do with your hands or whatever you do. It ends up being a work of art that wasn't there before, or it's something different. That's what's so cool about writing songs. Before I start, I look at that blank page, and I wonder what's going to be on here. You go back later and there's this song. You watch it evolve. That song wasn't there before. I love starting with a new notebook and there's nothing on any page, and a few months later, you go back and look and go, "wow." You can watch it being born.

Pam Rose - Life force and spirit. I think they're all kind of the same thing. I really believe that everyone is creative. I just happen to write songs, but if I didn't write songs, I'd be creative some other way. I think it's just the way people choose to express that life force or that spirit. Or their soul energy or their creativity or love.

Joyce Rouse - I think it's honoring the emergence of any artistic endeavor, be it movement or something visual or spoken. But at the center of it is a real pure emotion.

Wayne Tester - Being a channel to the gift God has given you, which is music.

Trisha Walker - Whatever your art is, trying to present a unique expression of who you are, in the medium which you're gifted. Preferably with as much freedom as is allowed you, and hopefully that's unlimited freedom.

Kate Wallace - I think the greatest gift given to us all is the concept of creativity.

Kim Williams - I think it's wrestling that's got the term: no-holds-barred. That to me is being creative. When you sit down and you don't make a bunch of rules about what you're going to write. That's creative. We all sit down sometimes and say, "What will work?" And when we start thinking that way, there are certain parameters that immediately fly up and that you're not going to pass. But to me, if you really want an original song, don't worry about anything. Because if you go with a no-holds-barred attitude, you're probably going to do something different, and eventually somebody is going to recognize it. And when it does get cut, it'll be a great song. I like any song that gets people all torn up. If it doesn't turn anybody's head, it definitely is mundane. It's just average, the same old, same old.

2. Do you have a writing room or special place where you feel the creativity flows more easily?

Kent Blazy - Yeah, I think it is very important that you have some place that you can go to work and be left alone.

Rory Bourke - I have a writing room that's my office, down on Sixteenth Avenue. My friend Charlie Black and I share an upstairs of a house. He's got his room, and I've got mine and we've got a kitchen and a lounge. That's where I go every day.

Gary Burr - No. It really doesn't matter. Both scenarios have something going for them. There's something nice in my little office here where I have my little demo recording set up and I've got my guitars hanging on the wall. It's very comforting and I'm used to it and it's familiar. But there's something always to be said for going out into a new environment; that always sparks something. It doesn't matter. If your antenna's going to be up, antennae go up above roofs.

Kim Copeland - At the moment, I don't have a writing room. I would love to have a room set up just for writing, but I just don't have the space now. That would be a luxury, but it's not a necessity for me.

Gary Earl - Anywhere with a great big huge window and a nice view. Doesn't make any difference whether it's a city view or a pastoral view. Somewhere to look out the window and let my eyes go out of focus.

Robin Earl - A lot of times when I'm in the car and I'm hearing a song, I'll get ideas for another set of lyrics to the same rhythm and feel. Sometimes I pull over and write ideas down. I've had times when I've stopped the car to write down bits and pieces several times before I've gotten to where I'm going.

Kye Fleming - It is just the ultimate for me to have no sound. That's the ultimate for writing. You deal with what you've got and I always have, but that's my ultimate.

Lindy Gravelle - Yeah. Where my grand piano sits. This house is just cool. It's an old cabin. It has a lot of light and it shadows just right. I know I'm very light sensitive and that has some effect on the brain. That plays a big part in how I feel when I'm writing.

Al Kasha - Many times I go outside to write. I'll go out to the park and write because I think you need a certain amount of quiet and solitude. The other thing I'll do to keep my energy level up is (this is going to sound like a contradiction) I'll play quietly in the background some other music that excites me. It's very, very subtle, but just the energy of it translates when I'm writing at my home.

Mary Ann Kennedy - I did in my other house, and when I'd write at Pam's [Rose], we wrote around the kitchen table even though she had a studio. I am not a tech-head, but I consider myself a developing producer. I don't like to write with a whole lot of gear. To me, that becomes distracting. Less is usually more for me. I think I like the purity. Plus, it clutters up my brain I don't want to be thinking about pushing a button. I usually end up using a little tape recorder and whatever instrument I have in my hands or a keyboard. As far as a room, it really depends. Usually it is around my music room so that I have all those acoustic instruments.

Sandy Knox - No, I've never had a certain place that was my place where I went to work. A lot of times, like I said, it's the car or sitting in the tub or whatever. I do have an office in my house, but it's strictly for my office computer and fax machine. I haven't been in the house long enough to use it for writing. I've never gone up there to work.

I just did a duet with Neil Diamond called *Like You Do.* I was lying in the sun and got the idea while I was lying there. I got my notebook and started working. No, I don't have one certain place where I go. I know some writers do. I know writers who have one certain room in their house that has white walls and one chair. That would make me nuts. I'd rather have texture and things in the room that would spawn thoughts.

Jess Leary - Actually, it's right here. I've tried to write at home but I'm very distracted at my house. My animals distract me. I love them dearly, but they're just too cute. I can't work with them around. And then my phone distracts me and my dishes distract me, and there's always those bills that have to be paid. I have to get out of there. Even though I'm very comfortable there, there's always something else that I can find to do. I like to come in here at least three times a week and sit myself down, drink some tea and look out this window, and just see what comes in. A lot of times I'll meet a co-writer here, and we'll just sit and talk and see what's up.

Trisha Walker - I tried that. I do have a room out at my house, which is a really neat room. It gets a little bit too hot in the summer because it's not air conditioned, so usually that's the one season I don't work there. I can work pretty much anywhere if I feel like I'm by myself. It's hard for me if there's anybody else in my house or anybody else in my office. I'm still a little bit inhibited. But if I know that everybody else is gone, and it's just me, and I can really get crazy, that's better. So just about anyplace works if I feel like I'm isolated.

Marijohn Wilkin - Oh, yeah. I write in my front room.

3. Are specific activities such as driving, showering, or mowing the lawn catalysts for creativity?

Kent Blazy - It's funny, but even manual labor, like working in the garden or planting a tree, will bring my subconscious out. Song ideas will just start coming or a melody or a hook. It's like what driving does. You're concentrating on it, but still it doesn't take all your concentration, so I think your subconscious starts knocking then. I'll come in and sing something into my cassette recorder, and I'll keep musical ideas or hook and music ideas on tape.

Gary Burr - I wrote the first song I ever wrote mowing the lawn, so there is something to be said about that. I know a lot of people who have written songs mowing the lawn. There's something about that motor going.

You never know when creativity is going to hit you, whether it's in the shower or whatever. You never know when a line is going to strike. You just have to be open for it. After a while, if you get to the point where you've really got the mechanics of this down, then you don't really need to be naked and lathered. You can just do it sitting here in your office with a guitar in your lap. If it hits me, like I said, I don't insult the muse by not paying attention to it and just saying, "I'll remember it." I always try to write it down. I'm not the most disciplined guy in that respect. I've lost a lot of scraps of paper with good ideas. But you have to have a sort of Zen philosophy about it. If it was really meant to be written by you, you'll remember it again, or you would have kept the piece of paper.

Jill Colucci - Driving in the car I get a lot of ideas. I didn't used to write in the car. This is new in the last three or four years. Just taking the mind off of focusing on the melody.

I've gotten many ideas on my walks. I run them over and over till I get back because I don't carry anything with me on my walks. A lot of people are into "you have to suffer, you know, suffering is a part of creativity." I believed that for a long time. A lot of it was because it was true in my life. In fact, I remember in L.A. once, something had happened and I was really distraught and upset, and I was crying. And as I was crying, I was in this emotional uproar. I don't have a clue what it was about now, but this melody came pouring through my head. It's really distracting when you're trying to have a good cry, and here's this song pouring through you and you have to stop crying if you don't want to lose it. That's happened to me so many times. But I've written a lot of songs from joy too. I've never really thought about this till now, but the *extreme* is powerful. It's interesting that I find those two extremes very creative. But it's in the middle too. I pull out a guitar at night when I'm tired, and I can create then. So it comes from all places, but I don't believe in the suffering aspect being a necessity anymore. I'll take a song however it comes.

Kim Copeland - I think you're just listening to yourself more. Less interference. For me, it's not thinking. There's this daydream level that you get into. And if you're driving by yourself, it's okay to sing something that may sound really bad. It's a freeing time because you don't have to concentrate.

Kye Fleming - For me, it's whatever opens me up to that unconscious a little more. Whatever takes me back to that childlike state. That state of having no cares, no worries—whatever, whether it is driving along in a car or just being kind of zoned. That place keeps me from having the editor sitting on my shoulder, and then things can just kind of pop in and out. You pick them up or you don't.

Al Kasha - There's a kind of focus that you get to, kind of a meditative place, when you're in a shower. In fact, one time when I was writing a song in the shower, and I couldn't finish the song, my wife was concerned because I was in there for almost an hour. I just couldn't get out of the shower until the song was done. I felt almost superstitious. I felt that I would lose the concentration or the focus of centering myself in that meditative state. I think when you write a song, you are in some spiritual state. With all the hits I've had, sometimes I still look at them and say, "Gee, who wrote that song?" I don't know who wrote it. My name is on it. I'm the writer of it, but it was from some meditative state beyond me. You put a lot of information in yourself, and then suddenly two days later it comes rolling out.

Sandy Knox - I think it's what you're doing every day, mindless things that you don't give a whole lot of thought to. You don't concentrate when you're taking a shower. You're not concentrating on that scrubbing pattern that you're doing. Same thing when you're washing dishes or driving. It's very automatic stuff, which I think allows your mind to get freed up and thoughts to start moving.

Jess Leary - I'm usually not consciously thinking about songs. Probably trying not to. If I'm mowing my yard (I love to mow the yard), I don't want to be thinking about a song at that point. You've got to have life. You've got to have space in there. Yeah, I'm not thinking about songs. Weekends are sacred.

Jim McBride - Yeah, riding in the car is one of the best. Especially on long trips.

We bought this house about a year ago. A riding lawn mower came with the house. I should get out and ride around on that thing more. I was telling somebody else about that, and they said that had also happened to them. Working outdoors is good for me.

Pam Rose - All of the above. I got the beginnings of *Love Like This* on the lawn mower mowing this yard. I don't mow it anymore, but I've thought about doing it again because I came up with some of the best things then. Now I just get in the car and drive.

Wayne Tester - It's not necessarily a creative time, although a lot of creativity can come out of those moments, because you're not necessarily searching. You're busy doing something else. Sometimes those ideas pop into your head that way.

4. Are you aware of the cycles of creativity?

Pam Belford - Yeah. Plus my own life. Sometimes I get so busy. The last year or two, until very recently, I was so caught up in trying to go, go, go and trying to write every free moment. Saying yes to co-writers when I should have said no. I had no time for myself. I kept feeling like I was disappointing everybody, every co-writer and myself. I wasn't writing anything good. It was only recently when I just said, "Forget it, I'm going to take a few weeks off and not write or anything." That's when I got this energy back. That was the best thing that's ever happened to me.

Kent Blazy - I feel that, and I've gotten more aware of it. Maybe it has to do with getting older too. I hit spells where I feel that the well needs to be filled up again. What I'll usually do is cut way back in my writing schedule and just get with people I know I have to get with, or people that really inspire me. I'll take a month or two months and go out and buy books and try to read or listen to music, or even go back through the old books and the old tapes and try to find things that I feel like I want to write. Just bring that water back up in the well.

Gary Burr - I think I would feel it more if I was back writing by myself all the time. I think I would really feel that ebb and flow. With collaborators, if you're in what would be considered a well if you were writing by yourself, you've got someone else in the room to throw you a rope and pull you out. And sometimes their creativity is infectious and helps spur your creativity. So, I don't worry about things like that. It's sitting with a guitar making up a story. I see the ebb and flow when there are periods of time where what I write is good and periods of time where what I write can be great. I have a respect for *that* ebb and flow. I would like to be in a period where everything I write is great, but that comes and goes. The antenna goes up for a while, and then it comes down for a while. You never know when it's going to be up or down. I can always write a song. If the antenna's up, it will be a great song. If the antenna's not up, it will be a song. MCA has closets and closets full of songs, and they've got a little tiny shelf of my antenna songs. Those are the really good ones.

Jill Colucci - To figure out the cycle is kind of like hindsight to me. It's not like I see the cycles coming. I definitely feel that it's cyclical. And that makes sense. If you're going to the well, you have to replenish the well. You have to have time for each. It also has to do with stresses and what's going on in your life. Just a natural rhythm like the four seasons. You couldn't just be on an output of creativity all the time. You have to have a wintertime when you're more introverted.

Kim Copeland - When you learn to recognize the cycles, then you can learn to appreciate them and use them to your advantage. You learn not to panic when creativity is low and to know that the well is just refilling. And you can really enjoy the times when it's high without any fear of what will happen when it takes a rest. That's when you're at a place where you know you're doing what you need to do, when you can appreciate the cycles and understand the process of what you're trying to do.

Al Kasha - There's a time that you have to get away, and that's why I listen to other writers. I will listen to a potpourri of different writers to get different influences. Otherwise you sort of burn out. You need to go on a retreat for a week or maybe a few days of not writing at all. If I were to sum up writing, I'd call it three-quarters thinking and one-quarter writing. I really think it's three-quarters thinking about the song, and then the song should pretty much write itself.

Mary Ann Kennedy - Absolutely. It's very cyclic. That's why you should never believe that you won't write another one or that it won't happen again. It will come again. Don't push it if it's not there, and get your head right. Meditate. Get on the horse. Have some fun. Breathe, jog, exercise. Do whatever you do to feel those life forces and that juice flow. It will come again.

Sandy Knox - I'm normally pretty aware. I'm also aware that they come back, so I've stopped worrying about them. I normally just allow myself to read and watch movies and shop and just kind of shut down from all of that. I call it rejuvenating. I'm on down time right now. I think all writers go through them. You can't tell me that there are writers out there who are writing every damn day of their lives. There comes a time when we're just burnt. Don't forget, songwriting is very emotional work. I get really caught up in songwriting. A lot of things surface. Especially if you're writing love songs or he-left-me songs. It really can drain you. *She Thinks His Name Was John* was a really scary song to write. It was a big slap in the face of reality. You sit there and think, it could have been anybody. It could have been me. It could have been a lot of women that I knew. It was a very scary song because I had to take a really good, hard look at myself.

Jim McBride - Absolutely. There are times when I'm just on a tear, and I'm thinking that I can't believe that I've had this many songs in the last few weeks and I love every one of them. Then all of a sudden it's like, that's it. So that's when I get out of town and go somewhere. Or I want to read some books or watch old movies. And thank God, it's always come back for me.

Wayne Tester - There are certain cycles. Sometimes you do have to empty it and let it build back up. Sometimes it overlaps. You can empty it a little bit and then you get recharged. There are no rules to me. If you had a recipe for it, then everybody in the world would be a songwriter. There are certain mysteries to this that are undefinable. You just can't figure it out, and that's part of the beauty of it.

Trisha Walker - For me, it is cyclical. I know a lot of writers in town who get up and go do it every day, but I don't think that anybody's consistently creative on a high-quality level.

5. Talk about the role of your subconscious mind in songwriting.

Tony Arata - I don't know how in the world you can tap into what you have in the back of your mind. I don't know that you can be creative on demand either. It's like being funny on demand. Telling somebody, "Okay, make me laugh." It doesn't always work like that. I don't have many good thoughts at all, or many great ideas. They are very, very few and far between, so I would spend an unnatural amount of time worrying about not being creative if I let that get to me.

I think anybody who writes is always writing whether they have a pen in their hand or a guitar or sitting at a piano. I think there's some part of you that's always working on something. The creative process is spawned most of all by being around creative people. And nothing will stir up the creative process like hearing a great song.

Pam Belford - I've never really explored that. I'm sure that it plays a big part.

Kent Blazy - I would say it's the most important part. I've been amazed at the times that I can go out with just a hook and walk the dog and come back with a song, just because I've let my subconscious work on it. Or if you're stuck on an idea, and you go out and drive around or go out to Radnor Lake, the idea will be working even if you're not aware that you're thinking about it. I really try to keep in tune with the subconscious. I try to bring it out as much as I can, and I try to be aware of when it's tapping on my brain saying, "Let me out." There are times when a song idea will start coming to you, but you get distracted. There was a long period of time when I would let myself get diverted, but now I've got this thing going, and something else is going to have to wait. I've learned that you can't take that subconscious gift that's coming along for granted. At the time that it's decided that it wants to be there, you have to open up and let it out.

Steve Bogard - My goal is to be as close to it as possible. To tap into it as much as possible. To let the inner guy kind of come on out.

Gary Burr - I don't know that it plays much of a role at all, other than songwriters who work out their angst in their lyrics without even knowing it. It's all I can do to stay conscious, much less deal with my subconscious.

Kim Carnes - When songs or ideas just come flowing through, it's got to play a huge part. It's not a conscious thing really. A lot of times over the years, I've found myself saying, "Where did that come from?" It still amazes me when a certain line or idea pops into my head. I still wonder, how did that get in there, where did it come from? As a writer, you just pray, every time you finish a song, that that will keep happening. Day-to-day things that don't have to do with music take me very far away from the place I want to be for writing. So the goal is to get rid of those. I think that if you're a male writer, you have a big edge over a woman writer who is married and has kids. If I get up in the morning and have to go to the market and the cleaners, there's no way I'm going to write. For me it just isn't there.

Debi Cochran - That's the magic part. That's the wonderful thing. I think people should figure out ways to tap into that more. Little things like reviewing whatever song you're working on right before you fall asleep and hoping that something in your dream will help fix it. When you get your hands busy with something and your creative mind takes over, and your eyes glaze over, things are sort of automatic. There's a lot of songwriting that comes from the subconscious and not from just sitting down and trying to make it happen.

Jill Colucci - Boy, I think that's really important. Sometimes I'll be working with a writer, and we'll keep kind of beating at it. You've been working four or five hours and you're brain dead anyway. So what I like to do, instead of keep beating at it, is to just leave it. And even if you go back to it the next day, I feel that during that overnight sleep, during even your waking hours away from it, you're doing incredible subconscious work on that song. By letting it go and doing that, you come back to it and you're just right there. You're more there than when you left it. So, I really try to remember the subconscious part. I think it's very important. That's another reason I'm writing a little bit at a different pace. The way I was writing, I hardly had any time for subconscious work. I think it's super important.

Kim Copeland - I've just recently learned how big a part it plays. I didn't give it enough credit before. It's a wonderful tool, once you appreciate it and learn to use it. For me, it's very important. Sometimes I can throw a crumb of an idea back there and at the end of the day, without having consciously worked on it, have the whole story come into focus. Then I can sit down and write it.

Gary Earl - That's one reason I like to write at four or five a.m. At that point, there's more of a steady stream of consciousness that comes out. I feel like that's when my best ideas come. Then when I get a little more awake, I let the analytical side tie up loose ends.

Robin Earl - That's when ideas pop into my head from out of nowhere. I've awakened before with a line running through my head, and it was a line I needed to finish a song.

Kye Fleming - What I'm after is that open channel, and that's also giving voice to the unconscious. I find that I'm doing really well to get a grain of salt occasionally. Just a flicker of the unconscious is all I hope for. I don't think it takes that much to connect with the collective unconscious, yet we're so surprised and pleased when we do. Obviously, those people who can connect to a larger extent than a speck here and there are the greats—the great writers, the great novelists, songwriters, poets, artists.

Lindy Gravelle - It trickles down into your gut. It's like when people say, "What do you feel in your gut?" Maybe that's your subconscious. It's such a phenomenal thing to me, what can pop into my head. And I'm assuming that must come out of the subconscious, or that it's the muse dropping a great thing on me. It's that thing, too, about looking at a hook that you've had for months and seeing it differently. The subconscious must have been working on it. It sure is a necessary part of the whole process. And you're not even aware of it.

(IS THERE ANYTHING YOU DO TO ENCOURAGE IT?) I like to reduce all the stimulus. Unplug the phone, get rid of distractions. Maybe that's a little too much to expect, especially if you're working in an office building where there are other writers next door. But the ideal way to allow that to happen to me is just to get down to a meditative state about your music. Focus. (SONGWRITING IN THE SHOWER. WHAT DOES THAT MEAN TO YOU?) That's that time when you're feeling pretty good, you're relaxed and letting that subconscious kick in. You're letting those thoughts roll around. Water ... there's something about water, isn't there? There's a healing thing and a stimulating property about it. Maybe it's because we came from that. Our bodies are, ninety-eight percent water. Maybe we should all try co-writing in the shower.

Janis Ian - Tons. Every time I haven't written for a long time and I come back to it, I will spend about a month being really irritated with myself till I remember that it doesn't happen by magic. I do have to work. When you look back on it, it seems like magic, even to the writer. I look at something like *Some People's Lives* or *Seventeen;* it's magic to me too. It's only if I go back to my notes and I see the process that I remember that it was a three-month song. I think for me, and most of the writers I work with, the subconscious works more at what we call the back of our brains. You may spend an hour writing and four hours talking or having lunch, walking around the backyard when you get stuck. Somewhere your subconscious is working overtime while you're doing this other stuff to keep it distracted. In that sense it's really important. I feel like God gave me the gift and said, "You'll have to work for it."

John Jarrard - They say you use two or three percent of your brain. It's a big advantage if we can enlist the other ninety-eight percent to help us. I think the way you do that is just by opening up.

Al Kasha - I think it's very important. In the Bible it says, "Meditate day and night and you will prosper and have success." The subconscious mind is very important. Before you go to bed at night, think of a problem. During our dreams we solve our problems because it's quiet time. I think the subconscious mind can pull out things from our childhood that have to be expressed.

(DO YOU REMEMBER YOUR DREAMS?) Yes, I do. And I will get up in the middle of the night and actually write them down. It's hard, but if you can get yourself up, I think it's important to write down your dreams. That might be the very best song you'll ever write, because it comes from that honest place that you might be blocking. You can get away from that block by writing down the dream because that's when the subconscious mind takes over. Christians call the subconscious the Holy Spirit.

Mary Ann Kennedy - That's probably what I use more than the conscious. That's whatever comes through to bring those influences out that are in there. Pieces of things that you've soaked up forever, but especially the most recent stuff that has registered as cool or positive. A neat thing. A neat way to convey a feeling through a melody. I think it plays a big, big part for me.

Sandy Knox - We kind of touched on that with the sleep thing. Oh, I'm sure that it plays a great part. I also think writing can be very therapeutic. There are songs I look back on and I realize, you were sending yourself a message when you wrote that about that guy or that situation.

Kostas - It probably works, I'm sure. You know everything is connected to the subconscious, so the role it plays is the same role that night plays to day. I don't try to be too analytical. I'm more philosophical.

Jess Leary - There's a lot of stuff going on in the subconscious mind. I guess it's working. I guess that my head's usually in a song, just in general. If I'm doing something else, there is a little corner back there that's still working, I'm sure. I might not be aware of it, but I'm sure it is, because you can be sitting there and all of a sudden you'll go, God, why am I thinking of that? Where did that come from?

Jim McBride - Curly [Putnam] told me a long time ago, "This job is twenty-four hours a day," and now I know what he means. I go to bed thinking about it, I wake up thinking about it, and I probably dream about it. I think that my subconscious must be working all night. It doesn't sleep much. I'll wake up in the morning and it's just amazing. I'm almost afraid to move. I've got all this stuff and it's just been waiting for me to wake up. I'm afraid if I move, I'm going to lose it. I try to say it over and over to myself, until I can get up and write it down. It's like the subconscious is waiting for me to wake up, so it can tell me all that stuff.

Wayland Patton - The subconscious mind is very important in what I do. I have some sort of a mechanism that picks up what people say. It's some sort of thing that goes off and says, "Write a song about that." It's how I express myself. The subconscious mind is always working, and having my conscious mind doing tasks helps me get away. It allows my subconscious to work on it. So maybe creativity has something to do with being able to allow your mind to go wherever it wants to go. Not being afraid to follow it, to go with it, regardless of outside influences. Just being able to allow your mind to dream. I dream in songs; that's how I express myself. That's how I'm able to understand how I feel about things. It's saved me thousands of dollars of therapy. I think there's something about letting your mind go. Being truthful to yourself, being honest. I never try to write with an artist in mind. I try to write hearing my own voice. I think it's important to have rules. You need to understand the craft of songwriting, but once you understand that, then you can break those rules and go wherever. Being unafraid to write what you feel, the inner voice that you hear.

A great example of that would be an artist. I always think of Vincent Van Gogh. No one has ever painted that way. But that's what he saw. He only sold one painting in his life- time, but he kept going. That's what he had to do. Not many people follow in his style, but that's an imitation, isn't it? I'm sure that like everyone else, he had to like the technique, he learned the brush stroke, he learned how to mix paint, the composition. Creativity would be taking all those things and making it something uniquely his own.

Pam Rose - I think it's a pretty powerful influence, because I feel like the conscious mind is purely the translator. The interpreter maybe. I don't believe the inspiration is a conscious thing. I believe it is a subconscious thing. What's conscious for me about the process is having the presence of mind to know what it is. Having the patience to grasp. Having the acumen to know what is what, what's a verse and what's a chorus, or what it means to say or to give it shape or definition. I use my mental faculties to maybe figure out which piece I am missing. The conscious mind just helps to get it out. It helps to manifest what's in the subconscious.

Joyce Rouse - I think that's one of the layers that creativity emerges from. And I know that to keep my pores open for the creativity, I need to stay open and listen to what's going on inside as much as I can. And to accept any messages my subconscious is sending me, like through dreams.

Wayne Tester - Well, if you say subconscious mind, I say it's your spirit. So, if we define it as the spirit, then that's where your inspiration comes from and your creativity.

Trisha Walker - I think [the subconscious counts for] a lot more than we give it credit for. I think that's one of the reasons I'm trying to move toward a more free writing style, is to try and really release the subconscious. There's so much that goes on underneath the surface that we don't ever tap. Either we're afraid to, or as we've grown into adults, we've lost that innocent piece of childhood. It takes a lot of courage, I think, to dig down into that subconscious.

6. What about dreams?

Tony Arata - I think that maybe when you're dreaming and in touch with some other part of your brain that you can't get to when you're awake, something is being figured out. And in the light of day, without your realizing it, it will come out. But I've never really woken up in the middle of the night and furiously written something down.

Pam Belford - They don't really help. I've never woken up and tried to write down what I dream. Usually it strikes me in the middle of the day.

Kent Blazy - I'm not much on dreams. I don't usually remember them, and I've never worked on trying to keep a pad by my bed so I can write dreams down when I wake up. When I get up in the morning, I usually "get up." I'll get up and take care of the dogs and then I'll go meditate. So whatever dreams are hanging around, unless they're really strong, they'll be gone. I'll get back in the subconscious through meditation.

Steve Bogard - I don't really use dreams. I know people do, but I don't need them.

Kim Carnes - I've never dreamed songs. When a song is, for lack of a better word, channeled through, it's like that. It's like a dream.

Debi Cochran -Yes, I do [use dreams]. There's a wonderful story: the guy who wrote *Sweet Home Alabama* dreamed the entire song. I don't know him personally, but he said he woke up and he had the entire song, the lyrics and everything. The guitar riff too, which is in a different key from the rest of the song. He had to argue with the producer that it had to be that way. I dream about songs that I'm working on, and sometimes wake up with a brand-new idea

Jill Colucci - No, I haven't. My friend Chapin Hartford did with *Shake the Sugar Tree*. I dream, but I don't remember them much. But for me, it's that time right before I go to sleep or sometimes first thing in the morning. It's in that unaware, unawake state.

Kim Copeland - I don't remember dreams per se where I wake up and remember having dreamed the vivid scene, but I do have dreams where I'll wake up and have a whole song ready to be written. I don't remember them like a movie or see myself writing them or anything like that. I just wake up in the morning with a knowing that there is a song to be written and, when I sit down with pen and paper, it pours out.

I've just learned in the past year or so to use my sleeping time to write. If I have an idea, I try to think about it just before I drift off to sleep and ask myself some questions. Where is this story going? What does this character want to say? Then I go to sleep without consciously trying to think about it and when I wake up in the morning, it will be very clear to me. Sometimes I'll wake up with exact lines. I can write them down in order and they rhyme and are there. Other times, I'll wake up with the story. It's a neat thing. It doesn't work one hundred percent of the time, but sometimes when it doesn't work, I'll wake up knowing that that particular idea doesn't need to be written. I can't package this method of dream writing. I'm still exploring it. But it's great when it happens.

I'm very good at problem solving in my dreams too. If I go to bed with something on my mind that I'm feeling overwhelmed or confused about, I can go through the same process and when I wake up the next morning, it's all in focus and I know exactly what I need to do about it. It gives new meaning to the phrase "sleep on it."

Lindy Gravelle - I don't think I've utilized the dream thing for my creativity.

Mary Ann Kennedy - Generally, I do create more in my dreams when I'm not creating really satisfying stuff in my conscious. However, sometimes if I am doing well and writing neat songs and they're almost done, it drives me crazy because I can't sleep well. I'm trying to finish the song in my dreams. I don't like that.

Kostas - I don't remember them too much, but once in a while there will be melodies and something said in a dream. It goes back to that subconscious thing you were talking about. There have been songs and ideas that were born in dreams. That may happen four to six times a year. I take them when they come.

Pam Rose - I also have a tape recorder by my bed. Unfortunately, there's somebody in there who, during my dreams, tells me I've already woken up and put it down on tape. That's happened so many times.

I think they're all connected. I think dreams are really just the rumbling of the subconscious, and I think I'm even more affected by my dreams than I could possibly even mention.

Joyce Rouse - I don't think I use them for song ideas, but what I use them for is my own growth, spiritually and emotionally. That can only help what I'm doing creatively.

Wayne Tester - I have dreams that might be an inspiration every once in a while, but not necessarily.

Trisha Walker - I don't know that they've ever had a direct effect. I don't seem to dream a lot. If I do, I don't remember a lot of dreams.

Kim Williams - I can't ever remember writing a song from a dream, but I do believe in them. I have had things pop into my mind, solutions to songs and stuff that just came out of nowhere. I've actually always believed that you solve those in your dreams. I've woken up and songs almost totally come out, and I believe that they're written in your sleep. Somehow or the other, we're working on songs all the time. Not just in dreams. I know songs come out of nowhere, and I don't think they happen instantaneously. I've had verses and choruses just fall right out on top of me. I think they were already written when I sat down.

7. Have you ever experienced a period when the flow of your creativity seemed endless?

Tony Arata - No. I wish I could say yes, but I think there are times when, very definitely, it comes easier. You're working on several ideas at a time, and all the ideas seem to make sense and you can see where they're going. You can tell what the song's going to be about, and you already have it kind of mapped out. That makes it seem like you're a bit more creative, just because you have a guide to go by. For a short span of time it seems like you're being overly creative. But what is really happening is that ideas are allowed to take root. You're able to nurture them over a period of time and they come together and then you put them all down in a matter of a week. It may seem like a very quick process but, at least for me, it's always been something that I've been working on for a while.

Pam Belford - No. Never.

Steve Bogard - Yeah, I'm in one right now. It's really spooky. I can't stop.

Gary Burr - I never feel like it's never going to stop. I never take for granted that I'll even be able to do it tomorrow. I think I'll be fine. I've never really had a block, because I think where you get a block is if you think that everything you write has to be great. I'm too fond of the goofy stuff that I write to ever have to worry about that. I can always sit down and write something about some guy picking his nose. That's no problem.

But there are times when you feel like you can write through a brick wall. When I went to the songwriting retreat at Miles Copeland's castle in France last spring, I was there for two weeks writing every day and sometimes at night. And if I wasn't writing, I was in the studio recording what I wrote or helping someone else record what they wrote. By about five days in, I couldn't *not* write. By about the fifth day, I was like a big Roman candle of creativity. Just so hot I was on fire with it. It was amazing. So was everyone else who was there. That was an amazing feeling.

(WHAT DO YOU THINK HAPPENED?) It's a muscle, and the more you use it, the stronger the muscle is. The more golf balls you hit, the easier it is to hit them well. That's all it is.

Kim Carnes - Those are my favorite times—when I just can't write enough songs. But it can't always be like that. There's no way. No matter what you try to do, until it's time again, I can never force it. I've learned that. Again, there are things that take away from it. If I've just finished an album, there's no way I can start writing again. So much energy and focus has been spent on that album, writing for it and the preparation. If I'm on the road touring, I can't write.

Debi Cochran - Yeah. When I was writing with those three other people in Decatur, we were on a roll and we just cranked out the songs.

Kim Copeland - It's great. It doesn't happen often enough, but it's great. I've had rolls where two or three or four or five songs would come out back-to-back. I would just write them as fast as I could, without really taking the time to think about them or appreciate them until later. I was too caught up in the moment writing them. And at the same time, I may have great ideas for other areas of my life and solutions for problems just come to me. I've got all the answers! Of course, it always passes.

Gary Earl - Yeah, I've had a few of those periods. It usually seems to be when I'm feeling more physically energetic and healthy, and I've got a good mental attitude.

Robin Earl - Getting a lot of exercise is important to me. That's when I feel most energetic and most creative, or when I'm in a good mood and laughing nonstop.

Kye Fleming - No. I don't think [I've had endless creative periods]. For me, it kind of goes as life does. You've got some good days and then you go through a lull. The creative process is a similar process for me.

Lindy Gravelle - No, I always seem to have to turn it off, to go to the next appointment or whatever. I've heard about writers who'll go hole up in a cabin or a condo by the beach and write. I just heard a story that Vern Gosdin went and wrote twenty-nine songs in twelve days. It's because they isolate themselves from responsibilities. Yeah, I'd like to try that, but I've never been able to.

Janis Ian - Oh sure. What a great feeling. I firmly believe in keeping your motor oiled.

John Jarrard - Yeah, but I don't know what started it. There are times when it comes really easy and times when it won't.

Mary Ann Kennedy - Yeah. You're just the lucky one that it's coming through, for whatever reason. It's your time. Timing is everything, I believe. Just because you're having a great creative flow doesn't mean it will be accepted by the masses at that point in time, but boy, if you feel creative and it feels good to you, just go with it. Don't stop.

Sandy Knox - There are times when you've got so many ideas coming, you can't wait to write them all. I think sometimes it's there and it just flows. There are times when I'm highly creative and writing and singing, and also I'm getting lots of stuff done around the house, and deciding to change my hair and buy a bunch of new clothes. It's just there. And then there are times when I don't want to do my hair and I don't want to put on a bunch of makeup and I don't want to wear anything but tennis shoes.

Kostas - There are times. Whenever you find yourself alone and have the time to think, that's one situation. Another time is whenever you throw yourself into the midst of it. Sometimes I used to come down there [Nashville] and write for a month, day and night, by myself and with other people. Those are the two scenarios for that kind of flow. (DO YOU EVER FEEL LIKE YOU HAVE TO BACK OFF AND LET THE WELL FILL UP?) Yeah, you always have to do that, no matter what you do in life. You can get tired and get worn out; we all experience that. That's true in songwriting as well.

Jess Leary - Creativity means more than just writing songs, so yes [it can be nonstop], because I have other outlets for creativity. I like to paint. I like to sculpt my yard and I like to plant, so those are all creative things to me. I live for creativity. I live in it. And when I'm feeling un-creative, it's okay. There are so many times when I am [creative], that it's okay if I'm on a flat line for a while. I just go to the movies or watch TV.

Joyce Rouse - That happened with this album project, which is why I have ten more songs ready for a second album. I just got going, which was, to me, the sign that this is what I'm supposed to be doing. Because not only was the creativity there, but all these doors opened busi-ness-wise. Contrary to everything else that was going on, the pathway was opened, and that's when you know that this is what you're supposed to be doing.

Wayne Tester - Those are the times that you wish would come more often. Those are the times when you really need to take advantage of your creativity. The up cycle. You work as hard as you can in that cy-cle.

Trisha Walker - Yeah. I don't know how long it lasted, but it does seem to a lot of times, come in spurts. I heard Kevin Welch say that he thinks of it in terms of input and output. During those times when he's not writing, he considers himself on input. You're just storing up, looking at things, reading things, thinking about things. Then all of a sudden when it's time to be on output, you go. I can't say necessarily what accounted for those times of the endless stream, but the input-output thing seemed to fit pretty well.

8. Someone once told me that if he feels uncreative in the morning, he goes fishing. What do you do?

Steve Bogard - If I don't feel like it's happening writing-wise, I blow it off in another business way. I'll pitch some songs. I'll go look at guitars. Stuff like that. I keep it going by coming in. I miss the office when I don't come in. I'm really happier working than not.

Rory Bourke - Every morning I go kicking and screaming into work. It's hard and there's a part of me that can feel the tension and resistance to having to put it on the line.

Debi Cochran - I go from one extreme to the other. Some days I feel like just laying around the house and watching soap operas. But also I have a wonderful backyard here in Nashville, so I can take the cat and the dog and a book and just totally remove myself from any thought of songwriting. I go read a good book sitting out in that big backyard in the sunshine.

Jill Colucci - Just a change of environment is the key for me. I think just taking the focus off what we were doing is more important than we know. That's the benefit. I don't even think it's important *what* we do, maybe it's just cooking. It's changing the direction of the mind, so it's focused on something else. I think that's more important than what we do. It's releasing the pressure from it.

Kye Fleming - Those first six years or so, I went ahead and worked through it. I felt I would get something out of it, even if it wasn't a song. I would have at least oiled the wheel or whatever.

John Jarrard - I usually come on to the office. Most days I have a writing session set up with somebody. There are days that I call it off early, but that's, more often than not, in cases where I haven't taken care of myself in terms of getting enough rest, or if I over-schedule myself or something like that. But if I make writing a priority, more often than not, I'll be productive.

Al Kasha - Well, I'm a jogger, so I'll jog in the morning. Jogging is very good because when the body walks or exercises, it gets everything going and sort of clears things out. And you're alone at those times. I think that's very, very important.

Mary Ann Kennedy - Mostly, I listen to something that inspires me. If I put something on that I'm fed by, it inspires me to go for that energy within myself. I'll run out if I'm just trying to get it from myself. It's the same old stuff.

Sandy Knox - I can blow off the day beautifully. I'm a professional at blowing off the day. Renting movies. Getting lost in movies. Going to essential therapy is my favorite: getting a body soak like a seaweed wrap and a full body massage. It's a good way to kill a day. Paying people to rub seaweed on you, getting massaged. I'm really into that.

Jess Leary - Anything in nature. Either go for a ride if it's cold out, or just get out in it. I can't be in it enough.

Jim McBride - You might as well do something else. If you're not feeling creative, then you're probably not going to be creative. And you can force yourself to sit there with the guitar, but after two or three hours of nothing happening, that's too much for me. There are other things to be done. Go fishing or cut the grass. That's one good thing about working with your hands. You write a song today and you may never see the results, or it might be two years before you get a cut. But go and cut the grass, and you can see where you cut the grass. And yes, it'll grow back, but there's the satisfaction of having done something where you can see the immediate results.

Pam Rose - Usually I just blow it off if I can. If I can't do that, I'll figure out some way to do the best that I can that day. Sometimes I'll sit with my co-writer, be brain dead. That happens a lot in co-writing situations. When I'm writing by myself, I go to the mall, or go to a movie or something. But if I'm writing with my co-writer, there have been times where I'll call them up and say, "I'm just brain dead. I'm fried." And we'll go eat lunch, and we'll both sit there and be brain dead. Sometimes you'll think of your best stuff when you think you can't do it at all.

Wayne Tester - You have to be flexible enough to say if it's not happening, do something else. And there's a point where you just have to start handling it. Get some ideas out or work on some more technical aspects of the business. Make a few phone calls, this or that. So, yeah, you have to jockey all those things and juggle them around.

9. Do you meditate?

Tony Arata - No. I pray daily, but I don't really consider that a form of meditation. And when I do pray, it's certainly not for songs.

Pam Belford - No.

Kent Blazy - I do. I meditate twice a day. Back twenty years ago, some friends of mine were transcendental meditation teachers, and they seemed so serene. My lifestyle at the time was a very intense musician lifestyle, so I decided that maybe I needed to try that. I've been doing it ever since, pretty regularly. Usually twice a day, maybe sometimes once a day. I think that has a lot to do with freeing up your subconscious. There will be things that come to me in the middle of meditating, and sometimes I won't write them down because I'll be pretty deep into meditating. But there'll be other times that I'll get up and come in and put it on the tape recorder. Other times, when I may have problems in my life, or a song I'm stuck on, a clarity will come in that period when I'm meditating, and I think it's that subconscious taking over. It's really helped me a lot to do that.

Steve Bogard - Yeah, but not much. I use the alpha state right before I fall asleep and right before I wake up. I do ten or fifteen minutes of just letting the subconscious come to the surface, and that's worked very well for me, in terms of ideas and things like that.

Rory Bourke - I have, but I don't now.

Gary Burr - No.

Kim Carnes - I've gone through times when I have, but I don't on a frequent basis. I don't have time.

Debi Cochran - No, I don't. That's one of the phases I went through, but I don't really meditate anymore. I think it's probably a good idea to do it; I just got out of the habit.

Jill Colucci - I don't do a specific meditation. Meditation for me is really just kind of my own thing. It's getting to a quiet part inside of me. I do other things as well. I've done yoga and many different spiritual things that enhance my writing. I use them for two things: one, to get in touch with my inner self on a deeper level than I might be at the time; and two, to get to the quiet. I need to turn off my mind. My mind is just always racing, whether it's with ideas or who knows. My mind goes a million miles an hour. That can get in my way. I try to turn that down, actually off, but certainly down, so that I can get to the heart and soul of that song. I kind of use it more to get to a quiet place, to the center of things, to start from there.

Kim Copeland - I do. I don't do guided meditations very often, but I meditate every day in my own way. I get to a meditative state every morning and spend time there.

Gary Earl - Yes. I feel that there's a benefit to songwriting and a benefit to the whole mental and physical health.

Robin Earl - Yes. It's important in helping me feel relaxed in general. I also take a yoga class, which I love. I really look forward to it; I've got a really good instructor. I try to spend some time every day at it. That's my time to unwind during the week.

Kye Fleming - I have [meditated], and I wish that I could say that I do regularly, because I think it's much more powerful than most people realize. I had much rather have my discipline in that area than in the writing area. I believe that if I were more disciplined in that area, I would be more creative, period. It's not just a belief; that's an absolute fact. It gets you in touch so that you don't eat the wrong things, so you don't bark at somebody. It levels out everything in your entire life.

Lindy Gravelle - Yeah. I need to get more disciplined about it though. I think that it's a wonderful thing not only for my creativity, but it spills into everything. Your health, your mental well-being. I live where I have to drive a lot, so I kind of meditate while I'm driving.

Al Kasha - Yes. I try to meditate. Some people meditate in the morning, but I meditate at night before going to bed. And, of course, I believe in God, so I pray every day. That's a form of meditating in the morning, but I'm meditating in a different sense. Meditating is more like thinking about things. Praying is a little different. In the morning, I guess, I talk, and at night I listen.

Mary Ann Kennedy - I don't think I do it in a structured way. I think when I'm taking my walks or grooming my horse, or I'm with nature, that's probably how I meditate. Sometimes I don't know when I need it until I've lost my temper or am jumping out of my skin or feel unsatisfied with myself or life. A phrase that my sister uses a lot is, "Go get grateful." I've found that if you get out there and think about how lucky you are, suddenly that just softens the edges and opens you up to receive even more.

Sandy Knox - Not consciously. When I say that, I mean I'm always thinking and pondering, but I don't like to sit down and burn incense. I'm a really deep thinker.

Kostas - Who has time? No, I watch other people and get the same effect. I think you have to find some way to release that energy. Recharge batteries.

Jess Leary - Definitely. I like to in the morning. I don't get to every day though. I go outside to where my little fish pond is, and the sun is shining there in the morning. I just spend about five or ten minutes and say some prayers and try to quiet my head. You just kind of open yourself up and let in the light. Amen. Feed the fish. Go to work. I kind of have a routine. I pray a lot anyway. Meditating is different, but it's also the same.

Jim McBride - No. Fishing is my way of meditating.

Pam Rose - I do. I'm just learning to meditate. I think I've meditated all my life, but I'm learning a new way to do it. I do t'ai chi; that's called "meditation in motion." I do t'ai chi every day, and I walk a mile every day, so that's not exactly meditating, but that's pretty close. I'm in a meditative state often. It's kind of mysterious because after I finish tai chi, I feel that kind of endorphin thing that you get when you run. My teacher has always said that t'ai chi is like aerobics in slow motion for the body. I do that for physical reasons because of the alignment of the organs and the body. It's hard to do too. It looks really easy, but your legs have to be pretty strong to do that for half an hour. It just slows me down and gives me time to just ponder. It gives me quiet time. I don't talk during that. And I don't talk while I'm walking, usually. I love quiet time. I love to just sit and receive.

Joyce Rouse - Yes. Not as regularly as I wish I could or did, but yeah, I do.

Wayne Tester - The way I define meditation is spending time in God's words and in the Bible and through prayer. That's my meditation.

Trisha Walker - Physically, I try to do a lot of things to stay in shape, and that seems to clear my mind. I pray. (DO YOU SET ASIDE TIME WHEN YOUR MIND CAN BE QUIETED IN ORDER TO LET THINGS COME

THROUGH?) On a daily basis, probably not. I can usually feel when my mind is so full that it requires a conscious effort for me to just stop and empty my brain. I probably do it more that way than I do on a daily basis.

Kim Williams - No, I can't be still that long.

10. If you ever find yourself in a rut, how do you shake things up?

Jill Colucci - I don't do anything about the craft of songwriting, but I do things to enhance my ability to be inspired as much as possible, and for me that's walking. I like brisk walking, or maybe even an aerobic thing to get that energy really going, and not smoking. I didn't realize it, but not having that cloud around me and that habit has just somehow opened my life more. I feel more healthy and I feel more tuned-in some-how. I can't really even explain it. For me, less alcohol, no cigarettes. Those kind of things, actually, are enhancing to my inspiration.

Kim Copeland - It helps me to put down the guitar. I write a lot of melodies without the guitar because if it is in my hands, then I'm limited by my playing ability. Most of the time, when I feel like I'm in a rut me-lodically, it's because I'm writing everything with a guitar. I feel like melody and lyrics are all married, and whatever I'm playing will dictate the flavor of the song.

Lyrically if I'm in a rut, I give myself assignments. I'll say, You have to write three songs without love being the theme. Then I say, Okay, it's just an exercise, so how silly a subject can I come up with? That gets my mind off of this other theme, and sometimes I can come up with some pretty good stuff. Then when you go back to the original subject, you're refreshed.

Lindy Gravelle - Get inspired. Then I think, You should go within. You should start this search into more of what you are, whatever that is. But I guess it's hard for me to figure that out too. Maybe it's the subconscious thing of being more observant of how you react to things, the feelings that you will feel and a lot of times are not even aware of. I keep thinking that I need to tune-in more to that part of me. I might find a whole treasure chest of things that I'm overlooking. Yet I'm always looking for a billboard or something that's just going to hit me. I've got to tell you something that happened. One morning on "Good Morning America", Joan Lunden was introducing this guest, and she was saying how this person did this and this and this, and it created success for them. She said one thing leads to another. And something in me said, My God, that's a hook. It ended up being one of my best songs. I just wrote it with Don Pfrimmer. One thing led to another, and the *another* turned out to be another's arms. Now, how many times have you heard, "One thing leads to another"? I thought, How many more of those are lying around? Songwriters, we're all exposed to the same stuff, and I can't tell you how many times I've heard a song title, and I say, "Well, I wrote that", or "I was going to write that". And you're thinking, don't bother now. We all like to think we know what's commercial. We all see the same thing or hear the same thing and all of a sudden there's a rash of songs with those hooks.

Kostas - It's like wearing the same kind of clothes every day. You just find new clothes. What comes in is what comes out. You're influenced by whatever is around you at the time. So if you're listening to one style of music, or one artist, get off of it; find somebody else. Something that is totally new and fresh, or totally old and forgotten, that you used to like. Their influence will direct you into a groove.

Pam Rose - Buy a new instrument. Buy a new toy. If I had to pick one thing, that would be it.

Wayne Tester - You go through that cycle too. You have to get away. You have to listen to some other kinds of music. That helps a lot. Listen to something totally different from what you're doing, and that helps.

11. Is there a certain time of day that you feel you write better?

Pam Belford - My best ideas and lines come to me when it's most inconvenient. Sometimes I do well on demand and sometimes I don't. One of the best times for me to write is when I come home at eleven-thirty at night from somewhere and have to wake up at seven. I go to bed, and as soon as my head hits the pillow, this line comes to me, and I get up and write it down. Or I'll be running late to work, and the lines will start coming to me. I'm trying to get dressed, and I have to keep stopping to write it down.

Kent Blazy - For most of my life I was a night person, playing in bands and all that. I would usually stay up till six in the morning then sleep till noon. But since coming to Nashville, and especially in the last few years, I've tried to make a point to get up earlier and earlier My Lab puppy is fifteen months old, and she wants to get up at six in the morning, so I've started doing that. To me the morning is pretty inspirational. I get up and walk her then come right back here and get into thinking about ideas and working on songs.

Steve Bogard - I'm better in the morning. I get a lot of ideas while I'm driving in the car on my way in and on my way out. I'm always jotting down ideas. Then I'll come in and prepare for a co-write. What I find is that the business part of it takes a toll. I can't go do that and then come back very well. The writing's the most important thing. The writing's what makes the other stuff even necessary.

I don't write past one or two o'clock. I work past that but do not write past that. I never ever write with someone on weekends. But if I get ideas ... We have a really big airy master bath that's open to the backyard, and I leave a pad and a tape recorder out in that master bath. There's a guitar sitting there in the bathroom. That's where I know I can go, and if I get an idea, write it down.

Rory Bourke - In the mornings. Mornings then up till about three o'clock. I'm not much good after three.

Gary Burr - I used to write more by myself, and that would come anytime. I used to not have much of a life, so sitting home at night in front of the TV writing songs was fine with me. Waking up at two in the morning with a song idea was fine with me. But I can do it from eleven to four. And now that I have a life and a fiancé and I'm happy, I pretty much try to channel it from eleven to four. If occasionally I bolt up in bed with a great idea, I'll jot it down and go back to sleep and work on it when I'm at work.

Debi Cochran - I tend to sort of burn out around three in the afternoon, although I often have a morning writing appointment and then one that begins at two. But I think I'm better in the morning. Also there are times sort of late at night, after everybody else has gone to bed, that are good for reflecting.

Jill Colucci - I like to start around elevenish. But if there's another writer who's really bent on ten, I don't have any problem with that. I'll just get up earlier so that I feel more ready by ten. This past winter, I was so busy that I was having a hard time finding time to write. I found myself doing paperwork and phone calls and stuff downstairs in my office all day, then I'd come up here in the great room at night and light a fire. I was so excited about moving into my house. My first winter here I'd light a fire and do some writing by myself. I finished some songs that I really liked. I don't think I could do that on a continuous basis, working left-brained all day and then work in the evening, but it was so great because it was cold out, and the phones didn't ring at night. It was extremely quiet.

I think I can write at any time. I'll take them any way they come and any time they come. If it comes at midnight, then I'll pick up the guitar. I've lost so many songs when I lay down at night and I'm just drifting. I'm at that point where I'm too far gone to get up, but I'm still not totally out. I'll get full choruses, lyrics, everything. I remember this happened to me a lot in L.A., and I would lay there thinking, I've got to sing it over ten times and I know I'll remember it by morning. I would sing it over and over until I fell asleep, and in the morning it was completely gone. So, after losing many, many ideas, I got a cassette recorder by my bed and a pen and a pad. That's one of my most creative times, when I'm in that relaxed state just before falling into a deep sleep.

It's so funny. I never know where or why. I think it was after Melissa Ethridge came out with *Bring Me Some Water*. I was riding in the car, and I was listening to pop music, and I heard that acoustic guitar. I got the title *No One Else on Earth*. I met her [Melissa] at Wynonna's concert, and I thanked her for her inspiration. I don't think she figured it out, but I tried to explain it and she said, "You know, it kind of sounds to me like you came up with that on your own."

Kim Copeland - Morning. That's when my mental and physical energy is at its peak, and I definitely write better when I'm rested. It's very hard for me to get into a creative mood when I'm tired.

Gary Earl - I like to write at about four or five in the morning when I'm still half asleep. No phones, no noise. Ideas seem to flow easily for me in early morning hours.

Robin Earl - I'm not an early morning person. I like to write in the midmorning or evening. The easiest times for me are evenings when I'm feeling relaxed, not overtired. Gary and I have lots of silly time when we laugh and talk together. Some good songs have come then.

Kye Fleming - I think it's more my frame of mind, because the inspiration itself can energize me.

Lindy Gravelle - I love twilight. I love it when the sun has set, and there is that soft shadowy kind of light. If I can be alone, in an environment where nobody's bothering me, that's primo. (HOW ARE MORNINGS FOR YOU?) My mind is probably fresher but my schedule isn't always conducive to working in the morning, especially if I have a gig the night before.

John Jarrard - I'm pretty much a morning person. My best time is way early. Four or five o'clock in the morning.

Al Kasha - I do discipline myself to get up early in the morning, and I try to take an hour every day for listening to someone who's not like me, so I don't get caught in the same chord progressions. I generally don't write much in the morning. I put a lot of notes down and a lot of titles that maybe come to mind by listening to other people's work, but I'm more of a nighttime person. Not that I haven't written at all times of the day, but it's quieter at night, and I think clearer at night.

Mary Ann Kennedy - Generally, I'm a night person. Mac McAnally said he just happened to be passing through town, or was the one who was awake one night at twelve-thirty, when a certain energy came down and poured this song out. He was the one who happened to be awake to catch it. It was some great song like *All These Years*. Just saying that title gives me chills. So, I feel like that sometimes too. Sometimes it just comes through, for whatever reason. It's just coming through and I happen to be the open channel. Most of the time that happens for me in the evening.

(DO YOU STRUCTURE YOUR DAY TO ALLOW FOR CO-WRITING?) There's that word: structure! No, I don't. It's so hard for me to commit to a structured, scheduled time, outside of the studio, which you have to do. Once I book that, I have to be there come hell or high water. So, I guess I have to be structured somewhat for studio stuff. The rest of it I just go with, and I've been lucky enough to be able to go with it when I really feel inspired. I've written a lot on the telephone. The last few years, I'm writing with someone who's doing more of the lyric, so I have the wonderful liberty of just doing the music when I feel inspired, and then giving them the work tape. We work back and forth on the song, scheduling very little time.

Sandy Knox - I used to think that I was more creative in the morning, but I don't think there's a set time. There were times when at three o'clock in the morning, I'd wake up with a song idea and write it. I used to think there was a higher energy at times, but now I just don't see that. I see it happen when it happens. There was a five-year period when I wrote most every day from ten till two. Then there was a period when I only wrote at night, when I got home from whatever. I'd start working at ten or eleven and write for an hour. I can get more done in an hour, writing-wise, than a lot of people can get done in a week. I'm quick at self-editing, and I don't dawdle once I get going.

Kostas - I write better when I'm forced to.

Jess Leary - Mornings. It used to be late night. When I was younger, I used to stay up all night. I didn't care what time it was, and I would just have a pen and paper or a guitar or both. I would drink some wine or something, and sleep late the next day. But it's all changed. It's all reversed. Now, I'm more of a morning person creatively and by midafternoon, I'm in my late afternoon thinking spell, and I kind of have to stop. Get out and move around. One thing I've found, too, is that when you're writing, you're so still. You're so stuck in your chair. Hours go by and you're just sitting. To have that motionless thing where your brain's racing, but your body's just sitting, I haven't figured out how to fix that yet.

You're so immobile, and sometimes it would be good to just take a little break and get up, but then you'll lose your train of thought. So, there are definitely things I can't figure out yet. How to make it better or easier. Maybe they're just not supposed to be. I mean, if it were easier, everybody would be doing it.

Jim McBride - I used to think I couldn't write unless it was late at night. Now I find that I work better in the morning. That's something that's changed over the last few years. I'll wake up in the morning and sometimes before I even move, ideas are there.

Pam Rose - When I have the business to contend with, I seem to respond to the creative early in the morning or late at night. But if I'm in Arizona or I'm in Florida, it doesn't matter. It really doesn't matter. Allen Shamblin said something that I don't think I'll ever forget. He said, "Writing is more a question of making yourself available." And I don't think anybody could say that better as far as I'm concerned. And so, whenever I'm able to make myself available, it's there.

Joyce Rouse - Mornings and evenings. Sometimes very late.

Wayne Tester - Just depends on the day. Sometimes I'll go in in the early evening when everybody's gone from the office and stay there a little later at night. A lot of times I'll get really creative then. But that's not necessarily the rule.

Kim Williams - I think early. I run on a treadmill for a couple of hours each morning, then I hit the office. It seems more creative, but I've written some really good songs at night too. When I first came to town, I was going about sixteen hours a day. The ideas, to me, are the most important part of writing.

Tony Arata - I think creativity is in taking those basic elements that already exist and making them into something.

Lindy Gravelle - It's a phenomenal thing to me, what can pop into my head.

Pam Belford - My best ideas and lines come to me when it's most inconvenient.

CHAPTER THREE

THE PROCESS

Steve Bogard - I'd rather be bad than mediocre.

Wayne Tester - Every day is a blank sheet of paper to me, and that's the neat part about songwriting.

Pam Belford - Usually, from playing songs that came from my heart, I find that no matter how weird you think you are or how singular you think your experience is, other people have the same experiences.

Gary Earl - One of the reasons I want to write and perform is because I feel like music is a very healing thing.

1. You have an idea for something you want to say in a song. What process do you go through to develop the story?

Pam Belford - I listen and I talk a lot to people about relationships. I read a lot. I look at my own experiences. I say to myself, Well, how did it feel that time? And I say, Well, I couldn't sleep, and I was waking up at the break of dawn, I had a lump in my throat, I couldn't hold the tears back. You start thinking about how it felt, and that's how those lines fall out.

Steve Bogard - I talk it over with my co-writer, and it just kind of falls out of the sky. Once we agree on a scenario, then the flow starts and it becomes like a tennis game.

Gary Burr - I don't have an answer for that because that's where the gift comes in. I don't know why, if you give the guy in the street a song title, he can't look past that title. And I don't know why, if you give that same song title to Don Schlitz, he can sit there and spin this amazing tale of everything—from where the guy went to junior high school to what hospital ward he died in. I don't know what makes those two people different. I don't know what enzyme is missing in one guy's head that there is an extra dose of in Don's. There's a song title right there: *An Extra Dose of Don.*

Debi Cochran - I don't know exactly how to explain that. You just have to grope for it. In Nashville, in particular, where most people co-write, you have to keep talking to each other about the situation and trying to pull things out, until the obvious, bright shining diamond of an idea comes out of there. Or sometimes you both have to talk over the basic scenario and then just sit there, silently. Both of you just kind of wander around in your subconscious until you find it. And one thing you have to learn early on is that nothing you say is stupid. You have to say every idea that pops into your head, no matter how goofy, or how off-track, or even just plain silly. Because that may be the thing that triggers in somebody else's mind the perfect line. You just can't edit yourself and say, Oh, he's going to think I'm really stupid. You have to say, Okay, this is really stupid, but I'm going to say it. And everybody who does this understands.

Kim Copeland - Well, storytelling has always been my strength. I got a ribbon for winning a storytelling competition in the first grade. My grandfather used to pay me to stop talking—asking questions and making up stories, so storytelling and me go way back.

The first part of the process for me is to make up a story around the idea. I'll come up with four or five scenarios for it, playing different characters each time. Asking, "What if this happened? What about this?" I'll tell all these different stories and see which one feels the best to me. Once I hone in on the storyline, then I decide which point of view it will be written from, and I climb into that character. I try to live the story and see how that character feels and what they would be thinking in that situation.

The best songs are the ones where you feel what the singer is feeling. To me, the way to make it believable and livable is to write it in character. If you're writing it from the third person, just narrating it, it's never going to touch anybody the way it will if you write it straight from the heart of the singer. So I try to get into that character's mind and tell what they're feeling, to act it out and let the story tell itself.

John Jarrard - I don't know. Each one is different. You just have to step back from the situation and try to figure out what you need to do to support that chorus. What is this story about? Who are the characters? One of my favorite muses for writing a song is thinking about a roll of tape. You try to get your fingernail under just an end of it, and grab just a little bit of it, so that you can get it started. Sort of like a ball of yarn. You find the end and then you start pulling on it, and it'll come out from there. "IT" can be just anything. A musical idea, a guitar lick, a title, just whatever shows up first.

Wayland Patton - You have a line that's going to be the main point of the song. Then it's just a puzzle that you put together. What exactly is it that you're saying? And when you figure out what the point is, then that eliminates a lot. You build backwards from there. You start thinking, How can I best get that point across? If you're co-writing, it's something that you just discuss. You start throwing out ideas. I wrote a song that I started from an image. It's called *Blue Sunset*. I started writing, and I came up with a couple of main characters and decided it would be a story song. It's like people who write books—they do the story outline then do their character profiles, and pretty soon the characters begin to take on a life of their own. You've only got three or four minutes, so you can't get too far off track. You have to keep everything focused. If it's a less concrete idea, then you boil everything down to the bare essentials. What is the essence of what you're trying to get across? You've got to get your point across in no time. Then paint that picture so people can feel what you feel, not just say I love you, but make them feel the love.

Pam Rose - That's still all so mysterious to me. And when I worked with Pat Bunch, usually she did that. She did a lot of that. Mary Ann [Kennedy] and I would give our editorial comment, and we would talk about different directions to take and different approaches, but generally, our function was to get a compass setting. Pat would most times do the particulars, but Mary Ann was very valuable in that, too, and would oftentimes think of the lyric to do that with.

That is still mystifying to me. I kind of shoot from the hip. I'm not as able to think of different ways. I usually have to latch on to something that feels right to me and just kind of go. Either it's there or it's not, and then I may be able to help it along, little bit by little bit, but that's more my style. Kye Fleming is another person who can sit and think of eighty ways to do something and eighty ways to do each one of those. That's a gift. I don't see how that could come to me in this lifetime, but I have been able to pick up things from Pat and things from Kye and things from Randy Sharp and things from Jill Colucci and from Chuck Jones. I do learn. So, I aspire to learn more about that process.

Joyce Rouse - I just try and come up with a memory or an emotion from my own life that would support that [idea] and try and draw from that. I've kind of reached a spot where I just don't think I want to write, "I need you, Baby, Baby, Baby" lyrics for the rest of my life. I'm really enjoying exploring this whole other world of musical opportunity.

When you think about it, what have you got to lose? We're in a town where ninety-five percent of cuts on albums got there for political reasons. We're living in a time when many of the artists are writers. Many of the producers have their own publishing companies. And not only that, but also record companies put lots and lots of money into albums, and if it comes down to the tenth song on the album being written by somebody whose name they have never heard before or somebody who's already had four number one songs and all other things being equal, whose song do you think they're going to put on the album? I'm not saying that all of those politics are evil. I'm just saying that that's the way it is and so, battling those odds, I'd just as soon take my chances and write what I love to write. My chances of having some success with them are just about the same, I'd say.

Trisha Walker - I think whatever that *one* idea is that you want to get across, once you're completely sure of that in your mind, then the "how" you want to say it becomes more of the craft. An example is a story song. For me it's sometimes either writing it out or talking it out to somebody else. Almost like a movie script. Like writing reams of paper to get to this one idea and then taking what's best out of that. That to me requires a lot of effort and a lot of work. But that is not as hard as making sure you know what you want to say and making sure there is only one idea. A lot of times writers make a mistake, myself included, in that you say something, and yet you also kind of say something else. So your idea gets diverted a little bit. Make sure of that one thing you are trying to get across in that song, and then you've got some way to gauge whether everything else around that idea points to it.

Kim Williams - A lot of times you write a chorus that's really general, and then you can go a lot of ways with the verse. If we've written a chorus first, then I still feel like the most important thing is how that first line opens. That takes you to a lot of different spots.

2. How many songs do you generally have going at one time?

Tony Arata - Sometimes as many as three and sometimes the songs are written very quickly. I truly believe you know how to write a song and you know the elements involved and you try to achieve those elements the best way you can. But I think the stuff that's really good or magical to anyone's songs, that's from somewhere else. The lines in songs that I'm most proud of, I don't think I consciously sat down and said, What rhymes with this that I'd really be proud of? I think you're riding down the road, and it just comes to you. So, that's why I have to live with things for a while.

It's like being funny on demand. It's not the easiest thing in the world. Sometimes you get wound up and you might actually be clever. For instance the song *The Change* that Garth Brooks did on *Fresh Horses* was a beautiful melody completed by a writer named Wayne Tester. I rode around with the melody for days, and I never thought that I was *not* going to get it. It wasn't like in a fit of passion, where you have to sit down and complete the song right now. I just rode around with that song for a while, to see what I'd come up with. It's a wonderful thing to have a melody that beautiful and that complete and that potent. When you hear that, it's evocative and it's inspirational.

I don't know how much of your brain they say you can actually use. Three to five percent or something. And that's on a good day. And so, if you can free up that and you already know what the melody is, then you're just talking about the words. So that's a neat way to write as well.

A lot of the great writers wrote that way. The Gershwins, David and Bacharach, or Elton John and Bernie Taupin. One person did one thing and one person did the other. But when you hear it, you wouldn't even consider that two people wrote it. In many cases, they probably never even sat down and worked on it together. I'm not in that league, but I really see that as just a real, true writing style.

For others, it works very well to sit down, and two people or three people hammer out an idea together. That works for a great many folks and you cannot argue with that method. I've just never been very good at it. I've just never been a very good co-writer, because I'm too slow. I'm not quick on the draw. I wouldn't subject anyone to all the gibberish that I sing in between, hoping the right words will fall out every now and then.

Pam Belford - Right now I have about four or five going with other people, and I find it frustrating. It's even worse when it gets to be more. I always feel like I'm not done, and I want to have something to show for it.

Kent Blazy - I'm the type of person who likes to finish up things. I don't like to leave too many things unraveled. Maybe five songs at a time, but I would hope that it wouldn't even be that many. I'm always thinking about ideas for songs. But usually the people who I write with, if we sit down one or two times to work on a song, we'll get something done on that song, and if we don't there's probably a reason why we're not, and so we go on to something else.

Steve Bogard - Usually no more than four or five. I'd rather be bad than mediocre. I'd rather people laugh and say "what a stupid idea" than to say, "hm, nice." I either want them to be ecstatic or I want them to hate it. I write a lot of songs in one day, and then go back and edit them. I don't try to edit them in the same day

Rory Bourke - I don't have a lot of outstanding songs.

Gary Burr - To tell you the truth, sometimes I finish a song in a day. When I first came here, it was really important for me to finish a song in a day because I was in a hurry. I was in a hurry to get somewhere, and if I had to spend a second day with somebody, that was another song that didn't get written, so I fell a song behind my self-imposed schedule. These days I don't panic about it so much. If I write a song with somebody on Monday, I might have to come back and have a half a day with him or a couple of hours with him later in the week or the beginning of that next week. At any given time, I've probably got three or four songs on the shelf that are waiting for a day to come up on the calendar when I've got a couple of hours with that person. And generally, for songs that I write by myself, I've got two or three ideas that are sort of percolating, and every once in a while I'll be thinking of one and get a new idea. It will slowly start to evolve and when all of them start to get close enough to actually being identifiable as songs, then I'll put a concentrated effort into them.

Kim Carnes - I don't know. I'm such an unstructured writer. I don't get up every day and write. Maybe two or three in my head. Pieces of them on paper. If I get together with Greg Barnhill and Vince Melamed, we can write two songs in a day. If I write by myself, I string it out with rare exception. There's a song I wrote called *Make No Mistake* that was on a Streisand album. She and I did it as a duet. It ended up being a hit here with Ronnie Milsap and Kenny Rogers. I had gotten a call from Jon Peters asking if there was something I could write that the two of us could sing together. While being extremely flattered, I hung up the phone thinking, Our styles are so completely different, I'll never be able to do that. It was one of those rare times. Ten or fifteen minutes later, I went to the piano, sat down, and an hour later screamed, "Somebody bring me a piece of paper." I was afraid to get up from the keyboard, afraid that it might go away. That song just wrote itself. When that happens, it's a miracle. I always wondered where that came from. It has to come from some other special place, because it's like my hands were on the keyboard and it just came out.

Debi Cochran - I would say five or six. Usually about a week's worth. And then within two or three weeks, try to finish those up. On top of those, there might also be two or three things that I've been working on for a long time. Either the idea is so good that the co-writer and I don't want to press it, or it's an idea that's been rolling around in my mind and I can't quite get it into a song yet. But every now and then I take it out and start working on it.

Jill Colucci - In the past, I got really up there in numbers. I don't know the number, but let's just say that I had ten things unfinished. Boy, that got really difficult. I just didn't like that. I felt spread too thin. I try not to be working on ten songs at one time. That's when I was writing with a lot more people than I am right now.

Songwriting is so intangible. There's a part of me that would like to have it in more of a neat package. I work on this many songs a day and I work this many hours a week, and all these little boxes and compartments, but songwriting doesn't work that way. Life really doesn't either, so I try to just flow with that. If I had to guess, maybe I'd be comfortable with three to five things going on at a time. I'd like to keep it below five rather than to get up into the ten range. I know a lot of writers who write a hundred songs a year or more, and I'll never be able to do that. I mean, it's not even a goal of mine. I'm just a different type of writer. I think that's just amazing that somebody can do that. It's incredible.

Kim Copeland - I can be working on three, maybe four if I'm co-writing. I may keep several ideas spinning, but I don't actively work on usually more than two at a time. I'm compulsive about finishing them. I will have four or five ideas cooking at the same time, but once one of them comes into focus, then I become compulsive about finishing that one. It moves to the front burner and demands to be finished.

Gary Earl - I probably have about ten or eleven at any given time. If I get up with an idea already going through my head, I go with it. But if I don't, then I just grab my little bag and whip up the first tune that's on top and stare at it bleary-eyed for a few seconds. If nothing pops into my head, I throw it aside and grab the next one and open it up. Usually I'll open one of them up, and bang, there's something playing in my head. So that's the way I go for it.

Kye Fleming - I've got about four melodies that I'm working on with a couple of people. They're just kind of sitting there waiting for me to get them. I don't mind having a couple going at the same time, because if it's not working on one then I can jump off to the other. Coming to them fresh sometimes, a whole different thing comes through me than might have the day before.

Lindy Gravelle - It varies. I don't like to get a whole lot because then I feel strung out. I get so diffused. Probably three or four. But I've had more than that going at times. When I'm really booking co-writes, and we'll have a verse and chorus working, we'll have maybe a dozen. But to me that's too much. That's when I start going kind of nutty. I would prefer when I write with somebody to finish the songs before we move on to the next one. But the way it's done in Nashville, most people have quite a few songs in progress. I don't know if that's good or not. I think when I'm really excited about an idea, I prefer to just keep writing on it and not get distracted with another song. But that can change.

Janis Ian - Hundreds. I'm at the point now where I've got a notebook filled with notes from the last eight or ten years. Hundreds of bits and pieces. I've probably got about fifteen or twenty in progress.

John Jarrard -I guess five or six. I believe the process of writing is sort of like farming. If I came in here and spent three or four hours busting my ass on a song, just really thinking hard about it and trying out different possibilities, more often than not, I'd find myself being stuck. But still that's really productive time, and I could capitalize on that productivity by getting away from it.

I really believe that a whole lot of writing takes place subconsciously. So I liken that first session to plowing and getting the soil ready. Then I've got to give it time to grow and come up. When I come back, there will be some things that are really obvious to me. I think that process probably goes on whether I'm working on something else or not.

Al Kasha - The number of songs I'm working on may be four or five, even though that sounds out of focus. I'll get four or five drafts going and then suddenly may lock into one. This is why I think I'm so successful. I came out of the school of being what I call a casting director. I'll call A&R people and say, "Who's up for a date?" If you look at Al Kasha's career, it goes from Elvis Presley to Ronnie Dove, Freddy Jackson, Shirley Bassy, and Aretha Franklin. It goes from R&B to country. I'm sort of like a chameleon in a way. I don't have the answer totally for success, but I think that it's to be flexible with the times. I'm constantly studying. I read *USA Today*. Bob Dylan, who's a friend of mine, said that every day he reads *USA Today* and can write a song from it. That's how up-to-date he is, because he's looking at what's going on in the world today.

Mary Ann Kennedy - I was going through my work tapes last night and I have pieces from years ago that I hope to go back to. I weed through my work tapes fairly regularly, but there are a few little gems that hang in there, and it's like, "Don't drink any wine before its time." *Leaving Line,* which is a song that Pat [Bunch], Pam [Rose], and I wrote—I think I had that lyric in my folder for at least a year. And it was a great lyric. Pam and I were on the road with Emmylou Harris in Seattle. I went over to Pam's room with my guitar and my folder, opened it up in that fancy hotel, and boom. The way to write *Leaving Line* came through me, and then we finished it right there. So I might have lyrics in my lyric folder that I've had for a couple of years. And I guess you could say I'm working on those and waiting for the right time. If I feel forced at all, I just won't write. That is a rule for me.

(DO YOU PLACE ANY LIMITS ON THE NUMBER?) No. In fact, I'm probably more the opposite. I do have to force myself, sometimes, to complete it. And a lot of times, booking the demo session will encourage me to do that.

If we had had a gig coming up, we'd sit down to practice. The "P" word, which I hate because it's structured. It's not just free-form, spontaneous, creative energy. Okay, we're going to practice, we're going to rehearse. Every time I'd do that, I swear, I'd start probably three or four songs. We'd get in there and I'm supposed to be practicing, but I'd start playing this little riff and I'd say wait, wait, wait, I've got to get a tape recorder. It would drive Pam nuts, but I think she'd probably thank me in hindsight, because we got a whole lot of songs out of that. Can't stop it when it's supposed to happen.

Sandy Knox - I'm sitting here telling you that I haven't written in a year, but I have about ten or twelve ideas in my head that I've been writing for a year. I haven't put pen to paper yet, where I sit down and start structuring. There's always a song in the works whether it's just a thought or a title idea. I would say I average five or six songs at a time that are spinning plates.

Kostas - There's always a number of ideas in my head. And you just don't really do much of anything until ... they are like fruit on a tree. When they're ripe, they just drop. It's not an easy thing to explain. Every day is different.

Jess Leary - I usually have two or three that are in progress, and I'm pretty good about finishing them. Or if they're not worth finishing, which doesn't happen very often, thank God, letting them go. It usually takes me between one and two sessions to write a song.

Jim McBride - Maybe seven to nine. Out of those, I will ultimately decide that two or three of them are worth finishing.

Wayland Patton - No set number. I always have something going. Probably five or six at a time. I've got a file on my computer called "Under Construction." That's where I can keep the lyrics and things I'm working on. And I have tapes of melodies that I'm working on.

Pam Rose - Six or seven. Every once in a while, I have that cleanup time when I've got too many unfinished things and I really need to focus on finishing them. That's when I'll go away. I'll take all my work tapes and take my notebooks.

Joyce Rouse - I tend to work on a lot of songs at one time. In fact, if I'm in a really creative mood, I will sometimes be working on three or four songs at the piano at the same time. I know that sounds crazy, but sometimes it works.

Wayne Tester - It changes. There are no rules. I try to finish them up as soon as they're supposed to be finished. So I may have one at the time or I may have eight. It just depends. I want to always make sure I try to get songs done and demoed, because after a while you feel like you have this baggage on you that you have to get rid of so you can move on to the next.

Trisha Walker - Realistically, I could probably have three things going on. Although that's pretty frustrating. I'd rather work on one and finish it before I start another one, but there have been lots of periods of time when I have had three things half going. So if I start on one and that one's just not happening that day, I can go pick up the next one. But I'd rather just go with one and think it all the way through, make sure it's done and then move on to the next one.

Kate Wallace - I've had as many as eight or nine going at once. When you co-write, that's a really common occurrence. If I'm going to be really disciplined, I'm going to set up three writing appointments a week, with three different people. I don't want more than that.

Kim Williams - As high as seven or eight. (IS IT BENEFICIAL FOR YOU TO HAVE SEVERAL WORKING?) I think so. It's really easy to get myopic in this business. Sometimes I write a verse and a chorus and think, Wow, this is great, I can't wait till we get back together, and then a week later I think, this isn't killing me like it did last week. To me that's perspective. That's worth more than what you thought about it the first time. Time gives you perspective. If it's really great, then time is not going to wear it out.

3. What type of notebooks or idea books do you keep, if any?

Tony Arata - I don't have any. I have my songs in my head. I might scribble a line here or there. One of the bad holdovers from working on that magazine was that I'd write a song, but I'd never really write it down until I'd go to type it out. So I don't have that wonderful art, the scribbled notes that you see in the Hall of Fame and that kind of stuff. I don't have a mind potent enough to keep track of more than maybe two or three things at the most. They're all there and they're all squirreling around back there somewhere, but I don't keep a diary.

Pam Belford - I'm very disorganized. I just have one notebook at a time, and when I get a new idea, I scrawl it across the top of a page. Then when I sit down to write with someone, I'll go through the pages, and we'll start writing the song on the page where I've written that idea.

Kent Blazy - I keep a little notepad and when it gets full, I go through it and the ideas I think are good song lines or good titles, I put in the big book. That big book goes with me whenever I'm writing with anybody. I think the more you're doing it, even transcribing it from one book to another, lets you see it and maybe work on it in the back of your mind somehow.

Steve Bogard - I have big bags full of envelopes and credit card receipts. I just slash down ideas on anything that's around, and then I transfer them to a legal pad.

Rory Bourke - No, I never have. I've tried to keep them. Like all writers, when I started out, I kept hook books and everything, but around ten years ago, I decided that was just too much work. So the majority of my writing is done when I don't think about songwriting. I don't think about anything until I actually walk into a room with somebody. I listen very closely to the things they say and the things that seem to move their lives, then I try to write something that's close to their truth. Not necessarily close to my truth, but close to their truth. I think that in a way, co-writing is helping the other person be the best they can be. So I listen real closely and then I probe a little bit about people. Sometimes people will talk about something, then move on to something else, and I'll still be back there with what they said, because something in what they said either rings of pain or joy or something that's real for them. So I say, "Let's go back to what you told me about", and lots of times a song gets written.

I believe that if you're professional enough, you'll find the hook in the idea. The important thing is the truth of the story. Working with Mike Reid taught me that. I used to think a hook had to be a trick line or something like that. Mike taught me that if you have the right approach or if you have the right music and the right story, "I love this table" can be a hook. A hook is what the story rests on. Mike Reid taught me a different kind of hook, a different way of looking at what a title is.

Gary Burr - At any given time, I'll have six or seven lines of something tucked away in my little electronic organizer. Every once in a while, you flip through magazines or something and you get the titles. My fianceé showed me that. She sits on an airplane and flips through, saying, "That's a great song title. That's a good one." And she writes them all down. She's a great songwriter. I'd look, and she'd be filling these pages with these things, and I'd say to myself, You know, next time I sit down to write a song with somebody and they say, "What have you got?" and I say,

"Nothing, what have you got?" it sure would be nice to pull out that paper and say, "How about this?" So I've started to take longer plane rides.

Kim Carnes - Notebooks. But usually the only notes in the notebooks are songs I'm working on at the time. It's not like I have a million ideas that I write down, and then I go to them. I should; a lot of people do that really successfully.

Debi Cochran - People laugh at me all the time because I have this huge book bag, which has all the work tapes of current songs I'm working on. One notebook is full of song-plugging information, who's cutting right now, and my catalog of songs. And I have a notebook where I've taken notes, because I find the way that I learn and remember things is to write them down. If it doesn't go through my pen, my brain can't retain it. So when I talk to people about who's producing who or whatever the current gossip or big news is, I take a lot of notes about those things. So I have one notebook full of where so-and-so used to work and where he works now. Then I have this notebook which is full of snippets of songs and all the songs I'm working on. As I'm brainstorming about a song, once again, I'm writing it down. I'm writing down rhyme words as they occur to me, I'm writing down the scenario as we've talked about it. I'm writing down any catchy little phrases that we've talked about that might later apply to the song. And my co-writers laugh at me when a song file will be a quarter of an inch deep, because I've kept every one of those scraps of paper. But I just don't want to get to the point where we say, "This rhyme is not working here," and then we have to go through the whole deal again. If somebody says, "This song works for me except for that line," then I go back to the other lines we might have tossed out and say, "How about this or how about that?"

Kim Copeland - I like spiral notebooks, bound at the top, because it leaves me both margins open to scribble in. I have several of them. I like to give each idea a page, so that when I'm ready to build on it, it has a place. I have many, many notebooks, but I'll also write on scraps of paper or anything that's handy. And I keep a pocket recorder in the car with me all the time. I keep tons of ideas on that, and I'll play back through those pretty often, looking for pieces of ideas. If I find one that I feel like working on, then I'll transfer it to my notebook and dedicate a page to it so it will be ready to work on.

Gary Earl - I have a couple of those, sure. I write down ideas all the time. You know, you can't go to a movie or church service or anywhere without picking up ideas. I've left church in the middle of a sermon because I got excited about a writing idea I heard in the minister's sermon.

Robin Earl - I'm a little scattered in that area -- too many little pieces of paper around the house. Ideas often get written down on the first piece of paper in sight. I spend time rounding them up and making lists of ideas in folders, but don't get caught up, really. I have idea folders in the kitchen, in my dresser drawer, in the studio, and I keep starting new ones.

Kye Fleming - I really don't and I should. I would definitely tell my writers to. I guess back when I wrote more, I kept a notebook. I guess I kind of do that now, except that I don't come up with ideas as much any more. I tend to want to be inspired by the music and let something pop out. I might be having more fun, but I was more successful when I wrote it down.

Lindy Gravelle - I have a hook book. If I think I have a hook, I write it down in my book. It's funny that when you write it down, you obviously think you have something, but then a day or two later, you look at it and go, what? Or you can write something down and it'll sit there for months, and then one day you look at it and you see it with different eyes. All of a sudden this hook takes on a different shape that you've missed. And you feel like, okay, there is something there.

I don't trust my memory too much. I do write down hooks and lines. I have the pad on the night stand. I'm just never too far from a pencil. (DO YOU HAVE A COMPUTER?) Yeah. But I don't like to erase when I write. When I write with a pencil and paper I don't ever erase anything. I'll just write the new thought down. I think probably in the past I've erased something and then couldn't remember what it was. So with a computer, I find it too easy to delete and then you can't even tell what the smudge was because there isn't any. I know writers more and more seem to be using computers.

Janis Ian - I keep tons of books. That black book over there, about every four months I transfer all my notes to there. I've been keeping notebooks since I was a kid.

John Jarrard - I've got an idea tape, but I don't refer to it much.

Al Kasha - I carry a pen and paper with me all the time, because someone might say something to give me an idea. I'm terrible that way because I'm a twenty-four-hour songwriter. I drive my wife crazy. A writer has to have a third ear and a third eye.

I keep a title list all the time. I write everything down and then later, on my computer or in a book, I'll organize it. I'll say, this is a country title, this is an R&B title, this is a theater title. It's cliché, but it's so true: preparation saves aggravation. I'm prepared for the opportunity.

Mary Ann Kennedy - I really don't keep them anymore. As a younger writer or greener writer (not that I'm ancient, but I've been doing this a while), I did more of the searching through the rhyming dictionaries and the thesauruses and the books of poetry. I think now I try to grab more of the ideas from life. From looking at what a person's going through in their relationship with their daughter or a couple situation and the hurdle that they're jumping this year. And I read those kinds of books that help me with becoming wiser as I become older and with figuring out the whole mystery. So I think it's more the self-help books and soul-searching books, the real life in those kinds of books, that I get ideas from.

Sandy Knox - Spiral notebooks. I have stacks of them and periodically will go through them just to see old ideas that, a lot of times, are worth writing. I don't keep diaries. Actually, I've always said that my writing is my diary. Especially my dating diary. I can look back and say, Okay, I wrote that about Tony. I wrote that about Dan. I wrote that about this guy. Oh, I remember him. He broke my heart. Oh, I was so in love with him when I wrote this song. It's kind of like your basic dating diary for me. But see, the good news is the guy breaks your heart, but you get the royalty check.

Jess Leary - Boy, I used to have a lot of them. I sure have dipped into them, pretty much to their last little pages. Over the years, I've gone in them and found some neat stuff. I've found some other stuff that [makes me wonder] where I was, what was happening, what I was thinking. I sure do wish I had more of that, because nowadays it seems the hardest thing for me is to come up with the idea. You can have song titles and you can have musical pieces, but the ideas are getting harder and harder to come by, because sometimes I feel like, gee, I've written that three times already. Or how do I write that differently, or do I even want to? I think if you have a strong idea or a strong title, you're going to be off to a good start. It's always harder the other way for me.

(WHERE DO YOUR IDEAS COME FROM?) Song spirit! I pray to Song Spirit a lot. Song Spirit, come on down. Try to just open my head and tell me something.

Kostas - None [no notebooks]. I've got unlabeled cassette tapes and they're full of my ideas. I wonder some times, How will you ever find the time to go back and listen to all this stuff? (DO YOU CARRY A TAPE RECORDER WITH YOU?) A lot of times. And a lot of times I write it down and carry the melody in my head until I can get to a cassette. (DOES IT EVER COME TO YOU IN ITS ENTIRETY?) A lot of times it does. It depends. I've written songs while I'm driving. So between mile markers 351 and 374, I've got it.

Jim McBride - I generally try to keep one or two notebooks with my ideas in there. But what I find, is that once or twice a year, I have to gather up pieces of paper and napkins and matchbook covers and everything else and put them in a pile, and then put them in a notebook. I've tried to carry a little pad around with me, but I'm a little bit too unorganized to do that all the time. But I do try to keep them all together.

Wayland Patton - I have a ledger book; that I buy. It's a hard book, it has lines in it. They're about thirty or forty dollars. I can write and keep my songs in there. It's a lot easier to keep up with than legal pads. I know guys who write with legal pads. They've got pages and pages. I can't deal with that. So when I'm out writing away from the house that's what I use. When I'm at home, I'm on my computer. I always input everything into the computer, all the songs I'm working on. That way I've got it there. If I end up moving verses or lines around, it's a lot easier.

Pam Rose - I've just started keeping an idea book these last few years because when I was exclusively with Mary Ann [Kennedy] and Pat [Bunch], most of the ideas came from them. Usually I was figuring out how to finish things. I'm a good finisher. I was usually very busy with the finishing, so I was really not the initiator very often. I have started an idea book, and I definitely use my notebooks. I also use my computer.

Joyce Rouse - They're all over. They're on my piano. They're in my office. They're on the table beside my bed. There's one in my car. I've learned the hard way, thinking too many times that I'd remember this great idea. Then your child falls off the bicycle or you burn the dinner or something happens, and every idea you've had that day is out the window.

Wayne Tester - All the time. I use it a lot to jot ideas down. I refer to it when I have a co-write situation come up.

Trisha Walker - I've got two or three notebooks in there that are just crammed full of scraps of paper, napkins, matchbook covers, and all those things. Whenever you get that little magic spark, you write it down. A few years ago I was going through my notebooks, and I was going to organize and be disciplined. I was going to take all my ideas and write them out on a separate piece of paper and throw all those scraps away. But I realized there was some almost tangible magic about each one of those scraps. So what I did was to take a blank sheet of paper and whatever scrap I had, and staple it to the blank piece of paper and keep it intact. So I can go pull out a notebook, there's a blank piece of paper, and that little scrap. For some reason it jars the memory, and I can remember what I felt when I thought that. That has worked well. I tried carrying a tape recorder around and that's okay, but I seem to do better with writing scraps down. If it's a melodic idea, I'll draw out a staff real quick and write out the notes.

(WHAT DO YOU DO WHEN YOU'RE RIDING IN THE CAR?) You can tell by my scraps of paper when I was driving. I've got one of those little notepads that sticks to the window. And if I'm really getting something, I'll go ahead and pull over and write it down.

Kate Wallace - I have a file called "New Songs." My favorite place to jot down ideas is on the back of a deposit ticket in my wallet.

Kim Williams - I keep what I call a hook book. I have probably ten to fifteen. I always file and keep them. It's just where you write things and then you go back and say, why did I write that, it sounds so stupid. Then other times they turn into hooks that are great. It's funny; *Radio Active*, I had that idea for six or seven years. *Wishbone*, I had that for two or three years. Sometimes I go back to the old ones. But the good ideas, like *Wishbone* and *Radio Active,* those ideas have always been in my head, I didn't have to go back and read them in a book. I never forgot them. With *The Devil Danced,* actually what I had written down was *The Devil Dances in Empty Pockets*. I was hearing that real serious. To me that's like, anything goes when everything's gone. But I got to looking at this hook one day and decided the reason I hadn't written it was that it's *not* serious. You can't use the devil in that context. So we started a light-hearted song. It's just fun.

4. Do you like to read? What kind of books?

Tony Arata - I love to read. I wish I was more diverse in what I read. I tend to read a lot by the same people, which isn't very good, but I do love to read. There again, if you want to be humbled and you ever think that you've written something really good, then just go pick up any number of books and ask, Now where do I fit into this picture? It kind of puts things back in their proper perspective.

I think that the more exposed you are, to any number of things, the chances for turning that into some type of creative process works in your favor. I do try to read as much as possible. It's a very humbling thing.

Rory Bourke - I used to read strictly nonfiction, but I read a lot of fiction now.

Gary Burr - I love to read. I read stupid books. Well, not stupid. I got the new *Rolling Stone*, and there's this big interview with Mick Jagger. He's talking about how this song was inspired from a line from a French Renaissance philosopher or something. He's reading all these books, getting all these song ideas, and I'm going, "Oh gee, I got a song idea from the last Spider Man comic book I read." I feel very embarrassed, like I'm going to be found out as a fraud. I just read what's fun. I like to read a lot of magazines and a lot of newspapers and Larry McMurtry. You get great imagery from stuff like that, especially for country songs. I've gotten a lot of mileage out of books like that.

Kim Copeland - I love to read. I don't spend as much time reading now as I used to, but I like to read a variety of styles. I like Natalie Goldberg. I like some self-help books, if they're not too technical. They have to be an easy read, and I have to be able to apply it to my life. I'm reading *The Artist's Way* right now, and also *101 Ways To Be Happier Day By Day*. And *Writing Down the Bones* again. Those are kind of reference books to me, and I may be reading or rereading two or three of those at any given time. I love biographies and Stephen King mysteries. I just don't find as much time lately to read those, so I read the books that you can pick up and put down quickly and still get something out of. I just finished reading *Ellen* and that was a fun distraction.

Gary Earl - I read a ton and listen to books on tape. I'd say probably at least a book a week. Everything from classic novels to current fiction and nonfiction.

Robin Earl - I read a lot of positive-attitude books and informative books. I like books that get me motivated. Many times they say about the same things in different ways but I still enjoy them. I met my husband at a positive attitude seminar!

Kye Fleming - What I tend to read is probably very telling because it's usually psychological books. Joseph Campbell, *Followers of Carl Jung*. My life is kind of busy, so when I've got that kind of time, I probably sit down and write or something. But I read an interesting quote, and I can't remember who said it, but it was, "It's really arrogant of man to think about sitting down and to think of writing when he hasn't lived." So I think I would like to take more chances with my life. So I've got some place to come from. I think my writing would be more interesting. To be a little more spontaneous with life. To say what the heck and throw a couple of things in the car and drive to Colorado for however long. Or decide to get to know somebody who you wouldn't normally get to know, and really put time in on it and really try to care about that person. Try to get to a deep level with that person. Go out of your norm. I tend to get caught up in the routine of every day, so that I don't have, or take time, or make room for those life experiences that make for a richer existence.

Al Kasha - I love southern writers. I think Pat Conroy is a great writer. I think Faulkner is a great writer, and I like Tennessee Williams. Being a kid from New York, I have a good sense of what I call dialogue language, but I think the Southern writers and English writers especially have a great sense of pictures. The only one I can think of from the West Coast is John Steinbeck. I actually go to the store and look for writers from the South for the majesty of words.

Mary Ann Kennedy - I like to read more than I do. I don't have enough quiet time in my life. I guess that says something. I don't read enough, but I do the movie thing more than a whole lot of my friends read.

Sandy Knox - I read all kinds of books. This weekend I bought a book called *An Unquiet Mind*. And I bought a book on the Boston strangler and a book on Walter Wenchel, the reporter in the fifties. I bought a book on Noel Coward and Cole Porter. And I bought a book on motherless daughters to give to a friend of mine, and last night I finished a murder mystery called *The Body Farm*.

I just read lots and lots of books. I think it's really important for songwriters to read because we need fresh ideas all the time.

(DO YOU GET A LOT OF IDEAS FROM BOOKS?) Yes. I was reading a biography on the virgin queen, Elizabeth I. In this book, she was making a speech to Parliament about a treaty that they were trying to instate between England and one other country, which I can't remember. She said, "What are you trying to do? You would have a better chance at weaving a rope made of sand to the moon than you will have of getting this treaty out." I went to bed that night thinking, "a rope made of sand." What a visual that is. You can see it, but you know it will fall apart. It won't stay. It's tangible and it's the impossible, basically. I went to bed thinking about a rope made of sand. It was one of those things; I dreamed I was writing this song and I actually was writing it. I was awake in my dream writing it, but I was asleep. I woke up and wrote what I had been writing in my dream, and that was the song that became *Ropes Made of Sand*. It's a song that, once it gets cut, will be a classic forever. I feel it very strongly. But I wrote like the first verse and a half in my sleep in that dream. I was watching myself sitting there writing it, reading the lyrics I was writing, going, these are very good. It's happened about two other times. I'm watching myself work, and I'm over my shoulder reading the lyrics that my other physical person is sitting there writing. Then I wake up and write them. It's a weird thing. It's a really good feeling. This is great—I can sleep and work. What a job. Kind of like sleeping for a living. Read a book, go to bed.

Kostas - I read quite a bit. I enjoy the Bible a lot. I'd have to say that it's written not just from a spiritual point of view, but from a personal, day-to-day level. It's beautiful to read about peoples' lives in such a pure way and see the good side of life as well as the bad side of life. It reveals both sides of human nature.

And I love old histories and westerns.

Jess Leary - Yes, I do. Unfortunately, I don't have as much time to read as I'd like. So a lot of times I read magazines, just flipping through them sometimes, because things might jump off the page at you.

I'm usually reading a book that somebody just told me about. I have such a wide variety of things I like. I don't like scary books, don't like scary movies either. I like love stories, of course. I like spiritual stories, *The Celestine Prophecy, Dancing in the Light*. I think I've already read them all. I have a couple of books around my bed, and I try to read a little bit before I go to sleep. Then I usually fall asleep with the book on me.

Jim McBride - I try to read a lot, especially when I'm not writing a lot. When it kind of goes away or I'm taking a break, I try to read. I've read all of Grisham's stuff. Generally whatever is on the best-sellers list, I'll give it a shot.

Pam Rose - I love to read. Sometimes I'm influenced by books either directly or indirectly. I love psychology and spirituality, but I also like murder mysteries, so somebody might think I'm a really fragmented individual. And I usually like to read two books at a time. I may be reading *The Tao of Negotiation* and *Silence of the Lambs.* I love Michael Crichton, John Grisham, Deepak Chopra, and I like to read Native American material. I can get stuff out of the psychology books. There's a song on our second CD, *Walk the Line,* called *Real World;* that was influenced by a book called *Beyond the Power Struggle.*

Joyce Rouse - Yes—actually, just about everything except science fiction. I've just never gotten big-time into that. Novels, biographies, history, current events, and I also tend to be reading three or four books at one time. I'm finding that my reading choices come out of filling a need somewhere emotionally. For instance, I've been reading *Women Who Run with the Wolves* several months. It takes such concentration to read it because the information is so excellent and it's so beautifully written that I really have to be in the right state of mind and have the right concentration to read it.

Wayne Tester - I've never been much of a reader. I've always liked to watch the news. I like short articles. I always used to read the Cliff notes instead of the novel.

Trisha Walker - Not as much as I'd like to. I bet I don't get through three or four books a year, if that many. But I feel like I'm constantly reading something. I'm always picking up magazines or newspapers, anything to read but the things I'd like to read. I'd like to read more novels and more history. I grab for anything if I've got a blank minute.

5. Do you feel different about the songs that just seem to pour out, as opposed to those that you struggle over?

Tony Arata - *The Dance* really was written very quickly, although it was written quickly over a long period of time. I had the melody for a long time. I had a whole other set of lyrics to the song, and fortunately those never saw the light of day. I was inspired enough one night to play that melody, and it became very clear what the idea of the song was. So those lyrics were written in the matter of maybe an hour.

Emmylou Harris recorded a song called *I Hear a Call* which was really written more as a prayer. It wasn't until after the lyrics were completed that I even went back and tried to add any music. I wrote the song a cappella and didn't even think about it. There was enough going on at that time to be inspired to write a prayer. So that's how that happened.

The only difference in the process is the time frame. You're still concerned about making sure that this will mean something. It's pretty neat, and I have learned that there are times when that will happen. So I try, when I am singing gibberish or just working in my office or whatever, to leave a tape player going. I think when you do get a chance like that, and the words just come out, then you were meant to write that on that day. There's usually some element of those spontaneous lines in every song. But there are only a few that the whole song is a result of one sitting. I certainly have learned enough to know not to sit around and wait on those things.

Pam Belford - Those are real gifts. It's almost like I didn't write them. It's like someone was dictating them to me. But they are very few and far between. I love it when that happens. I think the ones that have come to me that way are my best ones.

Kent Blazy - We write that way a lot. It's just amazing, especially with Kim [Williams] and I. We both start bouncing ideas off each other. There are times when it's like somebody must have been sending that song to us. It just kind of fell out. It's like that song wants to be born.

Steve Bogard - I get really inspired by co-writing relationships. Lots of things come out in big pieces especially if the whole idea warrants it.

Rory Bourke - I haven't had many of those. Generally it's a couple of sessions with somebody. When I first became a writer, you could write a song this afternoon, get somebody to like it tomorrow, get it cut two days from now, and it could be out in two weeks. Today that's pretty rare. If you write it today, someone likes it three weeks from now, it gets cut five months from now, and it comes out a year and a half later. It's like there's no need to get this done in fifteen minutes. That doesn't mean that if one came in ten or fifteen minutes, I wouldn't take it, but that hasn't been my experience. Usually the whole process for me takes a pretty long time. It takes a long time to write them; it takes a long time to get them cut.

Charlie Black and I had a song recorded by Dan Seals that just came out. It's kind of about my daughter. We wrote it when she was sixteen, and she's twenty-one now. So it's nothing for he and I to wait five years to get a song cut.

Gary Burr - Yeah, I've had three or four of those that are great. It's an amazing thing, almost like you're writing it long-hand as quick as the words are coming. They just flow. Then you sit there and write one and you're picking each word individually, and it takes forever. You just wonder why some days it goes like that and some days it doesn't. I mean, two of the best songs I've got I wrote in one night. At about three in the morning, I just woke up and wrote them both. Boom.

(WHAT ABOUT THE SLEEP FACTOR?) The less sleep I get, the better. It never bothers me if I've got a writing appointment at eleven and I go to bed at three in the morning. I wake up at eight-thirty and only get five and a half hours sleep, and I feel crappie all day. Sometimes it puts you in that little, weird alpha state. Sometimes it's good to be a little zoned.

Debi Cochran - That's always a wonderful thing. And you just wonder where they come from. I have a friend who I have known a little bit. He was having problems with his girlfriend. So when we sat down to write together, I said, "So how are you, what's new?" He said, "I'm still moving my heart around." And then we took a couple of beats and we just looked at each other and said, "There's our hook." He started playing this blues riff and I just started writing. I said, "This is it, that's the melody, this is the song." We were so excited, we didn't even stop when we went for lunch. He took the guitar in the car and we went through Burger King drive-through, still singing and talking out lines, and by seven o'clock that night we had a work tape that we were playing for his producer. It's one of his favorite songs and one of mine too. It was just so easy. It was a gift.

Jill Colucci - I wrote all through the seventies, and I thought I was working really hard. I wrote maybe five songs a year; I thought I was really jammin'. And in 1980 was the first time I knew I was a songwriter. What it took for me to realize that was that I had this song come through me. I don't know how fast. It was a time warp. Somewhere between five and twenty minutes. I had a pen, and I was trying to keep up with the music and the melody because I didn't even have a guitar in my hand. I got on the floor and I was writing on my coffee table, and it was just pouring out. Everything came through but one verse, and it was a challenge to meet up to the expectation of that inspiration. It was almost like, who wrote that? I'm clearly the vehicle, but where did this come from? It was so amazing to me. It happened with such gusto and such speed. I was very thrilled with the parts of it that came. I made many stabs at that last verse, and I remember trying all kinds of things. Everything that I was coming up with paled in comparison. It was more crafted. It wasn't the heart and soul that had come through the inspiration. So I kept trying. One day, I remember I wasn't even into meditation, but I was trying to get in some exceptionally relaxed state. I turned the lights out and I lit candles. I was just trying to get a certain vibe going, anything to try to pull the rest of the song through me. I finally managed to do it again by being still and listening to what's to be said instead of trying to force it. That was the first time. That song's called *Something's Different Tonight.* I knew then that I was a songwriter.

That was such an inspired experience that I looked at it more seriously, and I've been writing much more ever since. There were two things in my songwriting career that really were significant changes, and one was that experience in 1980. Then in 1984 Merlene Travis, who is Merle Travis's daughter, was a publisher in Los Angeles at Columbia Pictures. I had artist deals and I wrote for me, for my record deals. I never really had a publishing deal, nor did I want one. Merlene started wining and dining me to sign with Columbia Pictures. She says it was for four years. I think it was more like two or three, and the story keeps growing. Each year it gets a little longer. Pretty soon it will be ten years, and that I wined and dined her! But she really pursued me and wanted me to sign to Columbia Pictures. She said she could get my stuff in films and just help me as a writer. I resisted her and resisted her. I wanted to keep my own publishing and just write. She finally persuaded me to do that in 1987. I don't know how, but she did, and it was the best thing that ever happened to me. It was a huge turning point in my career. First of all, she did get some of my stuff in films, which was really inspiring, but basically, I was being paid an advance. I was getting money for what I did. I had a quota, which I really don't like. What it gave me was this deal, getting paid for it and having a publisher, knowing that they can't wait to hear the next song that I finished. I really started writing more. I really became more professional. I got really excited, really inspired, and so 1987 was a huge change in my career, and I've been with a publisher ever since. It really changed my whole attitude about writing. That and that other song coming through me were two really major changes. Okay, let's do three: my first number one. I wondered what I would do the first time I heard a song of mine on the air. I had written album cuts but I hadn't had a single yet. Then Travis [Tritt] heard *I'm Gonna Be Somebody.* Stewart Harris played it for him, and he said, "That's my life story. I'm going to record that song," and he did. He heard just a guitar/vocal. I thought when I first heard a song of mine on the air, being the extrovert that I am, that I would jump up and down and scream, and if I was sitting in an intersection, I would get out of the car, blow the horn, scream, tell everybody I wrote it, point to the radio and just act like a complete idiot. I was walking through my den when *I'm Gonna Be Somebody* came on the radio. I just sat down on the couch and cried like a baby. I was home alone. It was so emotional. It was such an incredible experience, but that is not how I would have guessed it at all. If you had asked me a long time ago what it would mean to have a number one record, well, I would have said that it would mean a certain amount of success in your career, certainly you would get money. But it turned out to be really, really different, the impact that music has. I was reminded with my first number one, and every one since, how powerful music is. How healing, how powerful. If you've got a number one, you're in heavy duty rotation. It's playing all the time. More people are hearing it and being affected. That's why I started out to become a songwriter, to affect people's lives emotionally. Whether it makes them cry or makes them happy, that doesn't matter. To bring out some emotion in people's lives and have a positive effect on them.

Stewart [Harris] went to ship me a gold record in L.A., and the girl behind the counter said, "You wrote this?" He said, "Yeah, I'm shipping this to my co-writer in L.A." She said, "Oh, my sister sings that as a lullaby to her child every night before she goes to sleep." A lullaby of *I'm Gonna Be Somebody*. Stewart and I both were in tears, it was so meaningful to us. So that's really what it's about with number one songs. You get more of that exposure. You're reaching more of the masses. More feedback. Touching more lives. A lot of things are turning out to be different from what I thought, but that makes sense, doesn't it?

Kim Copeland - I have had several songs that have come to me that way. It's great! They always end up being my better songs and the most fulfilling to write, because they're the ones that I'm just compelled to write. They are always the ones that, the more I live with them, the stronger they become, and they're usually the ones that other people respond to the most too. Those are always the strongest and live the longest.

Gary Earl - Actually, the ones that happened that way for me were the ones that sometimes pack the most emotional punch. I mean, not just for me, but I've had that feedback from other people too. Perhaps it's because they were pouring out of some emotion in me.

Robin Earl - Songs that come easily are also the ones that I like the best and have had more success with. Things just fall into place.

Kye Fleming - Not that often. I can think of one that I wrote alone that was pure pleasure, a gift thing. And one that was an absolute labor of love that went on for three days, pretty much uninterrupted. That was with Janis Ian, and the song was *Some People's Lives.* We had a mission in that particular song. Janis had this friend who had a restaurant in L.A., and we were talking with her one night. She was really down, and she was saying things like, "It shouldn't matter if somebody takes their life." She said that her life didn't make a difference anyway. The old *It's a Wonderful Life* syndrome. As much as we talked to her and tried to help her out of that, it didn't help. We left there and I said, "I've got to write something." Of course, Janis felt it too. We sat down and it just started at that point, and we finished the last line in three days. Most of it came that evening. It was like writing alone with somebody, because it was a mission together. We played it for my publisher and he cried. So we took it into the restaurant with a guitar. I wrote out the lyrics on a paper place mat, and we sang it to Janis's friend in her restaurant. I think it was about two days later when we went back in, and that place mat was framed, and it had made a difference. We said, "You didn't feel like your life made a difference, but look what came out of that one conversation. Hopefully other people will hear that song and be moved by it, and that was because of you." The interesting thing, as always, is that it then had a much more far-reaching effect, because it was absolutely from the heart. Can I point to many of them like that? No. Probably no other one that is that personal.

Lindy Gravelle - That hasn't happened for me that much. Probably *Exit 99*, because once I figured out the structure of that song, it wrote itself. But it was more than ten minutes, I know that.

I've always had a goal to take something into my publisher and to not have anything to rewrite. In that song, we changed a word or two. So I thought, Gosh, I guess I really did hook into something.

John Jarrard - One of the best songs that I've ever written, and maybe ever will write, is a song that I wrote with Mickey Cates. I'd been dating this woman and had left a guitar over at her house. When we broke up she brought my guitar back to the office and left it downstairs. Mickey and I had been writing, and when I walked back up here with the guitar, we wrote a song called *Katie Brought My Guitar Back Today* in probably an hour.

Mary Ann Kennedy - The ones that are truly inspired lyrically and that just kind of flow through and write themselves musically as well, I don't know if they're always better, but they sure do feel good. Maybe it's just the memory of how it happened that enhances it. I guess you'd have to ask the listeners.

Sandy Knox - Very few just really appear in their entirety. I think about them a long time, and then after I've thought about them a long time, I do write them quickly. But I've actually been working on them for maybe a year in my head, thinking about all the different angles. A lot of times I will sit down and it will seem like I zip through it in a couple of hours, but it's really been a process. Like *She Thinks His Name Was John*. I had that idea for so many years. I threw it up to other co-writers, and people didn't want to write it. By the time I sat down and put the pen to the paper, I had edited that idea and that song in my mind for probably a year or two.

Jess Leary - Yeah. I think I always wonder about that, too, because it's nothing I know the answer to. If I did, boy, I would bottle it and drink it every day. It is magical when that happens.

They're usually the ones that are really good. It's a weird thing. The song *Ready, Willing and Able* that I wrote with Jody Allen Sweet, I remember that day because we didn't really have an idea. We didn't really have a title. We were just sitting around drinking coffee and wanting to write something really good. I think I had said that. "I'm ready to write something good." I'm ready, I'm willing, I'm able, and he went, "to love." We wrote this thing in about an hour or an hour and a half, and it's probably one of the strongest songs that we've written. It's a Lari White single. I'm so thrilled that she's singing it, because she's just awesome anyway, a great singer and a great performer.

(YOU'VE HAD QUITE A FEW OF THOSE SONGS?) I feel like it's pretty balanced. When I do have those writer's blocks, they're killer. They are hard, and I don't like them because I get them sometimes for a long time. But I've come to find that, again, it's all in waves. I'll write six or seven really strong songs that I really like and that everyone seems to like, and then the wave will go to shore, and I'm sort of out in the harbor going, uh-oh, how did I do that? What was that? Who am I? Where am I? How do you write a song? And then I get in that thing where I just can't.

Jim McBride - I've had very few of those. Out of my career, I can only think of two or three times when I literally sat down and a whole song came at one time. And I probably spent two or three weeks looking at it, because I didn't believe it. It's not supposed to be that easy. To get a whole chorus, now that's happened a lot. Or maybe a whole verse. Generally for me, I don't get a whole song at one time. If you do, and it's what it ought to be, then that's pretty wonderful.

Wayland Patton - There have been very few songs that I would say I've not been able to improve upon. Usually I rewrite. There have been a few that write themselves from front to back. But it's not bingo, there it is. There have been songs that come very fast, but even those I set aside and let simmer. Then after I'm away from it, I'll go back and either say, that's pretty darn good, or here's what that needs to say, and fine-tune it.

Pam Rose - Sometimes those will happen, the music and the lyric together. Or sometimes a verse and a chorus will come just like that, and then it may take me quite a while to finish it with the same inspiration or to wait for the moment to be inspired to finish that. I just finished something that I started four years ago. And I think it's one of my best songs. For instance, *Safe in the Arms* and *Love Like This* or *I'll Still Be Loving You*, the music to those really pretty much came as one piece.

Joyce Rouse - With the ones that just come out, I find that the idea is there. It's just a kernel in the beginning, and I liken it very much to a pregnancy. The idea will be very small and very much just inside. I'll think about it sporadically as I'm driving or doing things, and then it gets to a point where all of a sudden I go into labor with that idea. It's excruciatingly painful and I have to get it out, and I have to cancel everything to write this thing. To write this baby, if you'll pardon the expression. Then there is just this high afterwards. I'm generally extremely proud and satisfied about those. And I think they are very often the pieces that touch people the most. They're the ones that came from the center of my soul and had to be written.

Wayne Tester - *Lifestyles of the Not So Rich and Famous* was written real quick. I had the idea and saw my co-writer, Byron Hill, in the hallway at MCA Music. He was getting ready to go home. And I said, "Byron, I've got this neat idea I want to run by you." And he said, "I'm tired. I've had a long day and I'm going to go on home." I said, "Well, let me run this idea by you. I think it's really good." I said, "What about, 'lifestyles of the not so rich and famous'? Make it a theme song for Bubbas who are proud of where they've come from." His eyes lit up and he goes, "Wow, Wayne, you shouldn't have done that to me, I'll be up all night now." So he called me the next morning and said, "Meet me at MCA." He had some ideas. We got together and had it written in probably two to three hours. It got cut within three to four months of being written, so that was a pretty fast one. I wish they would all go like that.

Trisha Walker - I've had a couple. One was a torchy song called *He's Not You* that really sounds like it could have been a 1940s ballad. It was one of those twenty-minute ones. When you feel that coming on, I think you can distinguish in the first twenty minutes that hey, this is done, grab a pencil. There have been a few like that that didn't take much re-writing. But they are few and far between. *He's Not You* is one of my favorites. I was literally the one holding the pencil, and that was it.

6. Do you try to write immediately when you get a new idea (while the inspiration is fresh), or do you like to kick it around in your head awhile?

Pam Belford - It depends. Usually there isn't time to sit and write it all down, but the best times are when you can keep having that thought and keep running back to write another line on it.

Kent Blazy - With me and writing, it's like no two times are the same. Sometimes I do it one way and sometimes the other. But a lot of times what I do is get the idea the morning I'm going to be getting with some people. And a lot of times we'll end up writing the idea that I run by them. I'll have some ideas about the song, maybe a musical idea, or some lines, or how I want the chorus to be. If it fires them up when they hear it, then they'll jump in and start throwing things at you. And before you know it, you've got a song.

Steve Bogard - I usually get it to the point where I have several options on how to write a good idea, in my own head. Then I'll come and beat it to death talking it over with my co-writer, and we'll figure out what's the best way. I try to always write to the song, not to the artist, not to what I'm in the mood for, but what's going to make it the best song it can be. I still love the experience of "wow, I wrote that."

Co-writing is important to me, so I try to form relationships where the two of us are way better than either of us alone. There's such a huge human resource in the communication and the dynamic between the co-writers. It's a resource that you can play and use, that goes into the songs.

Gary Burr - I like to throw it back there and let it percolate for a little while, because a lot of times if you sit down right away, what comes out is stream of consciousness and stream of consciousness is not necessarily good. The first thing that comes out of your mouth can sometimes be brilliant, but it can also be just the first thing that comes out of your mouth. Otherwise, we'd all be humming *Scrambled Eggs* instead of *Yesterday.* So I don't know. It depends on the intensity it hits me with, and it depends on where I am. I read about Yoko in an interview saying that John would wake up at two in the morning, and he'd have to go and pound on the piano until it was done. I just think that's so cool. Me, I'd just sing it into my tape recorder and go back to sleep and work on it tomorrow. What's the difference? I don't know.

Debi Cochran - Both. Whatever that first spark is that you get, you've got to write that down. If you trust yourself to remember it, you'll have lots of horror stories about wonderful ideas that you've lost. You've got to write that down, then just take it as far as it goes. If you get a whole song like that, or if you get a whole verse or chorus, you'd best drop what you're doing. If the muse comes and says "here's a song," then you'd better say "thank you," and sit down and put it on paper. Then that part may have to float around in your subconscious a little while, and some night when you're washing dishes, and you're singing the part you already have to yourself, the other part will come.

Jill Colucci - I'm an inspired writer, so I'm not going to have that inspiration every single day. Each song that I write certainly starts with some piece of inspiration whether it's a melody or a lyrical idea or whatever. So I'm not writing necessarily five days a week. I want to be available to inspiration, so it's not that I just go off to wherever for three months and not think about writing. I'm always coming up with ideas. I think part of my job is to be available for ideas. I like to show up, maybe not into the office every day, but I'll spend some time sitting at the keyboard.

Last year I did an album for Liberty. I went on tour for a couple of months. I moved across the country. I was in the earthquake at the beginning of the year in L.A. It was an incredibly different kind of year for me. I wrote less last year, in terms of finishing songs, than in any year in my whole life, but I had tons of ideas. I had full choruses, music, and lyrics. I had ideas all over tape cassettes, so when I went to the beach in February alone, it was so productive. I was ready to go. I find myself saying, gee, I didn't write hardly at all in '94. Well, that's not true. Maybe I didn't complete songs, but I was writing a lot. I'm writing at a different pace now. I've written seven or eight songs in the last three or four months, and it's a nice pace. It's very comfortable. I feel really good about every single one of them. I wasn't breaking my neck or rushing to be somewhere. It happened at a very nice pace, and I think that has something to do with the quality.

But I wrote some really good songs on that crazy pace. I would come in here from L.A., and you can imagine all the writers I wanted to work with. Some days I found myself working on two or three songs at a time. I'd do a ten o'clock and a two o'clock and sometimes I'd meet with somebody in the evening to try to finish something up before I left. I'll never work on three songs in a day again ever.

I wrote *Anymore* during that time. I wrote *He Would Be Sixteen* during that time, but this is more comfortable right now. Whatever works best for each writer. We're always finding new ways. Next week, next year, I might talk to you and I'll be writing seven days a week.

Kim Copeland - When I get a new idea, I always like to live with it for a while because I like to explore it from a lot of different angles. I like to be sure it still feels worth writing before I put it to paper and spend time on it. If it's meant to be written, it will stay with me and expand, and if it's not meant to be, I'll forget it or realize that it's just not that good of an idea.

Gary Earl - It's different every time. Sometimes we try to work on it immediately, and sometimes we carry the idea around for five years.

Once we got a phone call from an intern in a film company that we knew, and he said that the director just heard one of the songs that the music supervisor had picked for the film, and he hates it, and the music is supposed to go on the film Monday morning. So they were putting out a cattle call to everybody they knew to bring a song in Monday morning. They would just go through the pile, and the first tune that the director liked would go right into the film. It was like an emergency. So he described what kind of song they wanted, we hung up the phone and immediately started writing, and within four hours we had written the tune. I had played everything on it in the home studio, and we sang it and literally had the thing done the same night. We found the music supervisor's name in the phone book. The next morning was Saturday morning, and we drove down to Santa Monica and stuck it in the screen door to his house and drove back home. He loved it. He said, "This is it, I'm not going to listen to anybody else Monday morning."

Kye Fleming - If it's an idea that really moves me, I would probably sit down with it. If it doesn't move me that much, I'm just going to wait until I am writing and then come up with something. But that's a different approach than I used to take.

Lindy Gravelle - With my scheduling and the way things are, I collect the hooks until the next available time. And probably between the time I got the hook and when I'm going to sit down with it, how I'm going to treat it is circulating there in my mind. I'm one of those people who does write kind of simultaneously if I'm writing alone. The music and the lyric will kind of come out at the same time. So the whole song can develop right in front of my eyes like that. But when I co-write, sometimes there'll be a lot more discussion involved before we actually start writing.

John Jarrard - I probably tend to hold it for a while.

Mary Ann Kennedy - Both. Sometimes if the idea comes in the car, I have my little tape player and I'll sing until it's feeling forced, and then it might sit on a work tape for two years. It's just got to feel right.

I've had a couple of lyrics sitting around for a couple of months and the other night, it happened. I had looked at them before and it didn't happen. The magic wasn't there for me, even though I loved the lyric. I loved the titles and the lines were just great. But it felt a little strange, so I just put it down and waited till it was flowing out.

I have to know it's right or I just don't work at it.

Kostas - If I have the time to think about it then I will, up until the time I get stuck and say I'll get back to it, which I never do.

Jess Leary - If I think of a good idea, I write it down or I tape it and try, if I have time, to think about it a little bit before I write it.

Jim McBride - I learned from Curly Putman a long time ago to put some thought into it. Take the idea and think about it a little while, because there are a lot of songs that can go in several different directions. I think it's worthwhile to take some time to think about which is the best way to write an idea. Think about writing and then write.

Wayland Patton - I don't have to quit what I'm doing and go work on it. If I'm driving or doing something, I may want to jot down the idea so I don't lose it. If it's a good idea, I don't usually lose it. But I have pulled off the interstate to make notes. It's really easy for me to write in the car. It's almost like I'm more free. I think it's because your mind has a task. With the noncreative side of your brain, you have to concentrate.

You have to keep it between the lines, watch your speed. You're doing all these things, so the creative side is allowed to run free and be creative without you trying to harness it. I think that's one of the reasons I'm able to write while I'm driving. A lot of times if I'm stuck on something, and I can't figure how to get this a certain way, then getting away from it and driving home, running, washing dishes, or whatever it is, will jar that lose.

Pam Rose - It depends. If it's words, I usually need to write them down. I carry a tape recorder with me all the time, and before that it was napkins and paper towels and dry cleaning receipts or check stubs.

Wayne Tester - Depends on my mood. Sometimes yes, sometimes no. If the ideas aren't flowing, then I'll put it down and say, I'll come back to you later. You can't force anything.

Trisha Walker - If it's an idea for which I've got a pretty good sense of the direction it's going, I'll go ahead and sit down with it and start. I've got ideas now where I've got the phrase in my head that I know is the germ of the idea, but for some reason or another, I may not know really what I want to say. Or maybe it's a metaphor for something that I haven't really gotten a clue on yet. So those just get parked in the back of the brain, and they'll find their own time. Every now and then I'll pull it out and nudge it and see if it's ready yet, and if it's not, I just leave it alone.

7. A blank sheet of paper—now what?

Gary Burr - I love to do that, in an intimidated, awful sort of way. I like to sit down with somebody and just say, we've got nothing. Let's pull it out of scratch; out of midair. You sit around and you look around and you try to come up with something. Or you'll just sing something and the words will sound like something that you didn't expect.

I always remember Bobby Hart. I wrote with him, and he was telling me how years and years ago, a Beatles song came out and at the end of it they sort of do this sing-a-long vamp after the chorus. It was *Penny Lane* or *Hello Good-Bye* or something, and he thought that they were singing, "Take the last train to something." He thought that was so cool, and when someone told him that that's not what they were saying, he said, "Well, gee, that's still a catchy thing. We should do that." He sat down with Tommy Boyce and they wrote *Take the Last Train to Clarksville*.

Kim Copeland - I prefer to wake up with an idea and live with it for a few hours while I'm just going through my routine, daily stuff and then sit down midmorning or afternoon and do a cluster-write on it. But if I need to write and don't have an idea, then I'll sit down with a blank sheet of paper and make myself, just as a creative exercise, come up with something and then develop it. When I see a blank sheet of paper, it's almost inspiring to me, because I visualize those margins crowded with notes and the first verse line right here and the first line of the chorus there and the second verse beginning here.

I've started many a song sitting down with a blank sheet of paper and no ideas at all. I actually have a song called *What Can I Say* which came from just such a scenario. I was sitting, staring at a blank page, going, "What can I say that hasn't been said a million times?" and I turned it into a love song which says, "What can I say that you haven't heard a million times before?" It talks about how words aren't always strong enough to express the depth of love.

Sometimes if you can be silly enough and free enough, it will lead you to something good. Let your mind and spirit wander, and it's interesting to see where they'll take you when you don't have any preconceived ideas of where you're supposed to be going.

Mary Ann Kennedy - With *I'll Still Be Loving You*, Pam [Rose] and I had gone over to Todd Cerney's studio. He had just gotten a bunch of synthesizers and stuff, so we were all jamming a little bit. Pam started playing this pretty progression, and Todd was playing this cool guitar thing behind her. I just started singing the melody. It came out. And once we got to the chorus, we said, man, let's go to this chord for the chorus. It just came out and I started singing, "I'll still be loving, I'll still be loving you." So that was kind of like a blank piece of paper, but it was inspired by the music. I do it more that way. When I've come up with neat titles or pieces of lyrics, then I sit down and work with a lyricist usually. It's usually inspired by the music.

Jess Leary - I am inspired by an instrument. For me to grab a pen and paper scares me sometimes. I would rather grab my tape recorder or my guitar and just mumble into it and hope nobody finds the tape. But that works well for me and everyone's different. I guess that because I'm musical, I tend to reach for the music, and even just holding my guitar sometimes, I feel like I'm channeling or something.

Wayland Patton - I prefer that [working with a blank sheet of paper]. It's difficult for me to get into a situation where someone has a song almost finished. When I come in on that kind of situation, I can maybe help finish it, but not much of me is going to be there. If somebody has quite a bit done and they seem really happy with it, it may be something that I don't like. You get in a situation where the song is more on his side of the table. When I co-write and we're sitting across the table from each other, to me, the song has to be out here in the middle. We both have to be working on the same song. Sometimes it can be two people working on different songs.

I like to start with nothing or maybe just an idea. It's not always the fastest way to write. To have someone come in with nearly a completed song obviously is a faster way to go. But I don't necessarily enjoy it, because if something goes out with my name on it, there are certain things about the song that have to reflect me.

Wayne Tester - Every day is a new blank sheet of paper to me, and that's the neat part about songwriting. You always know that you've got something new coming.

Kate Wallace - I probably wouldn't sit down in front of a blank sheet of paper. I would probably sit down with a guitar and start doodling with melodies. One of my favorite songs that I've written is called *Your Love Is All I Need*. I wrote that with Frank Goodman. Frank's a great guitar player. We'd been sitting around, and he played this beautiful melody, over and over again. I said, "Frank, that song is called *Your Love Is All I Need*." Boom, out it came. What I like to do is think of it like those slot machines where the fruits are spinning. I've got a melody, and I allow words and thoughts to go through my head like that till one sticks in that melody.

I wouldn't allow myself to sit down in front of a blank piece of paper. That's the kind of thing that would send me into inner critic overload. Rory Bourke says that there are two kinds of songwriting. "Descriptive" songwriting, which is the story, the imagery, the pictures. Bob McDill wrote *Good Old Boys Like Me* which, let's face it, is a classic. He wrote *Old Coyote Town* and that brilliant thing that Dan Seals did, *All That Glitters*. That's a descriptive song. The other kind of song, according to Rory, is "teaching." What that means is that when you hear something, you go through your own card catalog of your own life experiences, and you come up with an emotion, a feeling, an experience in your life that that song punches the ticket of. Those are the two schools of writing.

One stimulates your own personal emotions, and the other one stimulates your ability to see something and be actually in the process.

Kim Williams - I like to have ideas, but with the writers I feel real comfortable with, we don't have to have an idea. Ideas and lyrics are my strengths. I've written melodies on two songs that got into the top ten. One of them is *Warning Labels;* the other one is *Haunted Heart,* which is more of a feel than a melody. When I write with Garth, he's usually the melody writer. My strength is lyrics.

8. Is there such a thing as "overanalyzing" an idea?

Tony Arata - I think that the way it becomes overanalyzed is that maybe there just wasn't much there to begin with. If it's truly a great idea when you get it, you can almost see the end of the song about the same time you get the idea.

That's why I have a hard time with co-writing. Two people can't think an idea. In some cases people who co-write successfully can banter and can parlay, volley things off of each other. And you have to be able to do that, but I think when you start going this way and that way, maybe the problem is that there's just not much there on the idea.

Pam Belford - Sure. I've written my way out of a good song before.

Kent Blazy - That scares me. I get really opposed to that. I think you can overanalyze your way out of anything. I just try to go with the gut feeling and the heart of it, and if it didn't work, then you go on to something else. I would rather do that than overanalyze it and get it where you might have it perfect, but there's no heart there.

Rory Bourke - I've done that lots of times. But I also think that if an idea can't withstand that, I wonder if it's really a great idea. I've gotten to the point with people where they say, "Rory, stop with it. You're analyzing it to death. Let's just write it like this." And when we do, it usually means it was a great idea. I think an idea has to stand up to a lot of scrutiny.

Gary Burr - Yeah. Generally it happens when it's a really cool, up-tempo song. We'll start to get into, well, the story's this and you've got to have the person do this, and it's got to be that, and why were they motivated to do this. And we'll say, "Wait a minute. It's just people out there dancing. It's just a fun song. Let's not worry about it. Let's just write it." The lyric should match the attitude of the music. So sometimes I get a little too deep and want to say too much when "all she wants to do Is dance." Sorry Don.

Debi Cochran - Yeah, that happens a lot. I would like to think that the more I do this, the less I'll fall into the trap.

Jill Colucci - I'm always at risk of doing that. I have to catch myself, just like I have to quiet my mind down to get in touch with the feelings. It is a challenge with the editor to not overedit. When I start overanalyzing, I like to just stop for the day. That's part of what I mean when I say, "Stay out of my own way." I'm very analytical anyway, just in general.

Kim Copeland - I naturally don't do that. If anything, I'm guilty of just the opposite: rambling and free-flowing; not thinking too deeply about it in the beginning stages of writing. I don't edit at all in the beginning. But that's okay, because I feel like I'm a good editor when I go back to do that.

Editing and writing are two different things to me. They don't belong in the same room. I write and then I edit. I think overanalyzing is just editing too soon. It can totally destroy creativity. To me, the editor is not a creative person. The editor is a businessperson who comes in and says, This is the craft. These are the ABCs. These are the guidelines that we want to work within. That's a whole different person from the one who says, Here's an idea, take it and run.

Kye Fleming - I do have an analytical mind and it's fun for me, so I do have to consider that and not take the spirit out of something just because it was fun to chisel at it.

Lindy Gravelle - I can remember somebody saying about songwriting that that's a danger you can always get into. But remember your audience. Somebody once said, "Go for the pelvis." If you feel good or you like a song, then your whole body is into it. Maybe they don't show it, but it's something they're in tune with. For me, anyway, I can just analyze the feeling right out of a song. It just defeats the whole purpose of what you're trying to do, to touch their body. I'll back up a little. The groove, too, the groove for me is the foundation of so many songs, even slow songs. There's this pulse. Make them tap their toe or feel it in their pelvis. They want to get up and dance or whatever. Their heads move and they're grooving with you.

And then you go look at your lyric. When you're looking at it on paper, you see things that you might not even notice just listening to the song. Sometimes it's better that you don't even look at it on paper, because that's when I think the analyzing can get out of hand. You're just looking at this group of words lying on a piece of paper, forgetting how there's the element of music that's going to make those words do something a little different.

John Jarrard - Absolutely. Give me a song anytime that's emotionally satisfying over an intellectual masterpiece.

Al Kasha - I have been guilty of that. As I said when you asked me about low points, I think I was overanalyzing. You've got to go by your intuition and just let it go and not analyze every line. Sometimes I've been writing when I've been given a certain assignment, and that's when craft really has to come into play more than intuition, because you're given a whole bunch of information and you're really just saying it back to them and putting it in rhyme and stuff like that. That's different, where you *do* have to analyze.

One of the greatest commercials ever written (I didn't write it) was, "You deserve a break today at McDonald's." The reason it's so great is that it's saying, tell your mother don't cook. Go out to McDonald's. You deserve a break psychologically. So there's a case of analyzing something to a good sense. I think a good writer intuitively analyzes, but again, feeling is so much more important than the mind.

Mary Ann Kennedy - Absolutely [I overanalyze]. Some people don't know when it's really there. They can't stop. You'll be in the studio, and you'll still be thinking about these little changes in a line or the melody. I'm a Virgo and I'm self-critical big time, but darn it, you've got to get into that feeling place and know when it's right. If you don't know that it's right, it's probably not. I can get in touch with making a decision and say, that's it. Try to get to that place and then stop and then move on to another song. That gets into that definition of insanity.

Sandy Knox - I probably am guilty of it only because I think about ideas for a long time before I write them. Only if it's a really potent idea. With *She Thinks His Name Was John*, I worked on that for so long in my mind, but I think I wrote it the way I was supposed to. I didn't ever want to mention death or dying or AIDS or gay or anything that really was obvious. I had to write around the target and still hit it. But if you have to think about it *too* much, it's not worth writing. I'm kind of from the school that says it should come somewhat easy.

Kostas - You have to sit down and think about a song, but generally it shouldn't require that much thinking. A song is only a reflection of life, so you should have that ability to look at it and say this is wrong or this is right grammatically, or the idea may be in three different tenses. You have to straighten that out. You have to be able to sort through those things, but it shouldn't be that difficult. Nothing should be that difficult.

One of my absolute favorite songwriters was Stephen Foster. He was so simple and yet so right on. One of my favorite songs of his is a song called *Some Folks Do*. What it has to say is so simple, yet so charming and so real to life. I like simplicity in songs. I like the idea expressed to come through, to be charming, and to grab you. To do it in a natural way, not in a contrived way. *Everybody* is capable of doing that.

Jess Leary - You can think about an idea so much that you out-think it, but maybe you came up with a better one because of that. Things like that kind of unfold.

Jim McBride - You can overanalyze and you can sterilize it. I've had to learn that if it makes sense to you, it probably makes sense to most people. And if you've experienced it, a lot of other people have too. So just say it. And if you can say it in a way that's a little different, then that's what you need to do.

Pam Rose - You're asking a Virgo? Let's just take it apart. Absolutely, I have overanalyzed things. I really try not to do that anymore, and I'm pretty good about it now. Especially for a Virgo, I don't like things to be perfect. I like them to be perfectly imperfect, because that's what I think we are as humans. We're perfectly imperfect. And I think to strive toward perfection--it's something you aspire to, but I just rebel against things being too perfect.

Wayne Tester - If you overanalyze anything, you're in trouble. So you want, at the outset, to make sure it's a good idea, and then say, "Can I move forty million people out there with this idea?" It's not about anything else except moving the masses somehow. You want to make sure that can happen.

Trisha Walker - The more you write, you develop a sense of, okay, you're beating a dead horse here. Back up, go to lunch, come back to it, or stick it in your notebook and just leave it there for a week or two.

If you start overanalyzing it, either you're really scared that it's not the best, or it may actually not be good.

9. We've all heard the phrase "from the heart." What does it mean to you?

Tony Arata - I think it means when you're sitting in somebody's office, and you hear it played back over the speakers, and whatever their reaction is, you're always proud of it. It's going to make you glad that you committed it to paper and to tape. That doesn't mean that everything has to be profound. It has to do with sincerity. You know that this is really good. It makes me cry. It makes me laugh, but it isn't just filler. I think "from the heart" means it is something you'll stand by and that you're proud of, but I've never ascribed to the thinking that it meant you had to abandon all other elements of life and get in touch with the muse and all this bunk. I think "from the heart" is the best that you can write.

Pam Belford - Something that you feel. Not some little story that you're making up. Not some line you're throwing in because it rhymes or because it would be clever. That has its place, and I admire people who can write those songs. Sometimes I can write those songs. But when you're talking about "from the heart," that's something that you've experienced with your emotions. Usually, no matter how weird you think you are, or how singular you think your experience is, I find from playing songs that came from my heart that other people have the same experiences.

Kent Blazy - I think every song has to be approached from the heart. Everybody goes through a time where they're trying to do what their publisher says, or what somebody is telling them to do. When I came to town, I had pretty much just written from the heart. But I don't think I had the capacity yet to write from the heart *and* write commercially. Everybody was teaching me how to write commercially, so I kind of got away from the heart of it. There came a point when I decided I was going to get back to that feeling that I had before I came to town. I needed to take what I had learned and the feeling that I had before I came to town and put the two together. If it doesn't hit you from the heart, then it's probably not going to hit anybody else.

Steve Bogard - It means that you respect your audience. It means that you love your audience. It means that you want to say things that are going to move them and make a difference to them. When a guy spends ten percent of his income, which may be one hundred and thirty dollars a week, on a CD at Wal-Mart, and I can give him three minutes of magic, then I feel like I'm the king of the world. That's my goal.

Rory Bourke - It doesn't mean anything to me. That's a thing that people make up to convince other people that they're really serious about what they're doing. Sometimes what I write about is from the heart, but most of the time it's just a craft. It's human experience, but it may not be my experience. We were working on a song today, and the thing that appealed to me about the idea is that I feel like it's universal, that a lot of people have asked this question, and a lot of people have wondered about it. Is that from the heart? I know people who write from the heart all the time, and after a while they're a little unbearable to be around. I think when a writer is writing something in a song that touches them, they know that this is part of their experience, part of their history. When that happens, that's from the heart.

Gary Burr - I don't think you have to write songs from real life, but I think you have to capture real emotions. I don't think you have to write your own life story, but I really do think you've got to write it in a way and paint it with the emotions that everyone can identify with. There was a time in my life when I wasn't happy, and I wrote a lot of really nice love songs. And when people would say, "I know that you're not happy, but you're writing these great love songs," I'd say, "Well, these aren't songs about how my life is, these are songs about how I'd like my life to be." So they weren't true fact, but they were from the heart. They captured something from the heart. You just want to be able to have the person say, "Been there, felt that."

Debi Cochran - That's where the best songs come from. There are a lot of light, up-tempo, for-fun songs, but I think that most people who become professional songwriters do it because there are things inside that they want to get out—ways of coping with pain, ways of expressing joy and love and passion. Things that they want to talk about and they want to write about. I remember that the first time I ever met one particular co-writer of mine, I ran an idea by him that was not really on the country market, but was a lyric I felt pretty strongly about. He started singing this melody, and he started crying, and so did I. I thought, Whoa, this is going to be good. We've written a lot of songs together. So it's not unusual to start crying when you touch on something that serious. The great thing about male songwriters is that they're not into macho and hiding their emotions most of the time.

Jill Colucci - "From the heart" is where I want to always come from, in my singing and in my songwriting. It's kind of natural, I feel, to come from there as a singer. Maybe it's a little more challenging to make sure you're always coming from there as a songwriter, but that's what I want. In order to touch people's lives and reach people, it has to be that way. It can't be from the mind, and it can't be shallow. It has to have the power and the passion of the heart and soul. That phrase does a lot for me. I think it's what the planet needs. It would be a completely different world if, in our daily lives out there in the world, we just all came from the heart.

Music is such a strong form of communication. That's my vehicle to come from the heart. The biggest compliment to me is when a listener, someone who's heard one of my songs, says, "You knew exactly what I was feeling." It's like you were inside my heart, my mind, my soul. That is the greatest compliment I can receive as a writer. And I definitely wrote it from the heart if somebody starts saying that to me.

Kim Copeland - "From the heart" means to write what you feel and feel what you write. To write an idea because it's something you feel compelled to say, and do it in your own way and with your own words. Then let it find its place. Don't try to please anybody else or match what's out there on the radio. It's a very freeing way to write and, in my opinion, the only reason to do so.

Gary Earl - One of the reasons I want to write and perform is because I feel like music is a very healing thing. It helps people release emotions, whether it be joy or sorrow, that you may be refusing to deal with in your personal life. Somebody may have never really cried over the loss of their father; They may have just tried to hold it in and be strong. But they can hear a song on the radio like *Where've You Been* and just break up and cry. They're not really crying about the people in the song as much as their own held-back emotions, the part of them they haven't released. I've always felt that being a good songwriter, you can help so many people, whether it's spreading joy or releasing sorrow or whatever. It's a very healing thing.

Robin Earl - I believe music "from the heart" can be experienced by yourself or vicariously through someone else; it's also, caring about what it is you're doing. I think it's important that people know that there are other people with the same feelings and thoughts they have, and that there's some hope.

Kye Fleming - I have written a lot of songs from my head, and it's important to know how to do that because of the craft. I even made a lot of money from some of those songs, so I certainly don't put that down at all. They definitely have their purpose.

When I am moved emotionally by the words or the music, then it must mean that my heart was open. There's nothing forced about it. I think in most songs that's the ideal, but the whole song doesn't usually come that way for me. There's that moment of inspiration, and then I do need to use my head to tie some of the inspiration to this earth, so the words can make sense on an everyday level.

Al Kasha - I think that's the definition of talent. Talent has to come from the heart and that's what makes you different. You have to have the natural tools, and that comes from the heart and from enthusiasm. To me, the most important thing is the idea of the song. I'm a person who thinks that if the idea is great, it should write itself. Sincerity, to me, is the key to being a great writer. Heart first, brain second. Is it relevant, does it deal with intimacy, is it happening in today's world? I like songs that solve problems. I like Alan Jackson's songs very much. It's very funny because people don't realize how good he is, because it's so simple, but it [his writing] deals with real problems. That's why he's so successful. Vince Gill is extremely honest, and one of my favorite writers as well.

Mary Ann Kennedy - It's just got to be full of feeling. This is a craft, so a whole lot of cerebral energy has gone into the song, but it's got to have heart and soul. It's got to create that kind of empathetic emotion in another person. Being a publisher now, that's the hardest thing to talk to the young writers about. Sometimes it's like, "Yeah, that's a really good second verse. All the twists are there, but you know, you didn't make me cry, or I didn't really, really care." You've got to go deeper into your heart to empathize with this person that you're writing about. You're telling their story, so that's I guess what it is, and it is tough. It's got to be there. All the great ones have it.

(HAS BECOMING A PUBLISHER AFFECTED YOUR SONGWRITING?) Yeah, and I'm just a young publisher. We have five writers now, so it's taking more time and I'm writing less. But I'll tell you what it's doing—it's pushing me to go even more "from the heart" on my own and to be less conscious of commercial [value]. When I'm working with the writers, they're kind of where I was ten or fifteen years ago, so we talk a lot about the craft and what's commercially viable, because they want to make a living. They're just getting going, and they're really going for combining all the elements to make their mark and get those cuts. So talking about all that with them is making my songwriting stronger because I'm telling myself all these criticisms. I'm really aware of what's being cut and all, but it's making me conscious about putting into the songs what's really uniquely me. I tell them that too. This is fine, but you've got to put a trademark on it now. Let's come up with something that doesn't sound just like what Craig Weisman is doing. This is witty, this is fun, but that's Craig Weisman. Now let's create that little trademark for you. It's really helped.

I spend so much time talking about the songs with them that I don't write as much because I get burned out. It's a real challenge, but I really enjoy it and I think the town is just so full of talent right now. All the publishing companies are just busting out at the seams, and there are not the places for many talented writers to go that I was able to go to seventeen or eighteen years ago. When I went to a small, independent company, I could go to the heads of the company and actually sit there with them. Maybe I didn't have a strong lyricist on the staff, but I did have a musician who could really, really help me. Hands-on criticism. Some of it was harsh as could be, but that's how I learned. But nowadays those kind of people aren't on staff at the Warner Brothers and the EMIs. I've been there and they're so busy just plugging and having their staff meetings and everything. Songwriters aren't running the companies anymore. That's why we started ours. Amanda Hunt was the first person we signed. I had known her for years and encouraged her to write. We set her up with Chuck Jones, and when *Your Love Amazes Me* was turned in on that little work tape, it wasn't the song that it is. They had some mature writers like Kye [Fleming] and me there to critique that song and say, "This is a classic, but the chorus doesn't have the heart, or whatever, and you need to change this and that." I helped produce the demo with those guys. They were young writers at the time and they had our expertise to help. It feels very satisfying to me to be able to pass the torch and help those kids.

Sandy Knox - Well, I'm real big on writing from the heart. It would be fraudulent if I sat down and wrote a song that had to do with my husband and my three children and woes that I'm going through being a wife and a mother, because I'm not a wife and a mother. It would show in the lyrics that they were contrived. I think it's very important to write what you know and to write what you're feeling also. To write what's going on in your life, and if it is sad or if it's happy, it's going to show in your lyrics. I think a song that's written from the heart screams compared to a song that's just, "hey, I've got an idea, let's write this."

She Thinks His Name Was John was written from the heart. I thought about that song for years before I wrote it. My brother died of AIDS, so I was close to the devastation that it causes. Once I put myself in the position of the character of the song, I really got focused in on the lyrics. I wondered, What if this was me who was getting the news? What would be my first thoughts? My very first thoughts would be, I will never have a baby. I will never know the love of a child. That's been taken from me. I will probably never be married. I will never really make satisfying love again without the shadow of HIV. When I started thinking about all these things, it became very real to me. I saw the character, the girl, very scared and just sitting there with all of those things going in her life. I mean, basically you're dead before you're physically dead. You're emotionally robbed and socially robbed before you die with that disease.

The song generated a lot of press even though it only went to number seven. With a song like that, you don't care if it's not a number one, because they weren't even planning on releasing it as a single. The radio started playing it and it snowballed. Then MCA got on the bandwagon and got behind it. It affected a lot of people's lives. A lot of young people have written Reba letters. It generated a lot of attention, which was good. Stories have been passed on to me from DJs, phone calls that they've gotten from women. It did affect their lives.

Anytime I've ever taught workshops, I've said a song has got to cause one of three emotions. It's got to make you want to laugh, cry, or make love, and if it doesn't cause one of those basic emotions, then you've just got a little ditty. I think that's really important for writers, that we know that the song affects people.

Jess Leary - "From the heart" means what's real. No cutting any corners, just the real deal.

Pam Rose - Well, that's how I write. Every once in a while, I'll use my mind, but only to get me out of jams. You know, I think as much as a song can be from the heart and inspired, the better.

Joyce Rouse - "From the heart" means from the center of your being.

Wayne Tester - It means being real and genuine, no plastic. No plastic coating on it. The heart is the soul to me. Whatever you write needs to be part of you. Don't try to make it something it's not. Make it you.

Trisha Walker - I don't know that every song I've ever written has a piece of my own experience in it, but a good percentage of them do—whether it's been a personal experience of mine, or it's happened to somebody I know. To me, songs that aren't from the heart are those that are just crafted, just fabricated. A lot of them are really good, but I heard somebody say one time that what those kinds of songs seem to lack is something called "the third dimension." You can have a great tunesmith and lyric writer craft a perfect song, but if it's not something that he or she's had some experience in, it lacks that third dimension. That something that makes it real.

10. Do you ever feel like everything has already been said?

Tony Arata - Well, sometimes when I'm sitting behind a guitar and can't think of anything, I feel like that. A sure way to get past that is just go visit one of the writer's shows or turn on the radio. Just get a real kick in the gut and go, "Wow, why didn't I say that?" Then you realize it has all been said, it's just that some people are able to say it differently.

Pam Belford - Sure. But when I'm with a co-writer, we just end up talking all afternoon. I could feel really guilty about that. We'll talk all afternoon, but eventually, somebody will say something, and we'll say, "Why don't we write a song about that?" And we do.

Steve Bogard - No, I don't.

Rory Bourke - I think that everything generally has been said, but I think today there's a new way to say what we said yesterday, and tomorrow there'll be a new way to say what we said today.

Gary Burr - Every once in a while you get these periods where you want to just throw the guitar away because you realize you're writing a song that sounds exactly like the song you wrote before, and they're not all that different in content. You're starting to forget if you said this line in this song or two songs ago. So that's when you just need to take a break. You need to turn on TV and watch "Murder, She Wrote."

Kim Carnes - Yeah, sometimes. When you are looking for that unique line, a way to say something, and everything you think of has been said before.

Debi Cochran - Yes, you go through that periodically. You think every idea's already been used. But you just keep plowing along anyway. A lot of things you write may be kind of mediocre, but once in a while you get something you think is truly wonderful, and you say, "Okay, I'll keep going until I get the next one of those." Because there is another one out there, somewhere.

Kim Copeland - It hasn't, but it can feel that way when you're in a slump. There's always a new idea or a twist on an old one that's waiting to be written. Usually when I feel that way, it's because I'm either in a rut with my writing or moving too fast, when I just haven't had time to sit down and be still and listen in a while.

Gary Earl - No. That reminds me of the guy in charge of the patent office about a hundred years ago who wanted the president to shut it down because he believed that everything that could be invented already had been. True story.

Kye Fleming - Well, I have that feeling, but I know that's not true. It has been said, but it hasn't all been said every way it can be said. So that's the difference.

Mary Ann Kennedy - That's the toughest thing after so many years of writing so many songs. It's all been said. But then, darn it, I get turned on again when I hear something that's a new way of saying the same old thing. That's what we're all looking for. And occasionally, you'll find a new subject.

Never lose hope that there is a space out there for your voice, because there is. Never give up hope of finding that way to do it. You can find it if you believe it, because there are infinite, infinite possibilities for combinations, and you can find one.

Sandy Knox - Yeah, sure. Everything's already been said. What do I have left to say? There's nothing for me to say. There's nothing going on in my life to write about. Will I top that? Will I ever write something as poignant as *She Thinks His Name Was John?* Yeah, I think you go through that every time you write a really good song that you know is a contender.

Kostas - Yeah, everything has. That's the beauty of songwriting. I see us as individuals who go up this mountain of words looking for little gems or ideas. I see us as being prospectors, so to speak, with words being the little nuggets we're looking for.

Jess Leary - If I did feel that way, I would be very gloomy. But I do feel that I've gotten with writers who may have had a title, or I might have even had a title, that sure has been done a lot. We'll say, let's just get off it. Let's do something else. Or let's just think of the most bizarre, different way to approach it if we're going to write it. Been done is no fun.

Joyce Rouse - I have felt that way. I don't feel that way anymore. I have moved through that one.

Wayne Tester - No. Never. The whole universe is open, and you can say something a little different than it's been said before. There are no rules.

11. Do you think of yourself as disciplined?

Tony Arata - No, other than the fact that I do write, and I do try to write all the time. I'm disciplined enough to be concerned with hoping that at some point when I look back over a body of work, to some degree, there was some element of style that was mine. I'll write anything, but there are a few things that I would like to have stay consistent. I've always tried, to some extent, to stay disciplined when it comes to lyrics. Whether or not they're the lyrics that everybody wants to hear, I don't know. I'm just saying that I've always been very concerned about that element of it. So that's the only discipline. But as far as any regimen or anything like that, I don't really have one. The discipline is toward the actual finished product and making sure that that's something you'd want to play for somebody. I can't think of anything worse than having a very specific ritual and coming out with a bunch of songs that you aren't really proud of. I think it's the end, not the means, that has value.

Pam Belford - As a rule, I'd say I'm very undisciplined. But I guess I have a certain amount of discipline, because I work a forty-hour-a-week job. I write now with regularity, because someone is paying me to do it, and I feel like I owe it to them. I work my forty-hour-a-week job, and that includes working at the library on Saturday so I can take a day off during the week to write on Music Row. I generally keep that day off filled up with one, if not two, writing appointments.

Kent Blazy - I think I am disciplined in an artistic way. Discipline for me is totally different than for somebody in another business. I try to listen to new stuff that comes out and keep up with who's doing what. I keep notepads in my car, by the bed, by the TV, in my room here, and anything anybody says that I think would be worthwhile in a song, I'll write down. I think I'm always trying to keep my mind open to thinking with that side of my brain, as much as it irritates some people. I try to work on it every day in some capacity, whether it's writing songs or trying to come up with ideas. I try to read. Reading is good a way for me to become inspired.

Rory Bourke - Yes. Generally speaking, I write four days a week with people, then I take care of plugging. Mornings, I take care of business. I'm in business for myself now, so I have to take care of all my computer work and getting songs ready that I'm going to pitch.

Steve Bogard - Yeah, I'm very disciplined.

Gary Burr - Yeah, I do. I'm very disciplined. I was just talking to someone about this last night. They were talking about how they had been in town for three years, and they were going out of their mind because nothing was going on. He sort of had the attitude of, what am I supposed to do during this time? I'm writing and I'm listening, but nothing's happening. I told him this is when you learn your discipline. You're going to need the discipline, because if things really take off, there are so many distractions that come with that, that if you're not disciplined, you'll be all done working. You'll spend all your time on the telephone and shaking hands with people and exchanging phone numbers. If you don't have some kind of discipline, you won't get new songs written. So, I'm really disciplined. I have no idea how many songs I write. Probably eighty a year. I've got a lot of songs, and I like to go to work. I work in some form, but I write several songs a week. My dad gave me that good Protestant work ethic.

Kim Carnes - I have discipline if I'm on a roll, in a super creative place. Or I have discipline when I have time to get together with writers like Greg Barnhill and Vince Melamed; I will definitely block out the whole day. When I'm in the studio making an album, I have complete discipline. My worst nightmares have been some producers I've worked with who have talked on the phone the whole time. Once I go in the studio, whether it's to make a demo or an album, I don't want any phone calls. We're there to do that, and I'm focused one thousand percent. When it comes to work, I'm disciplined.

Debi Cochran - No. Not at all. If I were disciplined, I would have learned to play guitar even though I seem to have no talent. Then this would have been much easier. But on the other hand, I am a person who drove up here every week for three years just because I had to do this. I'm driven, I guess, but disciplined, no. I come in here every day whether I have a writing appointment or not, just to hear what's going on, to see what may have happened overnight. I think of this as a job, and I do it every day unless I have some other activity that I have to do. You can't sit around and wait for inspiration. Now it happens, and it's wonderful when it does. Therefore, there are notepads and pens stashed in every corner of my house. By the bed, by the kitchen sink, everywhere. Those things are wonderful when they happen, and you have to have those as little seeds to start everything else. You can't sit around and wait to be inspired to write a song. That's a hobby. This is a career. You have to take it seriously.

Jill Colucci - I am at the beginning of a new period. I've got my moments when I am really disciplined. I did that whole very undisciplined lifestyle as an artist for years, and then I started singing in the jingle business. When I started doing jingles, they wanted me to be in the studio singing at nine or ten in the morning. The first day I walked in about thirty minutes late, and I caught the vibes in there. I think becoming a session singer in L.A. really helped me become more disciplined, because I saw that I needed to become more disciplined to be successful.

Even songwriters here, the people I co-write with, usually like to start a little earlier than I do. I've been known to write at ten, which is still early for me, but I still prefer eleven. I have a part of me that resists that. Maybe the creative part of me just wants to be more free-spirited and not really commit to such an intense schedule. I work really hard. The reason I got into the music business is so that I wouldn't have to work for a living but now I work longer hours and more days than I ever anticipated I would.

Kim Copeland - I can be. I know how to be, but I don't demand it of myself. That sounds suspiciously like a "no." However, I am more creative during periods when I'm more disciplined.

Gary Earl - I tend to be somewhat driven and can focus on one thing at a time very well, but I'm not always disciplined about what I'm focusing on.

Robin Earl - I can be very driven at times. I'm pretty motivated by deadlines. A lot of our work for films has been with a definite time-frame. The hardest part of being disciplined is when we're trying to do many things at once, and then it's harder to stay organized.

Kye Fleming - I go in and out of that. I think had I not been as disciplined as I was those first six years, I would not have had the success that I had. That worked really well for me then. And there are times when I need to back off of it and give myself permission not to be disciplined.

Lindy Gravelle - Oh, yeah. I just got my black belt in karate, so I know that I can accomplish something that requires discipline. People tell me that, so my lifestyle must reflect it.

(DO YOU APPLY THAT TO YOUR WRITING?) Yeah, but sometimes I think I could be more disciplined. I've just got so many things going on, it's hard to keep it all in check.

John Jarrard - Yes.

Al Kasha - Yes, extremely disciplined! I think a writer must be. The writer's job, every day, is not to have the ego to think he's more than a plumber or more than a person who fills gas at a pump station. I think discipline is vital for a writer. You just do it every day and you get better at it.

Mary Ann Kennedy - I'm very disciplined, but I'm very nonstructured. And I guess, if you wanted to sit down and analyze a lot of the stuff I've written, you could probably say the same about it. I'm conscious of great melody and form, or strong melodic verses and a strong transition into a solid chorus, which comes under the heading of craft, but I like to throw in surprises whenever possible. So I guess that is a "nonstructure", and I guess that's how my life is. I've been so busy with my private life the last few months, I haven't written a song. But I have a demo session coming up Monday, and in the last week I've completed three songs that I'm nuts about. So I am real disciplined and hard-working, but structure ... it's hard for me.

Sandy Knox - This is a yes and a no. Sometimes I'm very disciplined. There have been periods in my life where I've been very disciplined. I get up at the same time every morning and I go exercise. I don't drink coffee or alcohol or smoke or anything. I'm really good for a year and a half, really clean and pristine. Then I'll go, "I'm tired of that," and I'm very undisciplined. That goes into my writing too. When I'm being really disciplined and I've got everything working, I'm normally writing more and being in the studio more. And then I just get burnt out and tired and don't want to do it. I don't want to follow a regimen or a schedule. I just chalk it up to: it's rejuvenating me for the next go-round.

Kostas - I've spent my time being disciplined, and then I've spent my time being a free spirit. Now I'm just kind of hanging on the line, waiting to dry.

Jess Leary - I am. I like to work. I like to feel like I'm doing something and that I have a purpose. I'm not really good with vacations, although I'm working on it. I always feel like I'm missing something or that I could be doing something or that someone else is writing a better song today. I'm very much into that competitive thing, that "I know I can do this." I just really want to try. It makes me jump out of bed in the morning. I literally love what I do.

Some days I'm tired though, and I don't want to do it, and so I don't. I've learned that's the best thing to do if you're just not into it. Take a day off. Kye Fleming has been a big help to me. I've called her many times during my writer's blocks, in tears. "It's gone! I can't ever write again." And she's great. She's says, "Well, what are you doing? Did you take the day off?" And I say, "Yeah, I took the day off and I'm outside raking leaves, and then I'll run back inside and play my guitar." And she says, "That's what you're doing wrong. You came inside to play your guitar. Stay outside. Get away from that guitar. Don't go near it. Go play in your yard."

It never occurred to me that that was okay. It's a weird thing. I wouldn't say I'm a workaholic, but I could be. I don't want to be, so I try not to be, but I have little tinges of one.

Jim McBride - No. Bob McDill is definitely disciplined. Gary Burr is disciplined. Kim Williams is disciplined. But I can not go in every day at nine o'clock and sit and write all day long. Maybe I should try that one year and see what happens. I try every day at some point to pick the guitar up. It's amazing; sometimes you just pick it up and there it is. But I feel it when it's there, and I feel it when it's not there. When it hasn't been there for a while, I start to worry about it

Pam Rose - The "D" word. I aspire to be disciplined. That's about all I can say. I mean, that's a struggle for me. That's one of my greater challenges: the "D" word.

I'm not as structured about writing as some people are. I could never go in at nine o'clock and come out at five. I just can't do that. I rebel against that. I think there's still something so mysterious and exciting about writing that I'm not really able to put that structure on it. But that's just me. I'm not saying that something mysterious and exciting can't happen within a structure. Just for me, I like that seed to happen first, and then I'll put it in a structure.

Joyce Rouse - No. I'm very much an instinctual and spontaneous person. I've had to learn some discipline and along with the discipline, some organization. That's one of the things that I bad-mouthed myself about for years, how disorganized I was and how undisciplined I was. A really wise woman said to me one day, "You know, you aren't disorganized, you just have your own sense of organization. You know where everything is, and it may not be the same as everybody else's." I really think we need to honor our individuality.

Wayne Tester - Very much so. You have to be [disciplined]. You have to be a self-motivator in this business. I feel I have a really good work ethic, because I'll go in every day no matter if I have a co-write set up or not. I'll do something else, work on some melodies or work on ideas.

Trisha Walker - Pretty much. Again, it goes in phases. There are phases when I thought, Okay, at a certain time every day, I will sit down with a blank piece of paper, and whether anything comes out or not, I will be disciplined and sit there. And then there have been other phases in my writing career, where I think, Okay, I'm not going to even wear a watch. I don't care for the next five days what I eat or what I wear. I'm just going to be totally loose. And that worked. So it kind of goes in phases.

Kate Wallace - Absolutely not. I have no discipline at all. The only reasons I can think of for having a publishing deal (and they're very minor when you weigh them against not having one) are: if you need the two hundred and fifty or three hundred dollars a week; and second, the discipline of having an office, other writers there, and you book the time and go write the songs. Now without a publisher, I thoroughly enjoy myself. I write when I want to, with whom I want to, and if I write ten songs a year that's fine with me, because I'm going to like all ten of those songs. If you're in a factory situation, yes, there is discipline, but what you run the risk of is writing thirty-five songs a year, ten of which you'll like. It's just a question of how you want to go about doing it. But in terms of discipline, I have virtually none. It's not in my soul to be a writer; it's in my soul to be a singer. To me, an artist is a person who can take an instrument out onto a stage by themselves, play a song that they wrote, and knock the place down. That's an artist, and there are very damn few of them in the country music business.

Kim Williams - Yes. I definitely believe the difference in people who achieve a high level of success is not talent, it's the discipline. I know writers who are a lot more talented than me who haven't even come close to having the success, because they don't have the discipline to go after it. I know too many people who believe the solution to their problems lies outside themselves. That's got to be an awful feeling. If I want a George Strait cut, I know I can get one. It may take me a year or two, but I can get it. Any problem I might have getting one lies within me.

12. Is your writing style altered by writing on a different instrument?

Kent Blazy - I play a little keyboard, some bass, and mandolin. But my main instrument is electric or acoustic guitar. That's how I made my living. I used to keep my keyboard set up at the other house we were in. I used that sometimes because it does give you different sounds or voicings.

Gary Burr - I play a little keyboard. Two of the songs that I've had on the radio in the past couple of years were songs that I started on the piano.

(WHAT MAKES YOU CHOOSE ONE OVER THE OTHER?) Dissatisfaction with where it's going on the instrument that I first chose. I like to pick up an instrument that I'm not real familiar with. I'm real familiar with the guitar. I've been playing it for so long that sometimes I'll kind of go on automatic pilot. When I'm on a chord I'll just automatically go to the next chord that I've gone to a million times. You put me down at a piano, and because I don't know what I'm doing, I'm hunting and pecking, I might take it somewhere different. And there are times when I'll sit down and write a song on a mandolin or a bass or something that I'm totally unfamiliar with, because I don't have any signposts. What comes out is generally pretty interesting.

Jill Colucci - I play to write. When I do shows and play in-the-rounds, I play acoustic guitar. I'm a great little strummer and have good rhythm and a good feel, but I wouldn't record my guitar playing in the studio. I use it to write. What happens for me is I write up-tempo on guitar and ballads on piano. It just works that way. If I'm feeling a ballad, I want the keyboard immediately. I tend to just write up-tempo, groove stuff on guitar.

Kye Fleming - I play guitar and piano, but just enough not to do myself much harm. When I moved to Nashville, I started writing with Dennis Morgan, and he played guitar. I did more lyric and he did more music, so I just kind of let it go. I ended up forgetting most everything.

(DO YOU WRITE STRICTLY LYRICS NOW?) Every now and then I'll write one by myself. I'll still take a stab at that occasionally. I think I just enjoy being able to have a vehicle, to have somebody give me some music that turns me on and inspires me. Or the challenge of trying to come up with the concept without music. I write with Mary Ann [Kennedy] a lot now, and she needs it the other way. She needs the lyric first. But I usually like to write the other way. I like to be inspired by something.

Lindy Gravelle - Lately I've been really hammering on the guitar. It's different and new. You can't groove the same way on piano and guitar. They're two different kinds of feel.

Mary Ann Kennedy - I just have really good instincts and kind of a natural ability to pick up a whole bunch of different instruments and do what I do on it. I would say I'm not a virtuoso on any instrument. I have a style of mandolin playing that I developed that really is cool, and it works. It's my sound and my tunings and it's very rhythmic. Like with the drums, I studied a little bit in college, but basically I'm just self-taught. All those rhythms come to me. I just have a real instinct for the rhythm. As far as playing guitar and all, I'm a stylist more than a soloist.

(DO YOU ALWAYS WRITE WITH A GUITAR?) No. A whole lot of the time I do, though. I love to play unusual instruments. Not for the sake of being unusual, but it truly does give it a breath of fresh air. I like to keep all my stuff lined up and pick something up on a certain day and see what feels right. I probably use guitar more than anything, though.

Jess Leary - I'm a great piano player in the key of C. I wish I was forced as a small child to play the piano because I never got the lessons, and I wish I had some training. I've learned all of my instruments pretty much by ear. I did take a few lessons, but it was never on a page you know. So I have this little mental block with those notes. You might as well just teach me Japanese at the same time because it just does not compute. If you play it for me, I can learn it.

(DO YOU EVER WRITE ON THE PIANO?) I've written some songs on piano. In the key of C, of course. In fact, I think the piano is such a nice change. To sit down in front of this big, beautiful, wooden thing. I have all these candles on it, a candelabra, and I turn the lights out, turn on the tape recorder, and go away in my mind and see what comes out. I've come up with some neat things that way. Sometimes I'll transpose it over to the guitar when I don't know what else to do on the piano because I'm not that good on it, but it definitely has inspired me to write different styles. (COUNTRY MUSIC?) I don't think I look at it that way. I just try to write something that I like. Something that sounds good to me. In fact, that pretty much goes all along. I don't necessarily sit down to try to write country. I have in the past, but lately I'm in that place where I say, "Let's just write the best song we can write." Something that you just really like.

(DO YOU TRY TO BE COMMERCIAL?) I am still guilty of that, and it's okay to be, of course, because everybody's doing that. Sometimes you're just in that kind of mood. Let's write something that you hear on the radio, something that you really like. Something fun. It depends on what kind of mood you're in. Some days you're in a fun, silly mood. Some days you're serious, and you kind of have to go with how you feel because if you don't, it's probably not going to come out very good.

Pam Rose - If I'm sitting at the keyboard and something stumbles out, then it's pretty obvious. The same goes for the guitar. I may end up swapping those. A guitar thing may sound better on the piano. Sometimes I'll hear something in my head and if I go to any instrument too soon, it will go away. I'll lose it, so there have been times when I've taken days or a week or maybe even two weeks before I'm hearing the whole thing. I don't consider myself a great instrumentalist, although I love to play these instruments, and I have some skills on both of them. Sometimes it limits me. I'm confined by my knowledge of the instrument. And so a great part of my writing is what just kind of comes in there and what I work on in my head. It's convenient, too, because I can do it while I'm brushing my teeth.

Trisha Walker - Because I was schooled in piano, I can see the way things form on a keyboard better than I do on a guitar. Guitar is more by feel. I had a composition teacher in college who always used to admonish us to compose in our heads before we ever went to a piece of paper or instrument. Really work it out in your head, before you ever sit down with pencil and paper. So a lot of times I'll just groove. When I used to run more, I'd get out and run and do a lot of rhythmic grooving while I was running. When I drive, that frees me up. I like to get in the car and drive, just think patterns and things. But I'm a better rhythmic guitar player than I am a rhythmic piano player. So if I had to pick one or the other, it would probably be guitar.

Jill Colucci - I was reminded with my first number one, and every one since, just how powerful music is.

Kim Williams - I definitely believe the difference in people who achieve a high level of success is not talent, it's the discipline.

John Jarrard - Give me a song that's emotionally satisfying over an intellectual masterpiece.

Tony Arata - If it's a truly great idea when you get it you can almost see the end of the song about the same time you get the idea.

CHAPTER FOUR

THE SONG

Kye Fleming - I believe that if you don't have a great opening line, you'd better make up for it everywhere else.

John Jarrard - The basic skill of a writer is persistence. I thank God for all the people that are more talented than I am, that went home on the bus because they couldn't deal with rejection and the odds.

Kostas - It's no different than painting a picture with lines and colors, except that three minutes is your boundary and the words are the color and story.

Marijohn Wilkin - People write from where they come from. They write from their experiences, and it comes out in their writing even if they don't realize it.

1. How important is the opening line?

Tony Arata - I don't really think of it in terms like that, but going back to some of the songs that have been recorded, you can see that there was some thought put to that. You've only got two and a half to three and a half minutes, so I don't think it's *just* the opening line of the song that's important. There are only going to be twenty lines, so every line is important.

I think that in many cases, there are a lot of great hook lines and a lot of great catchy lines but the rest of it just seems to be filler. I'm not saying that every line has to be a quote, but every line should make some point and be important. Otherwise, you could stop after one line, just have music and then your hook line. Here's my big statement and that's all I've got to say and I ain't saying no more. So I think that every line should be important.

Pam Belford - I think that's the most important part of the song, as far as playing at a writer's night or grabbing the audience's ear. And as far as when you're pitching, when you get the opportunity to play your song for an artist or producer, they're listening to hundreds and hundreds of songs, and you're lucky to get them to listen to the first line. It had better be good if you want them to listen to the second line.

Kent Blazy - When I came to town, Tim DuBois was a really big help to me. He lived down the street, and we wrote a little bit. What he stressed to me was that you've got to grab them with the opening line. So I do try to think of something that hopefully will catch the listener and bring him into the song long enough.

Most country songs are four lines before the chorus, so if you can get them from that first line to the chorus, hopefully you'll have them. So I do approach it by trying for something a little different or something interesting enough to make the listener want to go further.

Steve Bogard - Very important. I like opening lines that make you go, "What? What's this about?"

Rory Bourke - I think we all know it's important. Most writers just instinctively know.

Gary Burr - That was something that I learned from Pat Alger. I think he's the king of that. He always comes up with a great opening line. I really didn't think about it that much. Whatever came up, came up. But listening and learning from him, I really see the importance of having that opening line that is just brilliant. It draws you right into the story. I'm not one of those guys that carries around a pad full of titles, but I'll have a few titles here and there. A lot of times, I'll take something that I think is a title and I'll make it the opening line, because if it's good enough to be a title, it will make a killer opening line. I just sort of forfeit it on the altar of short attention spans, just to make sure that I grab the people right off the bat because, frankly, a good opening line is just as important as a hook line. So I don't feel like I'm sacrificing much.

Debi Cochran - In the writing process, you have to start wherever you can get a toe hold. But yes, that opening line has to be pretty good, so you may go back and keep tweaking on that until you get something that you think is really going to catch the listener's ear. It's got to catch everybody.

Jill Colucci - I'm really into lyrics, so I think that every line counts. If that opening line doesn't make you want to listen to the rest, then it doesn't matter what I do after that. I think it's really important to draw the listeners' ears, so that they are attentive and willing to listen to the rest of what you have to say. No doubt about it, it's extremely important. But equally important, after you write that great line, is keeping the standard up to match that line, especially the second line and especially the second verse. You know, you can get lazy. Every line of the lyric is important. You only have a certain amount of time. It's not like writing a book. You don't have the luxury of all the pages. It's not like a film where you have two hours. You've got somewhere between three and four minutes and that's not a lot of time. In the early days of my writing, it might take me two lines to say something that now I can say in one and make that second line even more powerful. I don't know what you'd call that, economic writing or something. To put more power into it and say more in a smaller amount of time. I work very hard at that.

Kim Copeland - When I'm listening to songs, that's what makes me want to hear the story or not. In my writing, at first, it's just a way to get into the song. But when a song is in its almost finished state, then I do go back and look at the opening line and ask, "If this is the only line of the song I get to hear, does it pique my interest? Does it make me want to hear more?" You have to isolate that line and say, "This is all this person's going to hear. Are they going to say, 'oh' and walk away, or are they going to say, 'Hey, I wonder what happens next?'"

Gary Earl - I may spend more time on it than anything except the hook or the line that sets up the hook.

Robin Earl - Opening lines are very important. A good opener can really make me want to listen to the song, especially a clever one or one that paints a vivid picture.

Kye Fleming - I can't say that I always go with it, but I believe that if you don't have a great opening line, you better make up for it everywhere else. You've got to have just the right amount of "smack 'em in the face" to make it work. You can't let a lyric go very far without really engaging the listener or you've lost them. Make them feel something on that first line, then chances are they'll listen for three or four more lines, and then you can hit them again.

Lindy Gravelle - Boy, they sure say that's such an important line. And I'd have to agree. Some are better than others, but I wouldn't say every great song starts with a great opening line. I would like to always feel that every line, especially from the opening line's perspective, is tipping you off to what's coming up. It sets the tone, it keeps the interest from the get-go, and you're already giving them a clue. Hooking them in right there is pretty cool if you can do it.

John Jarrard - I think they're all important. I don't really think about the opening line.

Al Kasha - I think it's the most important line in the song. You have to work the hardest on it. It is the opening line that gets attention. To put it in a journalistic standpoint, without sounding too clinical, it's who, what, where, when, and why. I think it states the whole premise of what the song is about. When Cynthia Weil wrote, with Barry Mann, "You never close your eyes anymore when I kiss your lips," that tells me what the whole song is about. "There's got to be a morning after, if we can hold on through the night" tells me what the whole conflict is about. I'm a very big believer in opposite titles or antonyms, too, which a lot of country songs deal with. Berlin did a lot of that. The Bible deals in antonyms. Jesus preached in antonyms all the time: "If you lose your life, you gain your life."

Mary Ann Kennedy - It's definitely got to set the mood, and make you want to continue to listen, and create a wonder, but as far as knocking you out, no. To me, the ultimate, the most important line, has to be your payoff at the end of the chorus, and I am a sucker for that. You've got to feel your heart either rise or sink right there, or it isn't happening for me. I place more importance on that line.

Sandy Knox - I think, for the most part, that the first line of the song is the most important. That's the first thing that the listener, the artist, the publisher, or whoever, is going to hear. I think it's really important that it be something substantial.

Kostas - The opening line is pretty important. It is the beginning of the thing. It will continue. It's like a road. With your opening line, you just paved a few steps, and you've got to keep going from there. So it is pretty important. It's nothing that isn't natural though. Whatever comes out first seems to always be the right thing. There were times when we didn't pay much attention to those little details, but now we do.

I don't consider songwriting a craft. I don't care what other people call it. Some people have called it a craft. It's something that comes from within you. It's a labor of love. It's no different than painting a picture with lines and colors, except that three minutes is your boundary and the words are the colors and story. To me, a good song comes from the heart and from the soul, and somehow those elements, those spiritual elements, are involved. And that same good song will touch the heart and the soul of whoever is listening. That's how you can tell there is a song there. Because it goes to the same place it came from. Life is more than just eating at McDonald's. There has got to be more sustenance to our music than just these little three-minute ditties that mean nothing.

Jess Leary - It certainly is something that I like to hear in a song. Something that grabs you for whatever reasons right off the bat. I think it's important. It's not always easy to come up with.

Jim McBride - I love first lines of songs. I think it's very important. I look for the most interesting first line.

Wayland Patton - I think it's extremely important. It's like the opening sentence or the opening paragraph of a great novel. In a song, since you're looking at a limited amount of time, you have to catch the listeners' interest and say a lot. I think it's very important. If you're working on a commercial song, and you start from a hook, then a lot of times you're working backwards from there. You go back and try to come up with that first line. But I have written songs, and these are usually songs I'm writing on my own, where I have written from the front, where they just begin to come out. It may not come from a specific line idea, but from a general situation that I want to write about. A strong emotion or a person. I begin to write from an image and then the hook will come out of there.

Pam Rose - It was in the early eighties and Mary Ann [Kennedy] and I were going someplace with Larry Gatlin and Rudy and Steve. It was when *Ring on Her Finger/Time on Her Hands* came out the first time. Larry came up to us in this airport and said, "My God, what an opening line!" "She stood before God, her family and friends and vowed that she'd never love anyone again." He said, "I just can't believe what a powerful opening line that is." He said, "I always said, if you don't have a great, great opening line that will stop people, then your song will suffer for it."

I always tried to remember that. I think he's got a good point. I think there are exceptions to every rule, but it's always great to have that, and I really do feel that that's very important.

Joyce Rouse - I believe the first line of the song is just extremely important for setting the tone, and my goal is to come up with a killer first line every time.

Wayne Tester - The opening line is as important as the hook is. I don't have any steadfast rule. I start with the hook usually. And I'm the idea man on a lot of the songs that I co-write. I'll bring the melody and the idea, or just the melody or sometimes a partial lyric. So there are no rules, but I'm stronger melodically than lyrically. But I do write lyrics, depending on the co-writer and depending on the song.

Trisha Walker - The opening line is important, although that's not always the first thing I come up with. I may start with a little rhythm riff or a little melodic figure or maybe a lyric phrase that for some reason or another, just caught my attention. It may or may not be the opening line.

Kate Wallace - I come from the Rory Bourke school that says it's really important. It doesn't have to be the line that changes history, but it has to either inspire someone to imagine something or remind them of something or make them ask a question. I love that George Strait song, *The Chair*. "Excuse me, but I think you've got my chair," and then he comes around at the end of the song and says, "That wasn't my chair after all." That song gives me goose bumps. It is so beautifully written. The melody is so gorgeous. Start to finish, that is a piece of work. From that first line out.

Marijohn Wilkin - I think it's extremely important. It's "wow." I'll give you an example. When I was given the chorus to *One Day at a Time,* I was backed in a corner emotionally and drained spiritually. I had decided that I couldn't go it on my own any more, that I needed a higher power. I went to church, I sat down, and I talked to God. He gave me some pretty good advice, and although it was kind of dumb, it worked. He said, "Thank the Lord for your problems." That's not what you're supposed to do. You thank the Lord through them, not for them. But anyway, it worked.

So I drove all the way back to the farm, and said, "Thank you Lord." It was murder. It was the worst. My Mother had just died. My partner had just died. I was scared. I was backed in a corner. Everything was in a shambles, and I sat down with a pen, and that whole chorus came out. "One day at a time, sweet Jesus / That's all I'm asking from you / Just give me strength to do every day what I have to do / Yesterday's gone, sweet Jesus, and tomorrow may never come / Lord help me today / show me the way / one day at a time." I sang it out like that and I jumped up, because sure, I had just uttered a prayer, but I'm still a songwriter. I said, "My God, that's a hit." I grabbed a pencil and paper right quick and I wrote that chorus down, but I couldn't get the song started. And then a verse came. I thought. okay, that's a good verse, but that's not the first verse. And, because I am a professional songwriter, not a new songwriter, I knew I had to have a great opening line to go with this tune. Just think what I had been given there. Incidentally, some Christians didn't want to record it. "Well, Jesus, you know, if you're looking below," they said, is not biblical. They said you *know* Jesus is looking. I said, "Sing the song the way I wrote it." I was in a state of not too much faith at the time. "Sing it the way God gave it to me. It'll work." And some of them did change it. It's been recorded so many times.

So Kris [Kristofferson] was in town. He and Rita had just had *Why Me*, a tremendous hit. I said, "I've got a song and I can't get the thing started. It's just got to have a blockbuster first line." And again, extemporaneous, spontaneous, and always inspired, Kris just says, "I'm only human, I'm just a man / help me believe in what I can be and all that I am." I said, "You've got it." So fifteen minutes, and we had finished it.

Anyway, the opening line to me is as important as the hook, because you don't get to the hook for a while.

Kim Williams - They're so important. Some of the better songs start from opening lines. If the opening line and the opening scenario is good, it'll lead you somewhere. It'll make you work hard. The first four or five lines of *Margaritaville* get in four of the five senses. Maybe all of them. That's probably one of the greatest songs that's ever been written, as far as just getting you into it.

2. Which verse is hardest to write?

Tony Arata - Second verse. It's hard not to just tell the whole story in the first verse. I think that whatever follows the first verse is usually pretty tough. And I think that if a song requires a bridge, it shouldn't sound gratuitous. Every item is important.

Pam Belford - Actually, sometimes the first verse is harder.

Kent Blazy - The Beatles always used to say the second verse was the hardest, and I guess that it is. A lot of times you have so much detail in the first verse and the chorus that it's kind of hard to figure out which direction to take the second verse. So I would probably say that's the most difficult, having a second verse that's as strong as the first verse. A lot of times the first verse will end up being the second verse and we'll end up writing a new first verse.

Steve Bogard - I like to be as conversational as possible. So what often happens to me is that I'll be talking, and my co-writer will go, "What's wrong with that?" We'll write down what I said, and we'll work within that. Rather than trying to come up with an instant song, it's more conversational and story-like. My goal is to make everything not sound like a songwriter wrote it.

Rory Bourke - The second verse is usually the hardest, especially if you've written a great first verse.

Gary Burr - McCartney (I don't know whether this is just legend or what) was very into the "Nobody cares about the second verse, you finish it up." For a long time I had that attitude. I don't think you can have that attitude in country, because it's too much of a story. You can't start a scenario with somebody, get them up to a certain point, and then just blather on with the second verse.

Phil Spector always asked, "What's the second verse of *On Broadway?* What's the beginning of it?" "They say the neon lights..." Everybody knows the first. If you stop anybody on the street and ask them what the second verse of *You've Lost That Loving Feeling* is, nobody can tell you, but everybody knows the first "You never close your eyes."

I had that attitude too but in country, you can't get away with that. You've got to continue the story. So I think they're all tough in their different way. The first verse is tough because you've got to grab them. The second verse is tough because you can't leave your characters out there stranded in the desert.

Kim Carnes - The second or third verse. A lot of times you get that first verse and a chorus and then it's like, "Now what do we say to keep it fresh?"

Debi Cochran - The second verse. Mickey Cates, who writes here, says when he's a big famous songwriter he's going to hire a staff of people to write second verses for him. (HOW OFTEN DO YOU WRITE THE SECOND VERSE, ONLY TO FIND THAT IT'S THE FIRST VERSE?) That happens a lot. Sometimes it's just a matter of switching them. You suddenly see that the last verse is the first verse. Sometimes you have to wander on into the story, and then say, "Okay, all of this that we thought was the first verse was really just peripheral." Now we've got the story, and we start from here and try to finish up the second verse. A lot of co-writing is done because people say, "I've got the first verse and chorus to this song that I've had for a year, and I cannot finish it." And then you listen to it and say, "Okay I've got a different perspective that you haven't thought of. How about this?"

Jill Colucci - For me, there is not a set answer for that. It depends on where the inspiration for the start of the song came from, where that thread came from, as Kostas would put it. I've noticed that it's challenging to keep the end of the song as strong as the first. I'm not in a hurry. I want it to be as good as it can be and not be finished until it's done. Not be thinking or talking about how we're going to do the demo before the song is written. I just want to really concentrate on the song.

Kim Copeland - If I had to choose, I'd say the second one is hardest. Most often because in the interest of trying to say everything as efficiently as possible, you've given the whole story in the first verse and chorus. You don't want to be redundant in the second verse. You need to keep it new and exciting, and that makes it the hardest. But oftentimes, I'll find that the second verse is so strong that I'll go back and use it as the first verse and ditch the first verse that I had. Sometimes you can use the first verse to kind of warm up and get into the feel of the song, and by the time you're writing the second verse, you're more focused. I don't think it happens the same way every time for me.

Gary Earl - For me, the second verse is usually the hardest, because I've already got the concept which is going to be the hook or the first verse. And most of the time I know where I want to end up, but you still have to keep it interesting in the middle.

Robin Earl - The second verse. The first verse is often the original idea, and developing the story can be more difficult. Sometimes the second verse turns out to really be the first, so then I'll want to write a new second verse.

Kye Fleming - The first, because that's the first chance you've got at setting up the chorus, and if that's not done successfully, the second verse doesn't matter because they're gone. The second verse is like candy. It's like, "This is fun, the hard part is over." Bridges are fun. They can be frustrating, but they're fun sometimes because you get to kind of come at it from a different place than the verses.

Lindy Gravelle - Second verses are always a little harder. A lot of times, depending on the format of the song, you can say everything as far as the story goes in the first verse and chorus. It's like the second verse comes and you say, "Okay, now what?"

Janis Ian - I hate second verses. So does every songwriter. The hardest thing for me about songwriting is just getting to the place where it starts to flow. Especially when I'm writing alone. I'll come up with a great melody, then I'll come up with forty different alternatives for the words. Stella Ather used to say, "Your talent lies in your choices." As you set your standards higher and higher, it's harder and harder to match your own standards.

John Jarrard - I've noticed with a lot of things I write that what I thought was a good first verse turns out to be a second verse. I've heard people say that more songs get lost in the second verse.

Mary Ann Kennedy - Absolutely the second one. The dreaded second verse syndrome. You've usually used a whole lot of your pictures, that little movie's already rolling, and the story's been said. And then you have to enhance it and make it more. Give another aspect without getting too far away from what you're really saying. It's definitely the toughest.

Sandy Knox - Unless you've got a story song going, your first verse is a tough one, but the second verse is tough because you've already said a lot in the first verse. I've always kind of thought songs were like a jigsaw puzzle, and the songwriter is responsible for not only making up the picture, but also we're responsible for cutting up the pieces and then putting them back together. We're in charge of the whole thing. We've got to set it to rhyme and melody, and it's got to last three to three and a half minutes.

Kostas - The second verse can be harder to write, but the thing about getting yourself in a corner is that you just have to be a Houdini. You just have to figure out how to get out of those things. The joy of writing is that there's no set way of doing things. You get to create the way it's going to be. It's a beautiful thing whenever you do something that's totally unexpected, just because you couldn't think of another way out of the situation, and it just happens to be totally unique, and everybody else who hears it feels the same way. You've got something memorable.

Jess Leary - It seems like the first verse might be a little tougher because you're just figuring it all out. You're trying to put it together or let it put itself together. By the second verse, you kind of know what's going on and what needs to be said.

Jim McBride - Most people will say that the second verse is hardest to write, but I look forward to it. Sometimes you feel like you've painted yourself into a corner, but if you can get yourself out of it, then it's probably pretty good. I think the second verse is just as hard as the first. I can't tell much difference.

Pam Rose - For years and years, Mary Ann [Kennedy] and Pat [Bunch] and I were an exclusive team. Mary Ann would think of these powerhouse chords, and I would think of the verses. I was usually the verse person. Then again, there were times when Mary Ann pretty much wrote the whole musical thing—the basic outline of all the music, verse and chorus—and the same would be true for me. Sometimes I've done that and then we've both tweaked and edited, which is also an invaluable part of a team. But I love to do verses. I got used to that because sometimes Mary Ann would say, "Here's the chorus," and then that would be it. I mean, *Ring On Her Finger/Time On Her Hands* is a great example of that. That's Mary Ann's chorus. It's great, and it's a killer melody.

Joyce Rouse - The second verse! The second verse is always a bear. I believe it was Harlan Howard who said, "There are very few rules in songwriting, and the only one I follow is that the second verse had better be better than the first." That's a real tough standard to follow because the first verse usually comes easier.

Trisha Walker - Second verse, I'd say. You know what's going to happen and you know how it's going to end, but it's that development in the middle [that's difficult], to really keep it colorful, keep it interesting, keep your logic going.

Kim Williams - Probably the second one. It's awfully easy to drop the ball.

3. How important is imagery in songwriting?

Pam Belford - I don't use much of it. I would like to use more, it's just that I end up going more into thoughts and feelings.

Kent Blazy - I think the more imagery you can have in every song, the better it is. Certain songs require more than other songs. Anytime you can put imagery in there, something people can picture in their minds, then you're just that much better off. It's hard to do it and say it a little bit different than everybody else. That's especially where reading comes in, to see how other writers approach it and how they use words and imagery.

Some authors can blow me away with the detail they use in stories. It inspires you to try and use that in your songwriting.

Steve Bogard - I used to try. Now it just happens. I try to make sure the imagery is consistent, and I try to make sure that the guy at Wal-Mart understands it.

Rory Bourke - That's the hardest thing I can think of. Some people are gifted at that. I'll mention this guy, because I think he's the most gifted writer in this area that I know, and that's Dewayne Blackwell. Dewayne is the master, as far as I'm concerned, of being able to paint a picture and you get an emotion. To me, it appears to be such a natural technique of his. I think that's one of the few things that you can't teach anybody. That's a real gift. Dewayne says something in a song and you feel something.

Gary Burr - It's funny, the different imagery for the different genre. When you write pop songs you can get away with different imagery. When you write a country song, you'd have to use different imagery. Each one has sort of its own little niche carved out for what imagery is allowed. I love using imagery. It's that fine line of not becoming Donovan, but I always think that there's a better way to say, "This heart is broken." The trick is that with so many great songwriters trying to say, "This heart is broken," you're a little hard pressed to find that different way to say it. That's part of what makes it fun and part of what makes it intimidating.

Debi Cochran - Imagery is important because you need visual pictures. One way that I try to shift my mind to get an image is, after we've talked about the story that we want to go with, this is the emotion we want to tap, I say, either out loud or to myself, "Let's look through the window and see what these people are doing." Then you start to see it as a movie.

Kim Copeland - It's extremely important to me because all of the people who made me want to write in the first place are so good at it. That's what drew me into it. I think James Taylor is the absolute best at imagery in songwriting. He can paint a scene so clearly that you feel like you're right there living it. That's what makes the song to me. That's what personalizes it. That's been the most important lesson I've learned since I came to Nashville. Above everything else, the craft, the melody, the hook ... the imagery is what puts it over the top, makes it stick in people's minds. That's what puts the listener in the scene.

Gary Earl - I'll pass on that question, Bob, and take Medieval Castles for twenty.

Robin Earl - I think imagery is really important. I like songs that make good videos, tell good stories.

Kye Fleming - It's not the easiest thing in the world for me. I'm more of a psychological study person than I am this beautiful picture-story stuff. I don't do that well. But I believe that there's a reason that the great prophets, people like Jesus, used parables. And it's because it hits everybody, and it doesn't matter what stage you are at, you can still get something out of it. It's not somebody saying, "This is the way it is." It's somebody painting a picture, and you pull from it what you need and only what you need. No more. No less. That's what makes it so powerful. And I think that same power can be in lyrics in a song.

The best I can do personally toward that is to make what I try to say psychologically a little more colorful, or put it in a setting like *Give Me Wings* or *Some People's Lives*. You don't have to listen as hard to something that's got a lot of pictures in it because you see it. You have to listen a little harder to concepts, and therefore they may not be as entertaining.

Lindy Gravelle - Primarily, I've always felt stronger as a musician, so the music part of the song was easier, and I was more confident with that than the lyric part. But I have proven to myself that, when I feel that I have a really strong idea, I can come out with the lines. They don't come as easily as the music, but I know I can do it. That's what's neat for me right now; it's like I'm on a hunt, I'm hearing things, and reading more. Debi Cochran has really helped to pique my interest in reading good literature and exposing myself to it.

John Jarrard - Imagery is something I'm trying to be more conscious of. That's what they're looking for right now.

Mary Ann Kennedy - I think it depends on the song. Imagery made *Safe in the Arms of Love* a great lyric. It's a story song about a young couple, and the imagery is all over the place. That's what makes that song. The picture of Elvis hanging by the clock in the kitchen and all those kind of lines that describe this couple's life together are absolutely essential. Then again, in a heartfelt ballad, I don't think those kind of pictures are as important as relaying the emotion. So I think it just really depends on the kind of song it is.

Sandy Knox - Very important! Very important! I think that normally when I'm writing, I'm writing a little movie in my head. I'm seeing the video and the film. Anytime I do workshops, I stress that highly. Creating a visual image is really important. It's really simple to put in three words, "I miss you." But if you create an image of pouring a bottle of your perfume across the pillow where your head used to lay, that's a mournful image. That visual is a lot more potent than "I miss you." I'm real big on visual imagery, and I think most of my cuts have been due to that fact. Especially nowadays, I think it's important because of videos. Artists want stage potential, theatrical potential in the song. They want radio potential and video potential.

Kostas - I love imagery. Not only imagery, but I love mystery, and I love parables and all the cryptic stuff. It's like looking at a painting. You see one thing, but there are so many other things inside that thing. It should be the same with a song. Whenever I hear songs that I love, between the melody and what the instruments are doing, and the voice and the beat, man, there's plenty of imagery and mystical stuff in there that just touches me inside. I get a chuckle out of it, because I walk away thinking that only me and the songwriter know what's going on.

Jess Leary - I like pictures. I like to paint those stories as much as possible, and I like to feel emotion. To me, those are the two things: to get the emotional impact in there and to get the pictures with it if you can. With some songs, you can't. It's just emotion and you can't be weaving in the picture, but I prefer to do that if at all possible.

Jim McBride - I love color in songs. Every song on the radio doesn't need to be that way, but every song doesn't need to be a flat-out love ballad either. I like songs with houses and people and cars, cats and dogs, and stuff like that.

Pam Rose - Pete Drake was the man who I had my first publishing deal with, which is where I met Mary Ann. He always told us, "A song should be like a three-minute movie." And I feel like sometimes when I'm able to pull that off, it's a cool thing.

Joyce Rouse - Some songs are visual and demand that, especially in country music.

Wayne Tester - If it needs to be there great but don't overdo it. A lot of times, you tend to overdo it. Just be real in the song.

Trisha Walker - I try to pay a lot of attention to it. It's like some-body said about songwriting, "Don't write me a letter, paint me a picture." I think it's real important. Again, because the South is such a colorful place, and storytelling and the oral tradition is so important, people have to paint those word pictures. So I hope I've gleaned some of that where I come from.

4. What is the hardest part about writing a song?

Rory Bourke - Sometimes there's a point when I'm writing a song that I feel a mental dis-association with it, and I know that I'm going to need that other person to believe in this song twenty percent more than they need to for a while. That's a tough point in a song for me; I think, coming up with an idea that's not *just* a title, that has some depth to it and a solid foundation. Something that, not only by its title, says there's some truth in this, and it won't fall apart in a year or so. Actually as I go down the list, everything is pretty hard about writing a song.

Gary Burr - What I said about saying it in a new way. Everybody gets their heart broken, so at any given point, there are a million, there are a hundred million, there are a billion people walking around with their hearts broken. And they all expressed it in their own way. They've all heard it, and they've all related to it in their own way. So if you're going to sing a song about having your heart broken, then you've got to find a new way to say it, to make a reason for that song to exist. Otherwise, why write the song?

On any given day, in this town alone, there are fifty thousand heartbreak songs circulating on cassette and 49,900 have Schlitz/Overstreet's name on it. How are you going to compete? The only way you can compete is to have it be different. That's the hardest thing about it. I mean, forget that there are only so many notes. There are only so many words in the English language. There are only so many ways to say, "I love you," and yet we're expected to keep finding new ways. There better not be a finite number of ways to say, "I love you," or we're in deep trouble.

Debi Cochran - Getting started. I think starting with that blank piece of paper with two people sort of sitting in a room blinking at each other, and finding something that you're both excited about.

Jill Colucci - The hardest part for me is the business side. Writing songs and getting to go in the studio and record them, and the excitement of hearing them on tape when they're finished, that's my favorite part. The toughest part is the business. There's a part of me that, for years, didn't even know it was a business. But it's real important to know that it is a business.

Kim Copeland - The ideas. If you know the craft, you can pretty much construct a song around any phrase. The hard part is coming up with ideas and recognizing which ones deserve to be written about. Maybe that's the second hardest part. Maybe the first is beginning, just getting to that state of mind. Getting to that place mentally and spiritually to express yourself.

Sandy Knox - Getting started, probably. And the bridge is really difficult. The bridge is a difficult place sometimes because that's exactly what it is. It's a bridge that takes you from the two verses you've already written to the ending of the song; it's setting up the ending. Basically you've already said the whole song, and the bridge is where you've got to summarize what else has been going on. I find the bridge can be really, really difficult.

Jess Leary - I guess starting, because once you're in, you're kind of swimming. It's the jumping in. It's the beginning of the song that, for me, is a little harder.

Wayland Patton - I think one of the hardest things would be not sounding cliché. Maybe I can answer it this way. The most important part is to really capture the essence of what it is you're trying to say, to cut to the heart of it. If I write a song to say, "I love you," it's not enough to say, "I love you." You've got to write it in such a way that the listener or whoever you're singing it to *feels* the love. The song has to be alive, the words have to be living, and they have to move and also paint images. So if I'm writing a story song, I want to transport the listener to be there, to feel what I feel, to see what I'm seeing. One of the greatest lines is a line that Eric Kaz wrote in a song, "Love is blind and cannot find you." That's so simple but says so much. I think it's hard to capture that essence.

Wayne Tester - Writing a great one [is the hardest part]. Anybody can write a song that is pretty good. That's really good, but where are the great ones? I've written a few great ones, one being *The Change*, one being *Love By Grace*. That's Garth and Wynonna, respectively.

5. What are the basic songwriting skills? What makes a person a good lyricist or melody writer?

Pam Belford - I don't know. I think that we all have both of those. I feel like I have some really good and unique ideas, and I feel like I have some that have been done to death. I think it really depends on where you're coming from too. Some people just jump into songwriting because it's the latest thing or because they happen to be in Nashville and they know the right people. People who tend to write from a mechanical point of view tend to have boring ideas, I think.

Steve Bogard - Melody sense, lyric sense. To read, to have a flow of language.

Rory Bourke - Studying all the great writers, all the great records, all the great decades of music. If a person didn't do any of that, they could get a mediocre idea and think it was good. But if you have knowledge of everything great that came before you, there's a sort of mental yardstick that measures it to and compares it to everything else that's great. If you don't love writing enough to spend twenty-five percent of your time immersing yourself in everything that's been done and that's great, don't waste your time trying to be a writer, because you don't care enough. The person who has the great idea versus the one who has the not so great idea, I'm not so sure it's because one has superior mental capabilities. To me it's where discernment of an idea would fall under a good critical sense and maybe a little bit of a good editorial sense.

Gary Burr - I think the lyrics is what separates the men from the boys. I've always been pretty prolific melodically, coming up with grooves and things like that. The thing that's been so great about coming to Nashville, and such a relief, is to find out that there are so many great lyricists here. If there comes a time when I feel like I have nothing left to say, I can find someone else to figure out how to say it. Or figure out what to say. Lyrics are really, really hard, and when I'm writing a song by myself, and I have to pace this little room here to come up with them, it's tough. I have an incredible amount of respect for the people who are great lyricists. It really is the nuts and bolts.

The one thing I do not like to do, out of everything, is when someone gives me a track and says, "Here's a track, see if you can come up with words." Man, that is the hardest thing in the world to do, especially if there's not even a title and you have to come up with everything. It's tough when we go to lunch and we've got a song, and we know that all we've got to do is just write two more verses. I'm not happy at lunch because that's the hard part; that's not the fun part. The fun part is coming up with the melody and the groove and putting the song together and finding the way to make it start. Once the framework is there and all you've got to do is put in the little Lego blocks, that's not fun. That's where you earn your money.

People who play for a living always say, "I don't get paid all this money to play for three hours a night. I get paid all this money for all this other stuff that I've got to do. All the sitting around in all the airports, so I can get to play the three hours a night. I play the three hours for free. I get the big money to put up with all the other crap." We get the big money because we're patient enough to sit down and fill in those slots and not settle, because if you settle, you don't last. Your songs won't be sung twenty years from now.

Debi Cochran - A love for the language in the case of a lyricist, and I won't even say proficiency as a musician. Certainly complicated melodies are not a foundation for country music. It doesn't have to be complicated, you just have to be passionate about it. I think it depends on the individual, because there are some people who have the latest state-of-the-art computer and digital technology and that facilitates their writing. And there are other people—I have one co-writer who never even brings a pencil. He's one of the main reasons I'm sure to keep that guitar here.

Kim Copeland - You have to study the craft. You have to be good with words, with musical and lyrical hooks. In order to be a good songwriter, the most important criterion is being a free thinker. I think you need to allow your spirit to roam free.

That won't necessarily make you successful in the business, though. You have to really give some time to the business side of it. You have to be willing to shake hands with the right people, pick up the phone, go out to the right functions, work hard and be a real business person.

Kye Fleming - I think [the most important skill is] to be secure in whatever position you're in, so that you are teachable. By that I mean even going to the Bluebird or some place and sitting down and listening to other writers. I'm coming up with some of this from working with writers. I notice that the writers who are sponges tend to have more to give to their craft. Along with that, I think reading and filling yourself with other people's images and words can only help stir your imagination.

(WHY DO SOME PEOPLE SEEM TO HAVE BETTER IDEAS?) I think it's a difference in personalities. To some extent, you're either blessed with a vivid imagination or you're blessed because you haven't blocked it. I look at the different styles of different writers, and I will never put words together the same way somebody else does, perhaps because of my life experiences.

John Jarrard - I've always said that talent is fifth or sixth on the list. First is persistence, persistence, and persistence. The basic skill of a writer is persistence. I thank God for all the people who are more talented than I am, who went home on the bus because they couldn't deal with rejection and the odds. There is no substitute for determination and resilience and persistence.

Mary Ann Kennedy - You've got to have that gift. As much as I would want to be a ballerina, I won't be. My body isn't that limber. I'm not gifted with that natural ability and that kind of physical grace. And I think that as a songwriter too you have to have a certain amount of natural talent. It doesn't have to be musical *and* lyrical. It can be one or the other. Then having the discipline to develop it. And number three, which is probably the most important if you have the other two, is to be open to the advice and criticisms of those whom you respect, because that's the only way to grow. You don't go to therapy to tell your therapist all the excuses for why you're there or why you can't get better or change this bad habit. You go to change. To hear advice so you can better yourself. I know a whole lot of people who came to this town about the same time I did, and they came here with more tools, more experience, better songs than I had. And a couple of them I know didn't make it because of their attitude of not being open to learning from those who have been there. You don't have to agree, and you don't have to do it just like they did it, but be open to the criticism. If somebody who has written twenty songs that slay you says, "Man, I know you're really attached to this song right now, but that chorus didn't do it for me and probably won't for the other listeners because of this or that," you've got to let go of that and take that in, and just go back to the drawing board. If you've chosen to be among the troops out there who are making a living doing this and to compete with them, well, comrades and competition are side by side in this whole thing.

Sandy Knox - I think being conversational is really important in lyrics. Knowing when not to be too poetic or syrupy, sugary. Knowing when not to be clever. An overwritten song makes me crazy. I think being conversational and simple and from the heart.

Kostas - I really can't answer that. I think that each and every one of us has a place in life. We have a central theme, and then we have millions of other things that we do just as well. Things that are just as important to us, but perhaps we don't have as great an ability as somebody else. But our appreciation is there. And we appreciate that which other people do, and we specialize in something else. You've got to have a singer, and you've got to have a band, and then you've got to have those who listen and those who dance. It's part of the same vibration that we're all connected to. I think we all in life need to be expressive. When God had this desire to express, he created worlds. When man has this desire to express, he comes up with art, which is a reflection of life. We are just copying God. Love, the Bible says, is an active thing. Because love needs to express itself, it needs something to bounce off of. So he created all that he created, and he created us in it, so that he could see his reflection in us. Each one of us has a place in life.

Jess Leary - You've got to learn your craft. I have to say that in some writers it just flows out naturally, and there are some who have to work on it more. It seems like I have to work on it. I've read the standard books that you read when you move to town. Sheila Davis's books, and *Writing Down the Bones* [by Natalie Goldberg]. When I moved to town, I went to writer's nights six nights a week and tried to listen through all of it, the good and the bad, and find out what I did and didn't like. The harder you work at something, the better you're going to get at it, like any craft or any talent.

I guess it's who you are, where you're from, what you're all about. It's how you can express your emotions and feelings, because a lot of writing is trying to express emotion.

Joyce Rouse - Only God would have the answer to that question. I just have discovered that I have got to go with my gut feelings. I think the best thing we can do is know ourselves as intensely as we can and listen and honor that. If my gut told me tomorrow that the work I need to be doing is managing a bowling alley, I would have to do it, because I have learned that trusting my gut is of vital importance. When I don't do it, I get into big trouble.

Trisha Walker - It may be the difference between somebody who understands, and [somebody] whose desire is to write primarily for the commercial market, where it becomes almost a hammer and nails kind of thing. And that's not a bad thing. I think it's folks history, what their family was like, wherever they've lived on this earth, that contributes to the unique way that they see the world and their ability to share that. Some people probably see it in a unique way, but for whatever reason, they're not willing to share that.

Marijohn Wilkin - Number one, they've got to have a God-given gift. If they don't have that, I don't even know how to fool with them. I'm serious. What we're hearing a lot of today is somebody comes in to record, they're a singer, they're not a writer, and they get told, "You go get into that room with so and so, who writes, and write yourself an album." Give me a break. I took art lessons but there ain't no way in hell I can be an artist. That is not my talent and not everybody can write a song, regardless of what we've been told.

The only thing I can equate this to is that anybody can do anything, and the longer you do it, the better you can do it. In other words, when you drive a car the first few times, it's very erratic. But then you learn to drive because you learn the skill that it takes. So you can hone the skills to do anything.

What I'm hearing a lot today is not poetry. I'm hearing prose set to strange melodies. The older writers, like Hank Williams, wrote sheer poetry. He wrote poetry, and it didn't matter whether it had a tune or not.

Your lyrics should stand alone and keep your rapt attention. It all went downhill from, "You ain't nothing but a hound dog, crying all the time." We laughed at that because we had our criteria for what a lyric should be. *Achy Breaky Heart* is clever. "You ain't nothing but a hound dog" is not clever. But *Achy Breaky Heart* is a clever play on words. When I heard the chorus I said, "A soldier wrote this song," and later, when I read about him [Don Von Tress], I found out he was in Vietnam. I've forgotten the word he used in there—"might blow up this heart of mine," or whatever. It was a connotation of explosions that I would not have written because I would not have come from there. So, you see, people write from where they come from. They write from their experiences, and it comes out in their writing even if they don't realize it. The first time I heard that one, I picked it for a smash. Part of the hit potential of it was the simplicity of the song. Babies could sing it, and they did. That one and *Queen of Denial*.

Kim Williams - Ideas used to be one of my strengths early on, then I got to writing so much it's almost like I emptied the well. I think I saw where Don Henley said that the hardest thing for him is balancing the input and the output. It's like a barrel with water running in and water running out. If you look at creativity that way, the hardest thing is to keep the ideas flowing in as fast as you write them out. That's a problem for me, and I don't have a great idea but every now and then. But I can remember a time when my barrel was running over, because I couldn't write it. I literally had more ideas than I could write. Most of the people who I think have a lot of great ideas, I don't think they could be writing a lot. Because once you get to the point that you can write, an idea doesn't last long, because you can't wait to write it. I guess there are people who pay more attention to it. There are people who are more aware of an idea when they see one, of something different. But all of it is so subjective. I've heard guys say, "Man, I've got a book full of great ideas." And they come in here, and you go, "You've got a book full of ideas, but they're not doing anything for me." They may go to the next guy, and it just kills him. What an idea is is such a subjective call. And I don't know if you've heard it, but there are no new subjects. That's what's really hard. We're all writing about the same things, over and over and over.

Steve Bogard - My goal is to make everything not sound like a songwriter wrote it.

Debi Cochran - In the writing process, you have to start wherever you can get a toehold.

Jill Colucci - If that opening line doesn't make you want to listen to the rest, then it doesn't matter what I do after that.

Janis Ian - The hardest thing for me about songwriting is just getting to the place where it starts to flow.

CHAPTER FIVE
CO-WRITING

Jill Colucci - If we can't have a conversation together, more than likely, I'm not going to write a great song with them.

Jim McBride - Sometimes one writer can get this deep feeling within and if he can bring that out by himself, then it's going to be better than if he was writing that same idea with another person.

Kate Wallace - I think co-writing is almost like a marriage in a small sense. It's a very intimate experience.

Gary Burr - I always look at it like that song was not going to exist unless those people were in the room together. Therefore, it doesn't matter if somebody put in one word or all of them.

1. Do you co-write?

Kim Carnes - So many people here get together in a room and write. I don't usually do that. Donna [Weiss] and I have never done that. We just get together, take our tapes home, work independently, and call each other on the phone about a line. The process happens over a longer period of time. However, with Greg Barnhill and Vince Melamed, every time we get together, we write a song. I've written some songs with Susan Longacre. I like writing with her. And with her, we haven't gotten in a room per se. She'll give me a whole bunch of lyrics and one or two will jump out, then I'll write music to it, and we'll get together and hone in on everything.

Kim Copeland - Yes, some. I would like to start co-writing more.

Kostas - I have been co-writing in the last three or four years.

Jim McBride - Yes, but I am desperately trying to get back to only co-writing one day a week. What I had going for a while was that I would co-write one day a week, and the other mornings I would get up and write at home. I would sit there for an hour or two and see if I could get something started. And then that afternoon I'd go and pitch a song, or whatever. That was working well for me, because even if you don't finish a song, then when you get with somebody to co-write, you've got some ideas that you've put some thought into as opposed to walking into a room and nobody's got anything.

Trisha Walker - Some. It's not my first preference. The people I have been most successful and comfortable co-writing with are folks that I've already known for years and I have a friendship with. When I was writing for Word Music, there was one lady over there who I was very comfortable with. She and I just hit it off. We wrote several things together. Right now I probably only consistently write with maybe two folks. I don't know why. I guess I make a deliberate balk against what seems to be the Nashville mentality that you have to co-write. I realize that you double your output, and when you do that your percentages increase. But to me, songwriting is pretty personal. I heard somebody say one time that they didn't think it was a team sport. Personally, I prefer writing by myself, but co-writing has a lot of great benefits to it. You can really reflect and bounce off of somebody. But for me, it needs to be somebody that I've had some sort of relationship with. I guess it's almost like dancing. Somebody has got to take the lead. What I like to do when I co-write is come to the table with several ideas and just pick one that sounds good for that day. But even so, even if you've only got one phrase or one line written, I'll have a certain direction that I think it should go. So then a lot of the co-writing session is just pull and tug with your co-writer, all for the good of the song. I think a better way of co-writing would be to have an editor. Instead of co-writing, just bring somebody in to edit.

2. What percentage of your material is co-written?

Tony Arata - I probably don't do more than fifteen or twenty percent that are co-written. The reasons being, one, I'm not very good at co-writing. I don't write very well on demand. And, two, I wrote a lot before we moved up here from Savanna, and so whatever semblance of style I may or may not have started before I hit town. When I got here I just didn't actively pursue co-writing. As a result of that, I have a catalog of songs of which I'm sole writer, but it's not out of greed or anything like that. It just happens to be the way that I have written the most. So for good or bad, that's the style that I have.

Pam Belford - Lately it's been one hundred percent. I used to write only by myself, and I think I would like to do some more of that. I guess there's more discipline when writing with a co-writer. For someone who is undisciplined about committing to writing a song, if I set up an appointment to write with someone, I have to be there; it's both of our time, and I should use it writing.

Kent Blazy - Before I came to Nashville, I probably wrote over fifty percent by myself. But now I'd say that ninety percent of the time, maybe even ninety-five percent of the time, I'll be writing with other writers.

Steve Bogard - I wrote one song by myself in the last three years, and I turn in fifty to sixty songs a year.

Gary Burr - Unfortunately for my publisher, right now ninety percent of it is. I used to write a hundred percent by myself. And then it was one-to-one, and now with so many great, talented people here to write with, I hate to say it, but almost every day I co-write with somebody. A couple of times out of the year I try to take a month off and not write. That's gotten harder and harder over the last couple of years because people come to town and they say, "Well, I'm only in town these three days." So you say, "Okay, I was going to not work that month, but I'll put you in for two of those days." And then you look at that month and say, "Well, I'm already writing with this guy. Would it kill me?" Before you know it the month is gone, and I'm ninety-five years old, and I'm sitting at the Sunset Grill and my hands are shaking.

Kim Copeland - Right now, maybe five percent. It has been higher in the past, but I've been writing alone a lot the past two or three years, and it's been good. I think it's important to be able to do both.

Lindy Gravelle - Lately maybe seventy-five percent co-written. I keep thinking that maybe I need to get back to writing more with myself.

Janis Ian - In the last two months, pretty much everything. I've been on the road the last year and a half, and that's a good way to get back into it. I'll go through periods where I'll do a lot of writing on my own and periods where I'll do a lot of co-writing.

John Jarrard - Almost all of it.

Mary Ann Kennedy - For me, I have to say probably eighty to ninety percent of the time, but it doesn't mean that all of those songs were born in a co-writing situation. A lot of times I'll come up with the idea and a piece on my own, but then get with a co-writer to finish it.

Sandy Knox - Ninety-five percent. I still write every once in a while by myself.

Kostas - In the last six years, eighty percent, I'd say.

Jess Leary - These days, about ninety-five percent of it is. And a lot of times I'll come up with stuff on my own and then bring it in to co-write. I enjoy it. I'm lazier when I'm trying to write by myself. There's always those dishes in the sink. And it's funny, I used to write by myself. Before I moved to Nashville, that's all I did. I didn't know there was co-writing, so everything I wrote prior to 1985, I wrote by myself. And I'm glad I knew how to do it by myself, just to get those starts or go ahead and write a song. But I enjoy it. I enjoy the process.

Jim McBride - In the last year it's been one hundred percent. But I'm pulling back from that.

Wayland Patton - Probably less than half. I'm not a high-volume writer. I'm also a performing artist. I would probably write more if that's all I did.

Pam Rose - Ten years ago all of my songs were co-written. Now, probably seventy-five percent to eighty percent. It depends on the time period. I'm enjoying writing by myself because that's one way that I've been able to practice the unedited thing. I could never finish a song by myself before, because I would be saying it's not good enough. It's not as good as the songs I write with anybody else.

And now I really don't care. I just write them anyway and something may happen with them, or something may never happen with them, I don't really care. But I had to get to where I didn't care to be able to do it.

Joyce Rouse - Very, very little, but two years ago I was co-writing eighty percent of what I did. It's just that the projects I'm working on now don't lend themselves to co-writing. I still love co-writing. And for me, that also kind of goes in waves depending on what's going on in my life. There have been times when the co-writing has been just really smooth and wonderful and other times when it just feels better to write things by myself. Because if you know exactly what it is you want to write, and do it with somebody else, somehow that dilutes the theme of what you're doing. However, if you just want to sit down and write a song to pitch, I think co-writing's the way to go.

Kate Wallace - Sixty percent.

3. What is the maximum number of people you will co-write with on a song?

Pam Belford - My ideal would be to write with someone whose strengths are my weaknesses. I don't feel very confident about melodies, and if I could have it my way, what I would like to do more than anything is just totally write lyrics and turn them over to someone who writes melodies—someone with whom I have complete confidence that they're not going to step on my words and I'm not going to step on their melody. But I haven't come across that combination yet. It's still a very cooperative deal, and I like that too.

Steve Bogard - If there's a reason to do it [write with more than one co-writer], okay. I think it dilutes the dynamic, the fireworks, or the thing that can happen with a song.

Rory Bourke - I've done a lot of three-way co-writing. Some of the best songs I've ever written, I've done in threes. I think the best way to build up your catalog and really get rolling is to write in three's. This is a theory of mine. Lee Roy Parnell and Chris Moore write a lot together, and one day they asked me if I would like to write with them. I said, "Sure." I'd already worked with Lee Roy before, but I'd never worked with Chris. We wrote *Tender Moment,* which was a pretty big hit, and we wrote about five or six other things that Lee Roy's recorded. That was a three-way situation for them that was an adjunct to what they were doing. They write on their own together, but now they've got another situation where they're writing different kinds of songs. I write a lot with Charlie Black. Charlie and I have our own songs. We've written a lot of Anne Murray things together. From time to time I'll call Charlie up and say, "Do you want to get together with so and so?" We get together and write with them. So we've got a different kind of songwriting with that other person, and we've still got ourselves. That different situation adds to the mix.

Debi Cochran - Publishing companies really like to impose those limits, because of course if there are only two writers on a song, then they are getting half the publishing money, and if there's only one then they like it even better. But if a three-way thing works and there's something the three of you do together that the two don't have, then I'm sorry, you've just got to go with it. I have a couple of writing partners where it always works best if it's the three of us.

Kye Fleming - If five people started a song and brought it to me because they needed what I do, I wouldn't have any trouble with that. It has to do with whether it allows me to contribute what I contribute, and I tend to need to be in control of the lyric. So that probably tells you something. I'm a Libra, in case you couldn't tell. I have found myself in the last few years writing in three's a lot for some reason, and usually two people will work on the melody, and I'll come in and write the lyric. So, as far as a number, I'm probably more comfortable with two's or three's.

John Jarrard - From a financial point of view, it's better to narrow it down. But sometimes I like the energy of having three people, especially in situations where I write with an artist or the first time I write with somebody. I think it sort of depressurizes the situation to do a three-way. I feel like I write my best songs with people that I know and get together with on a fairly regular basis. But sometimes you have the opportunity to write with an artist, and that's a pressure-packed situation. It's just more comfortable with three in the room.

Sandy Knox - One other co-writer. I'm not doing threesomes. No point in it.

Jess Leary - Three [is the maximum number]. I can't say I like that as well. It doesn't work for me. I much prefer one-on-one.

Jim McBride - I've done a lot of three-ways and for the most part, I'm going to cut back on that too. Listen to most of the standards. They are written by one person. Yes, *The Tennessee Waltz* was written by two people, but most country standards were written by one person. Sometimes one writer can get this feeling deep within, and if he can bring that out by himself, then it's going to be better than if he was writing that same idea with another person or two other people. A lot of great songs are co-written, but a lot of great songs are not co-written. Some of my stuff that has done the best and that I like a lot is stuff that I wrote by myself. That's not being greedy, because I've written with some wonderful writers who are capable of writing a song on their own. My theory is that if you can write by yourself, then you need to do that. It's very lonely, so co-write once in a while. Co-writing is more fun and it happens quicker. But if you're capable of writing a song by yourself, then you need to do that from time to time, and I'm talking to myself right now. I haven't done it in about a year, and it's bothering me. How do I know I can still do it? Truth be known, in the last year, I've written some by myself with someone else in the room. Some artists I've been hooked up with can write and some can't, and it is terrible. The problem is that you've got these young artists out there who are twenty-one or twenty-two years old, and hell, they haven't done anything to write about.

Wayland Patton - The most I've ever had on a song is three. Co-writing is not my favorite thing to do, so to co-write, it has to be with people that I like. There are some aspects about co-writing that I like. It can be a lot of fun, but it can also be a nightmare. There are some guys who are great co-writers. They get in there and they're almost chameleon-like. I think it's a great talent to be that way, but I'm not that way. I have to really be able to respect that person and feel good about what that person is putting in, and love the idea; otherwise it's just an exercise. I enjoy some aspects, but I also enjoy sitting in a room by myself and working on it at my own pace, doing my own thing, writing what I want to write, and I don't have to run it by a committee. Let me go on record: I'm not criticizing people who co-write. The thing is, you get in a situation where so many people are competing for those cuts, and there are so many writers in town. The publishing companies have a handful of pluggers; it's their job to get out and pitch those songs. I came from a place that at one time had eighty writers. The mathematics are such that those pluggers can't keep up with the songs that are way back in the catalog. They have trouble keeping up with the songs that came in that week. Let's say you've got ten writers who write two songs a month. That's twenty new songs a month. So that's twenty songs that the pluggers are trying to hustle. The ones that float to the surface, that get the most interest, those are the ones they're going to work. Okay, they are stockpiled over here, and the new songs keep flowing in. So what happens? To keep up, you start co-writing more to increase the volume of songs. I know there are some very successful songwriters, and that's the way they work. That's their principle; they write them then push them out. They are going to write some that aren't so good, then they are going to write those special ones. It's a numbers game. But I write for my own. If I couldn't make a living doing this, I'd still do it. I'd find somebody to listen to my songs, because the people are out there. In the co-writing process, unless you get in there with somebody you really connect with, then the songs will be diluted. It's just another song. And there are plenty of those out there. I don't want to contribute any more.

Wayne Tester - I try to keep it at one co-writer and a third person if it works. It depends on the song.

(CREATIVE FACTORS, OR MONETARY?) All of the above. Financially, yes. Creatively, if there needs to be more than two or three writers, then it's probably not a great song to begin with. You need to move on to something else.

Kate Wallace - I will not write with more than two people.

Marijohn Wilkin - You're talking to a lady who started writing when the royalty rate was two cents, so money had very little to do with it. That was a penny for the publisher and a penny for the writer. We were some of the first people to be put in an office with a pencil and a writing pad and told, "Write!" But it worked out well for us. There were five of us on staff. Whichever one happened to be in that day and had an idea would say, "Do you want to help me write this?" or "I got this idea last night, you want to help me finish it?" But sometimes you're not tuned-in to whatever they're writing about at the time. Your own emotions have a big play in writing, and then again, some people you just write with better.

4. How do you choose a co-writer?

Pam Belford - I've gotten together with people that I thought were better writers than they actually were, and we couldn't communicate. There's a spark that you can feel with writers that you're compatible with. There are other writers who've written great songs with other people, but I get together with them, and I just feel like we're talking different languages.

Gary Burr - Well, there is a certain amount of up-front money involved. Basically, I put it in escrow and see how the song comes out. If it's a good song I give it back to them, and if it's a bad song they forfeit it.

When I first came to town, it was the same thing with everybody. You try to work your way up to the great songwriters because you want to work with people you can learn from. You want to find out what those secrets are. You want to learn the secret songwriter handshake. Which I know, by the way. It's a lot of factors. It's a successful track record. If I've written five songs with Bob DiPiero and three of them have already been cut, and one's been a number one, then I go back to Bob. If writing with Bob also happens to be a heck of a fun way to spend an afternoon, then he's top on the list. Another thing Pat Alger told me a few years ago, when he was on his incredible run, was I don't have to write with anybody that I don't just have a great time with. At my age, where I am, I just want to have a good time. That's the way I feel. I want to have a good time. So I've got plenty of co-writers out there that I not only have a good time spending the day with, where I wake up going, "Hot-dog, I'm going to spend the day with so and so," but I also know that the song we're going to write is going to be great, or at least it has the potential for greatness. Right now, because of all the hoopla of a couple of really good years under my belt, I've got a lot of people calling, people that I've always dreamed about working with and I'm suddenly getting to work with. They're calling me saying, "Are you interested?" I'm turning down things that I never would have dreamed I'd ever be in a position to say no to, but there are just so many hours in a day. This is not an altruistic thing, you know. I have two kids in college. I've got my days where I can maximize the potential. If someone calls and says, "So and so would like to write with you. Would you get on the band bus and go for five days on a run?" I've got to think, Gee, what if I sat here in town, and I wrote a day with Bob Depiero and a day with John Jarrard? If I add up the potential earnings for those five songs, as opposed to sitting on the bus for five days with someone with whom I don't even know if I can write a song, I'll stay home.

Jill Colucci - If people I've not worked with before want to write with me, and I don't know them, I would want to have lunch or dinner or coffee, just to make sure we can have a conversation together. If we can't have a conversation together, more than likely I'm not going to write a great song with them. I have to be able to say stupid lines to get to the good ones. I have to be comfortable. I have to trust. I have to be vulnerable and open. These are not little things. I don't necessarily feel safe with someone I've just met, so we get together first. And, if it feels good and we talk about songwriting, and I feel that our philosophies are somewhere in the same ballpark, then I might give it a shot. But boy, I used to say yes to everything, and I found it rather stressful.

When I started coming here in 1986, Barry Beckett signed me to Warner Brothers as an artist. One of the best things that happened from that deal was that Barry was playing my demos for all of these songwriters, saying, "I need material for Jill." I ended up meeting them and writing with them. They were people who I really admire—Charlie Black, Austin Roberts, Stewart Harris. It just changed my whole life. You work hard all your life and then you are in a position where the writers who you've admired over the years are willing to work with you, and it's really hard to say no. There are so many great writers here, and you're like a kid in a candy store. It's such a co-writing town that you can even feel guilty writing alone. I've experienced it. That's the reason I went to the beach. I got completely away so I could overcome the guilt. I've been scattered and spread too thin, so this year I can count on one hand how many people I've written with in six months. That's a huge change for me. There are more people out there who I want to work with; it's just that right now I needed to pull back a little bit. It's ridiculous for me to be writing with so many people that I don't have time to write with Stewart Harris, with whom I wrote *I'm Gonna Be Somebody, No One Else on Earth,* and the theme to *America's Funniest Home Videos.* That doesn't make sense. We have a chemistry. We have a history. We're like brother and sister. We're very deep friends. I get goose bumps talking about it, because we could hardly fit it in our schedules, and that just doesn't make sense for me to be writing with all of these new people and not with Stewart or Pam Rose or people I work with continuously. Also Randy Sharp, who's now in L.A. I need to write with the people that I have this chemistry and wonderful relationship with, and then other people, in addition, will be okay, but I had it out of balance.

Kim Copeland - I'm only a good co-writer when I'm writing with someone who is a kindred spirit. It can't be a comfortable co-writing situation for me unless you're both free to express any idea that comes into your head. I like to choose a co-writer whose strengths complement my weaknesses and vice-versa. I like to write with good musicians because I'm stronger lyrically and melodically than musically. My dream co-write is with someone who is totally uninhibited, a free thinker, because that's what I am, and we can bounce off each other and say the stupidest things in the world. That's the way profound ideas are born.

Mary Ann Kennedy - My strength is music, so it's got to be someone whose strength is more lyrical.

Also, it's got to be fun. It's got to feel great, and be such that you respect each other's opinions. Your ideas of greatness should be the same. Stylistically you turn each other on. It's not a tug-of-war. I don't like the tug-of-wars. They don't work for me. Some people like the tension there, but I don't.

Sandy Knox - Normally I like them to be really great at an instrument, whether it's guitar or piano. I prefer piano players. They have to have a sense of humor. I'm not interested in working with anybody who doesn't have a sense of humor or who's into corporate songwriting. I don't want to go write with somebody who's bitter and angry, and we've got to get this song done. I met with one guy once, a very successful songwriter. I had never met him before, and I said, "Well, what would you like to do? Would you like to play each other some stuff?" And he said, "No." I said, "You don't want to hear any of my stuff?" And he said, "No, let's start writing." I said, "You don't want to talk or anything?" It was about ten o'clock in the morning, and he said, "Heck, no. By two o'clock we should have two songs done." Forget that. I immediately knew I didn't want to work with him. I don't write like that. I take a lot of time with songs. I don't write ditties. I don't write something just to say I wrote a song that day or make my quota. I haven't made my quota in five years. I only write with about three or four guys right now. I don't write with a whole lot of women, never have. I'm more comfortable writing with guys, maybe because I can boss them around.

Kostas - I choose a co-writer by writing with them once. There are those that I'll go back and co-write with and those that I won't.

Jess Leary - The way I choose them at first, usually, is on a referral. So and so mentioned this one or that one. If it's fun and you're writing good songs, then hey, let's do that again. I do have a handful of writers who I look forward to getting with every time, and I know we're going to have a good time and most likely write something really good.

Pam Rose - Well, it's a kind of chemistry thing, I guess. I don't have very many co-writers. A lot of people I know co-write with lots of people, but I'm just kind of a quieter, shyer person. But the ones I do write with, we just have something really special, and I really like that. We resonate as people. The first day I write with somebody, I do have expectations of something to accomplish, and that is lunch. I feel we must eat lunch. That's about it and if anything else happens past that, great. And if it's somebody that I really like, then that's true for the second time. Chuck Jones and I, when we got together for the first time, we just expected to have lunch, and we wrote *Faithfully*, which is going to be Peter Cetera's next single. All we were really expecting to do was eat lunch, and we started that song.

Wayne Tester - Several things [determine how I choose a co-writer]. Placement in the community as far as reputation. A good chemistry is the most important thing. Somebody that's just fun to work with. Make it fun or move on.

Kate Wallace - I think co-writing is almost like a marriage in a small sense. It's a very intimate experience. It's cosmos from chaos. You're taking nothing and making it something, and you're bringing it through you. It's an intensely personal experience. I think picking a co-writer is picking someone you would want to spend an afternoon with.

5. Have you ever had a bad co-writing experience, and why was it so?

Steve Bogard - Yes. Lots. I felt he was patronizing the listener. I wrote enough to get out of the room and that was it. It's not good if your goals are not the same. There are writers whose goals are to play it safe, and I'll never get along with a co-writer like that.

Debi Cochran - The saddest thing, the hardest thing to deal with, is when you have a really good friend who you just can't write with. If both people realize it at the same time, it's okay. But if one of you has to say at some point, "This is just not working, I want to be your friend but our publishing company is just not buying it," that's hard. It's hard to turn down a new writer, a young writer who thinks that maybe your experience or your position can help, when, in truth, you know that you can't. A lot of this is so political. It's who you know. And if I wrote a song with a friend of mine down in Alabama who has no publishing deal, we could write a wonderful song, but there would only be my company pitching it instead of two companies pitching it. It would be more disappointing to write a great song and watch nothing happen than to say, "I can't help you." That's hard to say, because at some point somebody had to write with me and take a chance.

Jill Colucci - Yes, I have it was but not devastating. There were a couple of reasons. One is just where the chemistry isn't right, where it's not somebody you'd want to hang out with or be friends with or have anything in common with. What in the world are you doing in a room trying to write a song together? If you're going to affect someone emotionally, you've got to dig in there, right? So basically, you're exposing yourself. If you're going to write a great song, then you have to be really open and vulnerable. That's really hard to do the first time you meet somebody.

You've never met them. You open the door and they come in, and you're supposed to write a great, meaningful song together. I think that's one reason I cut back too. There's an intimacy about co-writing, and how many people are extremely intimate with everyone they meet on the street? It's just not that way. So I think that when the chemistry is not right, that's not been a good experience for me. You know you don't want to be writing a song wishing you were somewhere else or wishing you weren't writing that song. That takes all the pleasure out of it. If the two energies don't meet and have some kind of magic, then it's not a devastating experience, but it's not a good co-writing experience.

John Jarrard - I've had co-writing experiences that were just bad in the sense that it didn't work. I've had the opportunity over the years to write with some of my heroes. I guess I've had some bad co-writing experiences with them, probably due to the fact that I discovered that, without exception, they're all mortals. They don't have anything that's handed down on a stone tablet from Mount Olympus, or any particular songwriting wisdom. And they don't write a great song every time they sit down. When I first got to town, Kristofferson was a big hero. I had this picture that every time he sat down to write, *For the Good Times* came out. I was really intimidated by that, because it was clear to me that that didn't happen for me. A lot of times when I sat down to write a song, it was rough. I felt like here was a songwriting genius, and I was a songwriting clod. When I got to town, I had lunch with the guy who was pitching Kristofferson's catalog, and I was telling him that story. He said, "You need to come back to the office with me." He played me song after song after song of Kristofferson's that I would have been embarrassed to have my name on. They were some of the worst country songs I'd ever heard. They were horrible. That helped straighten me out, because I realized that we're all just stumbling around in this, and we all have to find what works for us and pursue that. That was real valuable to me.

Mary Ann Kennedy - Yeah, when there was a tug-of-war or when there seemed to be a powerplay kind of thing going on. You don't share the same vision. I've chosen not to pursue a few co-writing situations where the co-writing was okay, but not when it came to the studio. I'm passionate about that. The demo experience should be blissful. That's a continuation of the writing process for me.

Jim McBride - A good co-writing experience is wonderful and it's fun. But a bad one makes for the longest days and the longest hours and the longest minutes. You just wish that you hadn't gotten into it and you want out of it, and you swear then and there that you'll never do it again. I haven't had a whole lot of those, but I've had enough to know how it feels.

6. What are the advantages to co-writing? What are the disadvantages?

Tony Arata - The advantages of co-writing are borne out in the successes of how many songs you see on the charts that are co-written. A lot of those are from people who write together on a pretty consistent basis, and if you're a new writer and you moved here and you found somebody that you actually did connect with, that's all well and good. You may actually be able to develop some kind of style with that person.

The disadvantages are, I think, that too many people hit town and are immediately told that the only way to get ahead in this town is to co-write. I don't know that a lot of new writers ever get a chance to develop any style of their own, if the only time they're ever exposed to writing is with another person. A lot of the co-writing that I've done has been done by me only writing the lyrics. I'm just not very good at sitting in a room and writing. And I have never asked anybody. I've been asked, and I've done it, but there are so many great writers here that I don't know what it is that I'd exactly add to their work, and so I don't actively pursue that.

Pam Belford - The advantages are that you have someone who is strong where you are weak. You have someone who can tell you that you're getting too far out there. You have someone who has a totally different wealth of experiences to draw from, to throw in ideas that you didn't think of. You have someone who has, on the business end of it, a different set of contacts.

As far as the disadvantages of co-writing, I guess you don't always get to have the last word. There really aren't many disadvantages. Sometimes you have an idea that is really very personal to you, and you're really reluctant to share it with anyone, or at least I am. But I'll end up taking it to someone who loves the idea but doesn't want to do with it what I want to do with it, and that's really hard. I don't want to give up the idea, but I don't want to give up the relationship either.

Kent Blazy - The advantage is probably that two heads are better than one. It's a lot more fun. I usually just write with people that I like a whole lot. So when we get together we have fun as much as write songs, and that kind of takes the edge off of it being work. The creative process works better when it's fun.

One of the drawbacks to creating with other people is that maybe the idea that you had gets diluted. You have other people giving an opinion, and it might not end up being the same song that you thought it was going to be at the beginning. The other thing which bothers some people, but doesn't really bother me, is that the money gets split up more.

Rory Bourke - If a person has a style and they co-write and they begin to lose that style, it wouldn't be a particularly good thing. I don't consider myself to have a style. I sort of become whoever I'm with. For me co-writing or not co-writing is not an issue. For someone who is a great writer on their own and then starts co-writing and their own writing drops off, co-writing is probably not a good idea. When people come here, you have to learn a certain way to write. You have to learn the Nashville way of writing. You have to learn to make every line and every word mean something, literally mean something. You have to learn how to please fifteen zillion people with your songs. The good news is that if you get through that curriculum in a good way, you're probably going to be a hit writer; you'll get songs on the radio and make a lot of money. The tradeoff is that you will probably lose any individuality that made you attractive to them to begin with. So a writer has to really watch that balance, if that's important to them. It wasn't important to me, because I didn't have anything to protect to begin with. I just wanted to be a songwriter. You have to watch that you don't lose yourself in the process. What if you're talented on your own, and you can really write on your own, and you give yourself over totally to co-writing, then you make a lot of money, have a lot of hits, and somewhere down the line you go to push the "ME" button again and nobody's home? Real co-writing, to me, means that a song gets written that would not have been written except under those unique and special circumstances.

Gary Burr - The disadvantage is that if you're not careful, it can water it down. It is describing an elephant by committee. But if you write with people who are always as good or better than you, I don't think the watering down argument really holds. I mean, obviously, if you write with somebody great, then there's no down time. Any part of the song on which I'm stymied, odds are the other person is going to be able to carry the ball. There are days when maybe my antenna's just not up. I'd be glad to sit and take dictation while someone writes the song and puts my name on it, because I know there are plenty of days when I return the favor, when I'm hot and all they've got to do is just keep jotting down the words, and I'll write a song while they watch. It's both extremes. You've just got to be careful. I just don't want to ever write less of a song by collaborating with somebody. I always look at it like that song was not going to exist unless those people were in the room together, and therefore it doesn't matter if somebody put in one word or all of them. It's a co-write.

Kim Carnes - Yes, there are advantages. The songs Donna [Weiss] and I have written together are different than the ones I would write by myself. I love that. You can get into a rut. There's a style of song that I play on the piano and certain chords, and I get tired of that, so there's a huge value in co-writing. You find the right person and write a different kind of song. I think it makes you stretch out and that's important to do. I get bored with my same old chords. When I co-write, I really like to write with somebody who plays guitar, because I don't.

Jill Colucci - There are a lot of reasons why I like to co-write. One, I'm a people person. So I'd rather sit here with a friend of mine and co-write. It's a lot more fun. Number two, not that I'm into writing for speed or writing a lot of songs, because I'm not, but it does speed the process along and keep it more fun. Because if we're stuck, hopefully the co-writer's going to say, "Well, why don't we do this?" or I'll say that and you can keep going. It's a lot more fun with people and I love people. Another reason I co-write is that it's going to come out to be a song that neither one of you could have come up with on your own. That's the goal. When it's a good chemistry, both people can be inspired just sitting in the room. I also co-write if I have an appointment with just me to write. I will bump me for just about anything. I'm out of here. I tell myself, Jill, I can't make it. She'll get over it. I won't cancel so easily on my co-writers.

Those are some of the reasons, but writing alone is a wonderful experience as well. It's something very special, so I just needed to do it more this year. I'm not knocking co-writing. I think it's a wonderful thing. I may do more of it in the future than I am at the moment. I've certainly done a lot of it, and I've learned a lot from other writers. I've had great times. I've written great songs with other people. I have no regrets about co-writing.

Kim Copeland - I think the disadvantage is that if you have something you really have a burning desire to express, it can be diluted by another person's input. Not that it will necessarily make it a weaker song. Their vision may be great, but you may feel less fulfilled by the process.

The advantages are that you have two opinions on the subject, two people coming at it from different angles. Everybody says things in a different way, and you may come up with some things you wouldn't have on your own. If you're writing with somebody who's at a higher level than you, you have the benefit of their experience as far as the editing and the commercialism of it. You've got two people pitching the song, which is better representation for it. So it probably increases your chances of a cut a little bit. From the business standpoint, I think it's advantageous in that way. From the creative side of it, I think you have to pick and choose. I don't think I would co-write every idea I have. There are some ideas that I know need to be co-written—when what I'm feeling for that song is something that I'm incapable of expressing musically or something that someone else is a lot stronger at. That's when I really look for a co-writer. I think you have to treat each song idea individually and look for whatever will bring that song to life.

Kye Fleming - The advantage is that you've got somebody to share the ups and downs with. I can't imagine creating something that I thought was really great, getting it cut and having all this great success, and not being able to have somebody equally invested in it to go, "Oh, isn't this great!" I need and want to be able to share that happiness with somebody, and the only way that they would know the extent of that happiness would be if they had been there from the beginning. Maybe some of that's from being an only child. Maybe I cherish the being able to share, because I didn't have siblings with whom I could share my life. And obviously, the agony of defeat is a little easier when you can complain with somebody instead of everybody saying "she's a complainer."

The only disadvantage that I can see is if you are feeling extremely inspired and you don't have somebody to write with. Trying to find the right co-writer is the disadvantage of co-writing. The disadvantage of *needing* to co-write. Or maybe you start something with somebody, and you thought they would get the same vision, but it's not quite there. You finish it and it's not quite what you had hoped for. It's hard to find the right situations. I've never been comfortable with hopping from one co-writer to another. I would think it would be really hard to get to the heart of it with this other person. For instance, on *Some People's Lives,* that was like writing alone because we were on the same wavelength. That's the ideal in co-writing, and sometimes when you don't find those special connections, I think you can get songs that are not as deep as they would be or as emotional as they could be.

Lindy Gravelle - It's a good way to make sure you're going to write. If I book an appointment, at least I know I'm going to go and show up. I feel like it's a commitment. It's a disciplinary thing to co-write. In this town, I've learned that co-writing can be politically correct or incorrect. You get into this game of who you're writing with and what's their name and what's their company. That can work to your advantage or disadvantage.

Janis Ian - The nice thing about co-writing is that you've got somebody to back you up. You can get a lot more done. You don't get stuck as often because there's always someone to turn a right angle. I enjoy that. Right now I'm interested in turning out a large amount of songs as well as good songs.

Al Kasha - I think it's good, many times, to have a co-writer. It gives you another point of view on how to look at something. Sometimes you have magic with one writer. Of course, Joel Hirschhorn and I had some magic in our career, but I've written with lots of other people and I've had magic with them too. There's a kind of stability when you have one co-writer all of the time, but on the other hand, sometimes you stop growing. Either your partner stops growing, you stop growing, or you both stop growing because you're doing the same thing over and over again. I think it is important to hear a new voice come in. Now I've been writing with a whole bunch of different people. I'm writing with a guy named David Graham who wrote *To Be With You*, and I've been writing with Paul Williams and just a whole bunch of different people. Actually, it's been a new time because I'm hearing their points of view. I don't get stuck just looking at me all the time, which is very healthy for me emotionally and creatively.

(THEY SAY A LOT OF THERAPY HAPPENS IN SONGWRITING. DO YOU THINK THAT'S TRUE?) Oh, yeah. I think it's a catharsis, and it has to do with honesty.

Sandy Knox - Well, I think the advantages of co-writing are greater. You get a better song. I'm pretty much lyrics, and the other person is pretty much melody and music, and then we both kind of mesh in between. I get a much better song writing with somebody who's brilliant on the piano, and the chords are fantastic.

The disadvantages would have to be that you're dealing with another personality and we all have egos. The other disadvantage is that they get half of the money. I mean, you get a big check. After you've had a number one, you get a big old check for fifty grand and you look at it and go, "If I had written this by myself it would be a hundred grand." But for the most part, that song wouldn't have gotten cut without the contribution of the co-writer.

(DO YOU PRETTY MUCH WRITE ALL OF THE LYRICS?) My co-writers are pretty much hands-off lyrics. They will be the first ones to say if they don't like something. I've heard everything from "that stinks" to "you can do better than that" or "what's the matter, are you on drugs?" or "I hate that" or "that makes me want to vomit." They're very honest.

Jess Leary - Advantages, it's usually pretty fun. Two heads are better than one. The old cliché. A lot of times I'll be just on the edge of a thought or an idea, and I can say that, and the co-writer at that point will go, "Oh, you mean da, da, da." It's like throwing you a rope. You can grab onto it. I just find it's helpful.

I guess a disadvantage would be if you're writing with someone for the first time, and it's just not happening. That doesn't happen often. Everyone has different ways of writing, so how are you going to know if you don't try.

Jim McBride - If it's a good song, you can be proud. If you wrote it by yourself, you can be twice as proud. Co-writing is more fun, it's not as lonely, and it goes quicker. Notice that I haven't said you get a better song out of it. Maybe you do and maybe you don't. How did we get where we are now, where so many songs are co-written? I've got so many friends who are wonderful writers that definitely carry their load. I'm going to try and write with those people from time to time and then go back to writing by myself more.

Pam Rose - The advantage to co-writing is that you don't have to do it all yourself. And the advantage to writing by yourself is you don't have to please anybody else. I think they kind of wash each other out.

Joyce Rouse - The advantages are twice as many ideas—twice as much experience sitting in one room—and usually two instruments, which speeds up the editing and rewriting process so much. With some people there's a real magic that happens. There are some writers that I just love to work with because of the magic.

Wayne Tester - The advantages are you open up a whole new world that you would not normally see through your own eyes, and you build friendships. I don't really see any disadvantages unless you come across a hard head who's really inflexible.

Jim McBride - Sometimes one writer can get this deep feeling within and if he can bring that out by himself, then it's going to be better than if he was writing that same idea with another person.

Kim Copeland - It can't be a comfortable co-writing situation for me unless you're both free to express any idea that comes into your head.

Pam Belford - My ideal would be to write with someone whose strengths are my weaknesses.

Rory Bourke - If a person has a style and they co-write and they begin to lose that style, it wouldn't be a particularly good thing.

CHAPTER SIX
LOUDSPEAKERS IN YOUR MIND

Trisha Walker - I think the older I get, I realize the biggest failure is just in not trying.

Sandy Knox - My editor voice is real strong because I don't want to hear somebody else editing me.

Wayland Patton - If it's writer's block, don't let it be a stumbling block, or it will be a stone around your neck that you start freaking out over.

Pam Rose - When I don't have attachment to the outcome, then I truly do it for the joy of the work, and I can put more of that life force into it.

1. What about that "editor voice" that we all have in our head?

Tony Arata - In the back of my head, there's always an editor voice that says, "That just stinks." "That line fits in the meter, but it doesn't say anything." I think if you're going to sign your name to it, then you ought to have the wherewithal to really look at it and say, "Yeah, I want my name on that." So, editing goes on all the time.

Pam Belford - That's usually my co-writer. That's the reason I like to co-write, because I can really get out there. I guess I'm the editor for my co-writer.

Kent Blazy - I don't think I'm as good an editor as some people. I think Kim [Williams] is probably one of the best at that. I guess I'm more of an inspired writer, where what comes out is the subconscious coming out. A lot of times I go back and look at things and try to make it better. Sometimes what I end up doing is taking that heart out of it. There is a very thin line between editing where it's better and editing the heart out of it, and it's the same with going in and doing demos of a song. You might get a better performance on a singer the second time they do it. It might not be perfect, but the emotion will be there. Then maybe six times down the road, they sing it perfect, but there won't be any emotion. I try to keep a balance because a lot of my favorite records and songs aren't perfect.

Steve Bogard - My motto is "dare to be stupid." I think that's really important, or else I don't think you can find the "out there" things where people will ask, "Where did you come up with that?"

Rory Bourke - I have a highly developed editor and a highly developed critic. To me, they're different people. The critic is the part that says, "What you're about to say is stupid. Don't say it." You can't listen to that critic. You never know if what you're about to say is going to make the other person go off into something that's going to be good.

The editor voice is sort of a natural phenomenon, which asks a lot of different questions like, What's this going to be about? Somebody gives you an idea, and they start talking, and you add, Now what will that logically lead to next? That's the editor voice.

Sometimes people come into your life, and they're only there for three minutes, but it's as if they were sent to deliver a message, and you could listen to them or you could not listen to them. Someone who flowed through my life for just five minutes was a guy named Larry Brown. He wrote *Has Anybody Seen My Sweet Gypsy Rose* and *Tie a Yellow Ribbon*. It was probably 1975, and I'd not been writing that long. He said, "The key to great big hit songwriting is editing. The better the editor, the bigger the hit. And two guys working together, if they're both great editors, they can write some really big hits." I always remembered that. What that means to me is that I should be willing to ask, "Is this right?" all the way down the line. And the person I'm writing with needs to be courageous enough to ask that. We should be courageous enough to trash a line that I hate to let go of but is not right. If two people are working together in that sense, they can create something really fantastic. To me, a good editor not only can edit a song, but also can write a song to a different level. People who are editors in songwriting sometimes get a bad name. The implication is that they can't do anything else. I think we all know when we're in the presence of someone who's just a question asker. But I think a really great writer develops those editing skills, which also is a second sense of "this is right." Fortunately, I work with people who trust that part of me. That's not the critic, that's the editor saying this isn't right. The critic's job is to get you to give up. I think that's the hardest thing for people—is to give up that fear that they're going to appear stupid.

Gary Burr - While I'm working on something I think, I've got a really good editor voice. In this business, you either trust your instincts or you don't. I've gotten really comfortable. I've gotten on good terms with my instincts. I trust them. I'm probably a pain in the ass to co-write with because I want to follow my instincts. I'm sure they want to follow their instincts, so we'll probably clash. If we run ninety degrees to each other, we're in trouble.

But as far as an editor voice, and coming back to a song, I'm terrible at that. Once a song is done and I've filed it away, I like to move on. I'm certainly more interested in the next song I'm going to write than three songs ago. But while I'm writing it, I trust where I'm going with it, and I trust when I feel it's got to do something.

Kim Carnes - The editor voice is strong. It's important for me to write with people who have the same point of view, lyrically, that I do. The majority of my writing has been personal, so those I either write by myself or with somebody like Donna [Weiss]. Donna and I wrote *The Heart Won't Lie* together. She wrote *Bette Davis Eyes*. She's such a good friend, and we've written together for so many years, that it's like one person writing the song. That's what I like.

Debi Cochran - There's a balancing line. If the editor voice is telling you that this is a stupid idea, you might be wasting your time if you don't listen. But you also have to suspend that, and let the creative side take over. Then go back and edit. That's why I do all the free-form writing on all those scratch pads of paper, before I even start trying to put things into line and rhyme form. I want to get all the automatic stuff happening.

(DO YOU FEEL THAT DOING IT "AUTOMATICALLY" IS WHAT SUSPENDS THAT VOICE?) Yeah, and also activities like driving and washing dishes, or throwing the Frisbee for your dog. Things that occupy your body, so your mind can just start to drift, will allow the creative side to take over from the editor.

Jill Colucci - That was the breakthrough I had when I went to Florida to write by myself. It was interesting. I felt a desire and a longing to write alone. I needed a change. I needed to write some of my ideas. I needed some alone time and a new environment. I needed the ocean, and more sun. So I took off for the beach. I hadn't completed a song for a couple of months. I had lots of ideas and pieces, but hadn't sat down to put them together. I sat three days with an empty page. Day one I said, "It's okay if you have a bad day." Day two I was getting a little upset. I said, "Okay I'm here. I have no phones ringing. I have no distractions. I've got the most beautiful ocean for my front yard. What is the problem?" By day three I was really getting upset. I was struggling. That might be the first time I considered another occupation. I wondered what else I could do. I think that's the first time that that thought went through me even though I knew better. I took a walk on the beach the next morning. I took a walk every day. Some days it was foggy, thick fog. There were a lot of different atmospheres going on. It was very moody and inspiring, yet my paper was still empty, blank for three days. On day four I had an incredible breakthrough and, by the end of my stay, I finished four or five songs by myself that I was really, really happy with.

One of the main things that I was doing was that I was editing myself before anything could get to the page. I'm not really a journaler, or I wasn't, but I started writing something—anything—just to get some words on the page. Just by doing that, I was unblocking so many things. Through this writing process, I discovered the editor and sent her out to the beach to look for imperfect shells. So the editor was extremely busy for the rest of the trip because there were zillions of them out there. I put the editor aside, and then I was able to be still and listen more and let it come through. I was sitting there trying to make it happen, and it just didn't work. It was just very high after I broke through, but it was very painful and frustrating the first three days. It was a big lesson. Somehow I had to do that to be really aware of the self-editing I was doing.

Kim Copeland - I try not to let the editor voice in the room during a writing session. And I'm pretty good at it. The editor voice comes in when I'm doing rewrites. When I'm tweaking it. That's when you say, okay, this line is right on the fence. Is it profound or stupid? There's such a fine line between those two sometimes. But I really don't allow that voice in at all on the first write.

Gary Earl - I don't have a voice in my head that says that. If I'm enjoying writing it, I just go with it. Afterwards, if two or three people whose opinions I respect tell me it's stupid, then I'll put it away for a while before reevaluating it again later.

Kye Fleming - One of the reasons I quit after those first six years was that voice. It took years to get over that. That's one of the prices that I paid for learning to craft songs. I know I'm not bothered with it as much now because it has turned into a friend instead of an enemy. Now instead of saying, "You can't say that," I hear, "Does that really move you? Is that what you meant to say?" So it's more of a friend to me.

Lindy Gravelle - What I've found, for me, is that it's best to just sit down with my instrument and just start going for it. Don't interrupt if something's flowing. Just go with it. Sometimes it's stellar and sometimes it stinks. But I have to admit that I like to think, when I'm really writing a good tune, there is that force. It's a vibration, the music, the frequency, the pitch, the groove ... all that. When it's right, and when the words match up with the music, that's the force. That's the "flow," maybe. Trusting that is kind of scary, but maybe the more you write, the more you can trust it to be right.

John Jarrard - Honestly, I don't know. A lot of times, during writing sessions, I go unconscious. After it's over, I don't know how we got to it, but we came up with a song. I can't stress enough the idea of keeping it fun. I think that creativity and fun sort of gravitate towards each other. There were literally years when I thought I had to have one of those hooky, catchy titles to start, and I didn't write many songs those years. I didn't have a lot of fun those years. I spent most of those years thinking, I probably can't do this for a living.

Al Kasha - I think of myself as being my toughest critic. My wife is a good critic. She used to work for a music publisher, and I'll tell her to just be stone cold honest with me. Abraham Lincoln had a great saying: "Everybody has the right to criticize as long as they have the heart to help." So I tell her, "You can criticize me, if you'll only tell me you'll help me." She'll read something, or sometimes she'll play it in the other room, and when she gets some time to digest it, she'll come with some thoughts. I have some friends who I consult with who are fellow writers. A lot of songwriters tend to be jealous, but I don't surround myself with jealous songwriters. I surround myself with writers who I can help and, in turn, will help me.

Mary Ann Kennedy - I guess the bottom line answer to that would be to go with the feel. Step back and go with the feel as opposed to thinking, should I play the E minor here, or should I just stay on the C. To really step back, play it down and then listen. Open up that part of you that just says, that feels right or it doesn't. I try to make that editor be more of a heart than a brain.

Sandy Knox - My editor voice is really strong because I don't want to hear somebody else editing me. I want to get it done so that when my publisher hears it, they don't have to say, "You know, that second verse is weak," or "What was that line?" or anything. I'm really tough on myself. I'm really good about editing. I'm really good about talking to my co-writer. My co-writers are very honest. They'll say, "You can do better than that," or "That doesn't sound like something you would have said."

Kostas - That editor voice for me is a good thing to have. It gives you the ability to look at what you've done and see what's sticking out and doesn't belong there.

Jess Leary - I've learned to lighten up about that. I used to be kind of brutal, thinking about every little thing I'd write. If it sounds right when you're reading it, it usually holds up, or you can see little spots that you can polish up a little, or get rid of that extra word.

Jim McBride - The editor voice can stop you. I remember waiting two or three weeks, or a month, for one line. Maybe it was good that I did. Thinking back, most of those songs got cut. I try to be really honest with myself and give myself enough time.

Wayland Patton - I have to be very critical of the writing. And in collaborating, one of the important elements is being able to throw out anything, no matter how stupid it may be. I may throw it out and realize after I say it, boy, that's really stupid. Or I may say, "Now this is going to sound stupid, but—.". You have to have the courage to say it, because no matter how stupid it may sound, it might be the very thing that triggers the response from your co-writer. It might open that door, or lead your co-writer down the path to that right line.

Pam Rose - I've just now really gotten mine under control, to tell you the truth. I think it was so strong for so many years. Jill Colucci and I were talking about sending the editor down to the beach to pick all the imperfect sea shells. That's always something good for the editor to do. You can think of other things for the editor to do, because they're very talented, those little editor guys. They want to be busy, and you can't just snuff them out. They'll resurface as something else. Jill actually gave me, for a gift, a book called *The Artist's Way*. I haven't even read the book yet. I just read the forward and the introduction, and it changed my life. It encourages you to do an exercise called morning pages, which is uncensored, can't correct any mistakes writing. You can't go back and change it. You can't erase. That was so powerful, just learning to do that as an exercise. That set up a whole chain reaction for me. And it really reminds me of something that Mary Ann [Kennedy] shared with me. She was reading it on the airplane once when we were going some place. She had this book called *Writing Down the Bones*. She told me what it said, and that changed my life too. It is the uncensored part, because if you get a certain amount of that going, it unplugs everything. It unblocks everything, and then I'll end up having a choice about which road to take. Do I feel uncensored today or do I need to ask the editor to join me? Then it becomes a matter of choice. Then I'm choosing between the big, unedited self, and the editor, instead of the editor running the show. It's a matter of "who's driving this bus?" It makes me feel freer to make the choices.

Joyce Rouse - I just discovered over the past couple of years that my editor voice has become less critical and more loving and nurturing. It is very directive about using the things I know about the craft but is much less acerbic and critical.

Wayne Tester - I never try to let the editor come out in me. I always try to have fun with it, to worry about the craft of it, and the editing of it, way on down the line. I just try to get pure inspiration on paper and on tape first, and worry about the other stuff later.

Trisha Walker - I think that during the majority of my writing time, I've had a really strong editor voice. Some of this may be because my mother was the editor of the small town newspaper. The past couple of years, though, I've tried experimenting more with what I call free writing, and not letting the editor in too soon. If I've got an idea, or a picture, or a story line, I just write it out freehand, as if you were writing a play. One of the exercises is to put your pencil to paper and literally, for ten minutes, don't take your pencil up. Then go back and start editing. That's been real interesting, because I'm much more prone to edit while I'm going, but I realize that you lose a lot. So I do have a strong editor voice, and I have to fight it quite a bit.

2. Let's say you have just finished writing a song that you feel is really special. Do you ever experience (even for a moment) the fear that it might be your last?

Tony Arata - I would never say that I've written my best song. I think that would be kind of a dangerous thing. I can go back through my catalog, and I can pull them out and say, this one is worth it. This one is marginal at best and these are awful. But I know there are some really good ones in there, and they're scattered over a long enough period of time. There are periods of time when I'm just really not happy with stuff that I'm writing, but I never think that that's the last one. That would be up to somebody else to decide, you know.

(WHAT WERE YOUR THOUGHTS AFTER YOU FINISHED *THE DANCE*?) I knew that one. I wrote that not long after we moved up here. There weren't many places for anybody to get lost in that song. It's a very simple piece. I was pleased with that because that, to me, is harder to do than anything. To come up with something very simple that allows people to conjure up their own explanations of what this song is about. I can honestly say that I knew that song was special. That's not to say that it found a home immediately. It was pitched around for a while and turned down a few times. The greatest fortune that song ever had was that it was heard by another songwriter. I think it was understood from the ground level up. It was heard by Garth. We were out playing when I did that song, and it hit him then. I think he understood. His success speaks for itself. He's a huge talent, but I've never been able to get past the fact that I still think of him as a songwriter first and foremost. So I think that was a blessing for that song. He had no record deal when he heard that song. He was one of us. He was just out there trying to get somebody to listen to his songs.

Pam Belford - Sure, anytime I write something really good.

Kent Blazy - I've never experienced that. I've got books and books and books of ideas. I don't ever feel like it's going to be the last song. I want to be like Harlan Howard and be in my seventies and writing songs that people can relate to. I think it's just the process of keeping yourself open to the creative. It boggles my mind when people say they have writer's block.

Kim Copeland - I used to. I used to spend weeks after a song like that, worrying about it. Every idea I would write after that, I would edit too much, too soon. Now, I allow myself to just relish those songs a little bit. I'll keep writing, or I may not write for a few weeks and concentrate more on performing. I allow myself to enjoy those special songs, and I don't worry that there won't be more. Those feel so good that it seems a shame to diminish them by spending the immediate time afterwards worrying about the next great one.

Gary Earl - No, not really, because my wife Robin and I have written so many things on a tight time schedule for film and television.

Robin Earl - I think it's easy to feel that the song I just wrote is the best one, because I'm involved in the intensity of it at the moment. That seems to be the feeling, rather than that it's the last song.

Kye Fleming - There might have been some fear there about that, but the couple of times that I might have felt that I will never do this again, I was right. And I may not even do anything that satisfying again, but that's okay, because to have felt that great about something is success in itself. If you turn that into fear, then you've got a problem.

John Jarrard - My fears are more typically on the front end of a songwriting session. I think, how do you do this? I typically have to have this little talk with myself in almost every writing situation that I get into. I have to tell myself that if I will sit here, and if I will trust in this process, it will happen. There are a lot of life lessons that songwriting is sort of a cartoon of. Trust is one of them. Often enough for me to have a pretty good career with it, if I just sit with it, a song will emerge.

Al Kasha - Oh, sure. I've felt that many times, but as long as there are people walking the streets and as long as people have problems, there will always be songs.

Mary Ann Kennedy - It might sound cocky or something, but I really haven't had that. I don't expect to write another *Love Like This,* or another *Safe in the Arms of Love.* I have enough sense to know that I have a couple of killer jewels in my catalog, and whatever I contributed to that song isn't gone. My challenge is to do it a little bit differently next time, but to do it again.

Jess Leary - Absolutely. A lot of times when that happens, I really want to take a couple of days off. I want to relish the beauty of that, because if I write something tomorrow, I know it's not going to measure up to this. Let me just surf here for a minute. It's going to be in my head anyway for a couple of days, so let's just take two or three days and forget everything.

Jim McBride - There are times when it seems like there are ideas everywhere, and I'm trying not to miss any of them. There are other times when I wouldn't know a great idea if I stumbled on it and fell flat on my face. It's those times when I haven't had a good idea that bother me. At this point in my career, I don't worry about writing a song. If I can find an idea that I believe in and I feel strongly enough about it, I can write the song. I may not write it well enough, but I can write it. It is the ideas that are worth writing that I might be afraid I've had the last of.

Wayland Patton - Usually, every time [I'm afraid it may be the last great song.] It goes back to basic insecurity, that fear of being found out, or if you go through a dry spell. But I just have to get in and start working. Work through it.

Pam Rose - After *I'll Still Be Loving You* was so big, I was really very intimidated. I experienced something called "phenominalization." Performance anxiety, I guess you'd call it. Will I ever write another *I'll Still Be Loving You*? You know what I finally figured out? The answer is no. I may write something that's even better than that. So that's what it took for me. I will never write another *I'll Still Be Loving You*, but I may write something that's that good or better. That one has already been written.

Wayne Tester - You try not to let that happen to you or you'll get on that emotional roller coaster again. You'll get paranoid, and that's only detrimental to your creativity. You just don't worry about it, and say, "When it's supposed to happen again, it will."

3. What advice can you give on dealing with the fear of failure?

Tony Arata - I think that failure is really on two levels. One, somebody tells you you've failed. And two, you feel that you've failed no matter what anybody says. I'm very grateful to be able to say that I make my living as a songwriter, but long before I made my living at it, I dealt with rejection on a very daily basis. There were no open arms waiting for the next thing I was writing, but I didn't think I had failed. I think that too much is made of the thought that achievement can only come by someone else saying that you've achieved. I think that you have to write because you *want* to write, not because you want to have plaques on your wall. Most of the people you hear on the radio or at the top of the charts have all "failed" at one time or another. The important thing is whether or not you continue on after that. Ultimately, I believe you have to do this because you enjoy doing it. It may require that you do something else in addition to it, but you know, people can write novels while they write at newspapers. And you can certainly write a song while you're doing something else. I think it's a part of your life. I don't think there's any lifestyle you have to adopt in order to become a songwriter.

Failure can be caused by putting so much stock in thinking that everything is going to be taken care of by somebody else in this industry. In fact, it all comes down to whether or not you're willing to do something about it. When you turn off the light at night and, during the day, you wrote something that you're really proud of, you can't truly fail by doing that.

Pam Belford - I think that everybody has a certain amount of fear of failure. But I think this is not a good business to be in if you're afraid of failure. There's a lot more failure than there is success.

Steve Bogard - Take the "fear of failure," put it in your hand, and hold it right up in your face and stare at it until you really understand it. Don't try to avoid it; you're giving it power if you try to avoid it. Let it be there and then let it flow away. We all have it every day, and there's no place where you have to confront it more often than in songwriting. You have to believe in yourself and go on. Anything that you're afraid of, if you avoid it and go away from it, you're giving it more power than it deserves.

Gary Burr - There is a book out that says, "Feel the fear and face it anyway." I have a fear of failure. I think everyone has a fear of failure. I think that's healthy. Everybody wants to succeed. You fear what you don't want to be, or what you don't want to do, or you don't want to experience. Nobody wants to be afraid. You can deal with it in two ways. It can either make you not do it, or it can make you do it "extry" hard, as we say in the South. I want to be a success. I want to leave a mark. That's all I ever wanted to do. I just want to leave a mark. So the only thing that's going to make me fail is not working hard enough. When I feel that fear of failure, I just work a little harder. I think you can turn that into a positive thing. You can turn that into a great motivation, or it can be a wall that you never get over.

I'm making a living doing music when a lot of people I grew up playing music with got out of it, one by one, because they weren't willing to live out the struggle. It really just comes down to that; you're willing to put up with the struggle, and fight and outlast the aggravation. I read once that a hero is somebody who's just cold enough and tired enough and fed up enough to not give a damn anymore. That's basically what songwriters are. They've heard all the no's that one person can take and they don't care. One more no isn't going to kill them. I'm really critical of what I do. I can't even sit in a room and listen when my songs are played. I'm just sure that everyone hates them, but I do it because I know that even if they say no, one more no isn't going to kill me. I get no ninety-nine times out of a hundred. One person says yes and it's a number one, and I make my kid's college tuition. I mean, come on, it's even stupider odds than a baseball player. All he's got to do is hit one out of every three times, and he's in the Hall of Fame. He misses two out of three times, and he's in the Hall of Fame. I can get ninety-nine no's and one yes and be in the Country Music Hall of Fame. So if you look at those odds, what have we got to worry about? All we've got to do is find one person out of a hundred who will do it.

Debi Cochran - We're all afraid of it, so just look it in the face and keep going anyway. Just keep putting one foot in front of the other. There aren't any monsters in the closet, so just keep walking.

Kim Copeland - I think it can be a very debilitating thing if you allow it to. You have to decide how much power you're going to give the fear and if it's going to get the best of you. If it is, then get out now because it will be a miserable career for you. Success is a by-product of hard work. Work so hard that you don't have time to think about the fear, and you will outrun it. If you can learn to use it as a motivator, it can work for you.

Gary Earl - It's a tough line, but it would be easy to be glib and say that you have to have no fear. Charge right ahead. And that is important. On the other hand, you do have to be realistic. You're going to get a ton of rejection. You have to want it more than anything else in the world, to persist through all that fear and all those rejections.

If you flew an airplane from here to New York, ninety percent of the time your airplane is not pointed at New York. It's slightly off course most of the time. The pilot is constantly making little minor corrections back and forth and you really fly on a zigzag line to New York. And life is kind of the same way. If you want to get somewhere, you aim at it and you take a run for it, and you may hit a wall, so you twist that steering wheel a little bit and go around it and aim again. And each time you change your way of doing something, you're getting a little closer to your result until eventually you do get the outcome you want. I really do think that's true.

Robin Earl - Think of a failure as learning. Everything is part of your growth, and sometimes what you perceive as a big failure leads you to something that's better anyway. You realize later that sometimes these turning points that seem like big failures are really just turning points that kind of change your direction. At one point I was afraid of being in the music business because of the insecurity of it. So I became a partner in a restaurant, thinking that was more practical. I ended up working for a year for free and lost a lot of money. After that, music didn't seem like so much of a risk, and I was doing something I loved.

Lindy Gravelle - Friends [help in dealing with the fear of failure]. Try to find a sympathetic ear, verbalize your fears, actually say things out loud. And if you have somebody who's listening, boy, that's helpful. You can get stuck in a perspective. I came to town thinking, I've got to get a recording deal or I'm nothing. You can get an all or nothing attitude about this business, because there's so much emphasis put on being successful. If you buy into that, and you're not strong enough to realize how damaging it can be to you when things aren't going great, the fear can eat you alive. For me, it was more a matter of tapping into a spiritual power and realizing there was a life besides the country music world that actually meant a hell of a lot more.

I would tell young people today who come to town, "Listen to your body." I've seen so many, including myself, get so fraught with stress and working so hard to try to be successful, that you end up fried and getting sick a lot—just feeling crappy, no energy, getting colds, flu, sore throats. Couldn't sing or couldn't write because you couldn't sing. To me, it was all rooted in fear of failure. Then my perspective, thank God, started to change to, Hey, you can be a somebody and not have to be a star.

John Jarrard - Keep it fun. The atmosphere in which we do our best work is one in which we're enjoying ourselves. I've heard that fear and love are opposites, and fear and fun strike me as diametrically opposed as well.

Al Kasha - The most important things are to never give up and to stay in touch with the times. It doesn't matter how old you are, you can always have hits if you really analyze the charts and stay in touch with the charts and, most of all, stay in touch with your heart. Be honest and get with your feelings.

Mary Ann Kennedy - Fear is a poison. You just can't have it. That's easy to say, and I'm not saying I don't have it in my life and don't continue working on it, but I've never had it around since I've been successful as a writer and singer in Nashville. I kind of knew from the time I was twelve that this was how I was going to live my life and that I was going to make it. I've been blessed enough and worked hard enough that it's worked for me.

Sandy Knox - I've never had a fear of failure. I always felt I could do it. I felt like I had no choice, because it was the only thing I knew how to do. I always believed in myself, and I had family who believed in me. I never thought I'd fail. My fear, if anything, was how long it was taking.

Kostas - Don't be so much afraid to fail. Be more concerned with whether or not you're in the right field. A lot of people think that this is a glamorous lifestyle and what they want to do. TV, the movies, and the media have made everything so accessible and so unrealistic. They show the bright side of everything and never the dark side. So everybody gets out of high school and thinks what they want to do is move to L.A. or New York and become a rock star. Just because you can tap your foot and sing doesn't necessarily mean that's what your calling is in life. Time will take care of most things like that. Believe me when I say that this is not a Nazi idea. I'm not saying that this is just for the special few, but the special few who are good songwriters are not there because they choose to be there. They are there because that's what they were born to be. That's their calling in life.

There's no way anybody in life is going to fail. The only way we are going to fail is if we choose to fail. I think the very fact that you're born, that you, above all those other little sperm cells, were chosen to come out the winner [makes you a success]. God chose you to live, from the moment you came into this world, and you survived long enough to know the difference between right and wrong, and survived school and everything else. I think that everybody is born a success. Then it's a matter of what you do with your time and health to make the best of those situations. You can't expect life to be a gambling parlor. Yeah, we take chances and gamble, but you can't always depend on lady luck. You have to make your opportunities, and you have to take them when you see them. There are people out there who are great songwriters, struggling to be heard.

Jess Leary - Don't believe it. Don't put energy into the fear of failure. Turn it around and think positively and realize that you have a gift. Do the best you can and learn the most you can about it. Be sensible in how you're going to approach it and set attainable goals. I never liked feeling the fear of failure. There are enough negative things in the world without putting something like that on yourself. I can honestly say that I always knew I'd be okay, one way or another. I always knew I'd have a roof over my head and that I would be able to eat at night. I feel grateful for that. I would tell people to close that door and open a bunch of windows and think positively.

Wayland Patton - I don't have a fear of failure. I'm not afraid and I'm not going to be afraid. Maybe it's because I feel that success doesn't necessarily mean that I'm going to be the wealthiest, biggest name in songwriting that ever was. My success happens when I lift my pen off that page and I can sing that song, listen back to it, and know that it's a good song. A song that says what I wanted to say at that moment. Beyond that, it's out of my hands. But I'm not a success or a failure based on somebody else cutting my song, or somebody else liking my song. I have to please myself first. I have to be able to move myself first and accomplish what I set out to do.

Pam Rose - I'd like to tie a lot of the fear of failure back into what I was saying earlier about the concepts addressed in *The Artist's Way*. You deal with it by relying on yourself and connecting with yourself and putting the editor aside, letting the editor do the other editor's chores.

If you take fear out of your life, I don't think that anything you do is a failure. I think it's just the next step. That's easier said than done, and that's one of those things that looks great on paper. I find that when I'm able to do that, when I can truly look at a situation and not be afraid of it, then it just doesn't have the same meaning anymore. It doesn't have self-worth attached to it, and it doesn't have loss of self-esteem attached to it. When I don't have attachment to the outcome, then I truly do it for the joy of the work, and I can put more of that life force in it. Then it's just my work and it stands like what it is, and it's something I'm proud of. It's something I've done, and it's something that brings me joy. It's the next step toward being better at what I do.

Joyce Rouse - Get over it! Again, it's just part of that "do what you love." Write about what you love. My sense is that fear of failure comes out of much earlier fears. Fears from developmental years. And fear of failure is a learned fear. It's not a natural fear, so it can be unlearned.

Trisha Walker - I think the older I get, I realize the biggest failure is just in not trying. So what if you fail.

Marijohn Wilkin - Dallas Frazier was a great writer, and when he was interviewed and they asked him, "What would you have done if you hadn't made it?" He said, "I didn't have an answer, because I never thought about not making it." You can't do anything with the fear of failure, write a song or drive down the interstate.

4. When you first write on an idea, do you try to go from beginning to end without editing, or do you work more on the basis of one line at a time?

Kim Carnes - I really don't have any set pattern. A lot of times we just need one more line, but it has to be a killer line. Sometimes that's the hardest to come up with. Just that one line that's some place in the song that has to be right. Over the years, I've ended up being more and more critical. You have to be. You never let a song come out if you haven't honed in on every single line, no matter how long it takes.

Kim Copeland - I always cluster-write. That's why I like top-bound notebooks, so I have the whole page with both margins to work with. I may write down an outline. If I have an idea for a chorus or the hook line, or whatever, I'll write that in the middle of the page. If I have an idea of how the story is going to lay out, then I may write an idea for the first verse on the top line of the page, or a line to begin the second verse eight lines up from the bottom of the page, just to give myself some visual form to follow. Then, in the margins, I cluster-write. I write down every idea I can think of relating to the subject. Phrases, words, whatever. They don't have to rhyme. They don't have to have any form or even come at the subject from the same direction. I don't isolate any one direction to approach it from. Then, most of the time, after I've done that and have the margins completely filled up (and I can write really small!), I have the song. Usually, I can go back and read all of those scribbles, and the song is there. It's just a matter of putting it together like a puzzle.

Robin Earl - Every song is different. Sometimes we'll start with an idea and just brainstorm phrases. Sometimes it's the music, but a lot of times music and lyric ideas come somewhat together. It depends on the situation. One time we had a film supervisor ask for five songs to be written and recorded in two weeks. He said, "Oh, by the way, these are the titles we need, because the film's done, and the titles are already on the credits. And we need such and such a tempo."

Janis Ian - It totally depends on the song. Gary Burr and I just wrote a song called *Getting Over You*. We started out with the third and fourth line of the chorus, and somehow worked our way backwards. It was fascinating for me because I almost never work that way. Neither does he; it just fell that way. I used to worry about it. I used to think, if I could just get the right formula down, I'd be able to do it every time. I've discovered that there is no formula; there is no way to do it every time.

(DO YOU EDIT AS YOU GO?) It's rare that I'll let something go if it's more than half a line. I might let a word go because I'm not sure about it. I might have two lines where it's moving so fast I just jot them down and keep going, but in general, and particularly in co-writing, you tend to try and get it pretty right. I also think you hit a point as a writer where you have instincts and you have craft. At that point you have the luxury of going pretty quickly and editing pretty well. The only time that becomes a drawback is when you are working with a young writer who doesn't have the craft, and then you've got to stop and explain to them why things don't work. I think co-writing is one of the nicest things that Nashville does. Especially if you can write with people who are your peers or better than you. That's a real luxury.

John Jarrard - I'd like to [write from beginning to end], but that doesn't come naturally. Usually if I can get a chorus first, then that'll give me a lot of information about what the verses need to say.

Jim McBride - I generally just play the melody, which usually comes first for me, over, and over and over. Hearing that melody helps me to fill in the lines. If I get a line I think I like, I'll put it down. If I'm not sure about it, I'll put a little "x" by it, which means come back and see if you can beat this one. I put down words that are associated with it over in the margins. I generally do that starting out. Once I have the title, I think of all the words I can that would fit in the song, and put them in the margin.

Joyce Rouse - I tend to want to let everything come out, and then I'll rearrange it later if I need to.

Kim Williams - Brainstorming an idea is really important. Sometimes you don't have to, because it's pretty obvious where the song's going. First thing, you kind of talk about it. Is it this, is it that? Sometimes the idea is really strong, and I say, "I don't care if it's commercial or not, let's write this the way we feel it." Sometimes your best songs come out of that. The first thing is the brainstorming, and then you start writing. But I won't allow anybody to stop the flow to fix an adverb or a pronoun.

To me, if it's flowing, let it flow. You can polish later with the left side of your brain. To me, the writing comes from that right side, the illogical side of your brain. Harlan Howard says you've got to get to that part of your brain where the writer is. And the great writers, they know not to stop the flow.

5. Define "writer's block."

Kent Blazy - Writer's block is feeling like you're never going to write another song, or feeling like you've done your best work and you have nothing new to say. I really don't know what it is, but it seems like it's time to refill the well when that happens. Whatever works for you is what you need to do. I tell everybody that you need to start reading some books, reading some novels, or go out and buy some new music and listen to it. Go back to things that you love. That'll get you inspired again to want to write.

Rory Bourke - You're blocked and you can't write. I know people who wear that like a badge. Maybe writer's block goes to the question of how brave you are about leaving your mind open all the time to what might be lurking in the shadows. Maybe from time to time people aren't as willing to deal with the shadow stuff coming in, so they just shut the door and nothing gets in. Maybe you're afraid that you're not going to live up to the expectations of other people and yourself. You and I both know that if you wanted to sit down and write a song about this table, you could probably write a real good song about this table. But who the hell would cut it? Nobody, and then what would that make you? Nobody. The emphasis is on performance and not on the love of writing songs. Our business doesn't value that song about the table, because if it doesn't go on the radio, who needs it? So that's a tension that exists inside songwriting: how not to stop doing what you love. Charlie [Black] has got the great line. He says, "Rory, we write what we write. Sometimes we write it by not getting it cut for five years, but we were true to ourselves."

Debi Cochran - Writer's block is an absence of excitement. You come up with ideas that just aren't interesting.

Jill Colucci - I haven't put any thought to it much, but I guess it would be the inability to write. You are completely out of touch with your creativity. That's a pretty strong thing. Of course, as long as you could remember that, it would be a temporary and not a permanent thing, then you'll be okay.

I guess those three days I went with an empty page could be called writer's block, or you could just say that I had three bad writing days. I was actually sitting down, available, ready, willing to write, but I was blocked. And it was the editor in me that was blocking me.

Gary Earl - I think writer's block is the internal belief that you're unable to do it, or an internal lack of belief in your ability to do it. I think it always comes from within. Fear is one of the most debilitating things in life.

Janis Ian - Writer's block is when you *think* you're not working. I think you're working all the time on some level. Writers write, that's what they do. Whether or not anything is coming out in a usable form, it's in there somewhere. I think you have to be really careful to distinguish between writer's block resulting from thinking, "I don't feel like writing songs," or writer's block being mistaken for what is actually, "I need some rest time." That's different from writer's block that is a pathologic occurrence, which I don't run into very often, when somebody is scared to write. Everybody experiences that after they finish a really good song, thinking, I'll never write a good song again. It's always that way, but that's not a block. I try really hard when I feel like that to not play into the "I'll never write anything good again" and fall into all that negative stuff. I just keep going. I am a good writer and I will write when it's time. I cut myself a lot of slack. I'm just coming off a year and a half on the road and in the studio, where I wrote next to nothing. I might have written five or six songs, and I normally put out twenty to thirty songs a year. When I was teaching writing classes I didn't write a lot, but I learned a lot.

Al Kasha - Well, I'll quote someone else: "I don't have writer's block, because I write with every writer on the block." I think the way to get away from writer's block is to hang around with other people. Maybe go to some foreign place where you don't normally go, to hear another point of view. I live in a very beautiful place in California, but I find if I go into a diner and listen to some truck drivers or waitresses talking, that helps me a great deal because of their honesty. It gets me into a different place other than my own problems. Being a writer, you are a communicator of what's happening in the world. I like talking to women. I feel that women are much more honest about feelings than men are. Men are into facts and women are into feelings.

Sandy Knox - I think it's kind of a depression. For me it is. Although then again, I can't say that, because sometimes we write our best stuff when we're depressed. My publisher used to love it when I would break up with somebody, because he knew a whole new crop of songs was coming in.

Jess Leary - Writer's block is when you just need to calm down. You need to tune out. It's your body and your mind and your spirit all saying "chill, you're working me too hard." The more it happens to me, the more I find I'm in a frantic kind of state when that happens, for whatever reasons. If I got a phone call from somebody that was annoying, one too many bills in the mail, or just something that threw me off track. Sometimes that can start that process of staying off track. It's those biorhythms again. They're all taking their turns. Try to relax and be open to creativity again. I think that's what it is. You block yourself. It's not anything done outwardly—we do it to ourselves.

Joyce Rouse - That's when I go to work on getting my office up to date and doing the kind of rote things that I don't have enough time to do anyway. I very, very rarely have writer's block.

Wayne Tester - Writer's block is no creativity flowing through you. That's the time to move on to something else, another part of the business, or spend time with the kids, or do something else.

Trisha Walker - It may not be anything more than the cyclical going and coming around. Probably, writer's block is not being receptive enough to the ideas around you. For songwriting, [the hard part is] that first five minutes of sitting down. I'll wash the car, I'll wash the dog, I'll wash the clothes, anything to keep from sitting down and starting. But once I'm there for five minutes, I'm okay. Then you can't get me away.

6. Do you ever experience writer's block, and if so what do you do about it?

Tony Arata - Oh, sure. I don't know that it's necessarily limited to writers. I think everybody kind of goes through periods when, if they were forced to elaborate on what they've been thinking about for the past forty-eight hours, sometimes that would be a pretty full page and sometimes that would be a stark page. I think people make too much of it, and I think people make too much of how to get past it. They can't do anything else. It's really not worth it. I have to say this—ultimately, at the top of this field, this is still just songwriting. It's not curing polio or anything like that, and so to get upset because you haven't written a song is really not worth too much anguish.

Pam Belford - Yes. I used to not know what to do about it, and I think I accidentally stumbled upon an answer recently. I just said, "Who cares. I'm going to pamper me for a little while, and I'm not going to worry about writing, and I'm not going to worry about responsibilities to co-writers. I'm not going to worry about anything but me. I feel like living the life of a complete couch potato for a few weeks. I'm going to do that." I've found that was the best way I've had so far of getting over the pressure.

Steve Bogard - I don't think I've ever had it, but that's [because of] my collaboration ethic. I don't think you ever have writer's block. I think you don't keep score with your co-writers, you just bring your best ideas and try to write your best ideas every time. Then if I had a six-month period where I couldn't come up with a great idea, I'd have enough co-writers that I'd have stuff to write on. I would never even notice if I had writer's block.

Rory Bourke - I don't experience writer's block because I'm constantly working with other people. My job with each person is different. I've experienced bad song writing, but not necessarily writer's block. It seems to me that the only way around writer's block is to write. But I really think songwriters do have a fear that what they are writing isn't good enough. Something from a long time ago is at work, which literally shuts down everything. The fear involved with it is so great that it makes you stop writing. I don't believe that you have writer's block, and six months later you don't have writer's block. The only way to get around writer's block is to keep at it. You've got to say, "Okay, what I'm writing may not be the greatest thing in the world, but I'm writing." I write songs that are less than other songs, but I have to write those to get to the really good songs. If I wrote under the apprehension that everything I write has to be great, then I might have writer's block too.

Gary Burr - No, I don't have writer's block. I just can't see getting all that angst up about it. I mean, it's not like we have jobs or anything. If I'm in a period where I can't think of something to say, I'll go help other people say what they want to say. Then, hearing what they want to say makes me inspired to say something on my own. It's such a repeating cycle that a little writer's block never killed anybody.

Debi Cochran - Yes, I have. You just keep going anyway. You hope that maybe the person you're writing with that day is on. Or if you are sitting there and you've got a great melody that you know is going to work, and the story or the lyrics are just not coming, then you adjourn and you go to lunch, and sometimes on a full stomach things will be very clear.

Kim Copeland - The best way for me to get over it is to write through it. I make myself sit down with a blank sheet of paper and my guitar and give myself a time limit. Say I have to sit there thirty minutes. I'm too impatient a person to sit there that long doing nothing. I'll get restless and my mind will start to wander, and I'll start singing or playing just silly, little things and the next thing I know, I'll be working on something. If I take all expectations off of it being good, then something will be written in that time. It may be something stupid and terrible, but it will free me up and usually lead to something better.

I think to face the fear and to write is the way to get over writer's block. That's all I think it is: being scared or too intimidated to try. It's self-imposed, and you have to deal with it from within. I ask myself, what's the worst that can happen? I could write something really stupid, but I never have to show it to anybody. That takes the pressure off. If something really good comes out of that session, then you can tell stories about how you planned to write that idea from the start. No writer's block here! The plan all along was to sit down and write this masterpiece today.

Gary Earl - I don't think I've had writer's block. I've had periods of not writing for literally months, but I accept it. When I don't write, it's usually because I've been doing a whole bunch of it, and it's time to go do something else like coordinating or producing other music projects. For me, it's just that I like a lot of change. I think it does go through cycles, and I never give it much thought. It seems natural.

Robin Earl - I go through cycles, times when I write more than others. When I'm not writing, it seems to be because I'm busy with other things, or procrastinating, or not motivated.

Kye Fleming - I probably experience what I think people mean by writer's block, regularly, but not for any extended period of time. For me, it's that I have blinded myself. I don't even know what's wrong, and I need to get back to the basics of taking care of myself, whether by meditating or just getting in touch. I get in the now and live a little bit, then it takes care of itself and eventually, without even realizing it's happened, just like the same, slow process of getting blinded, I start clearing out a little bit. Then creativity comes.

Lindy Gravelle - I get idea block. For me, that is writer's block, because you've got to have a good idea to start with. I've relied so much on wanting to be inspired by a hook. I'm starting to think that I'll explore other ways of writing and not just have to have a hook. I've heard a few writers say that they can start with just an image of something, start writing, and then they'll end up with a hook. I get envious of writers who always seem to have lots of those.

John Jarrard - I don' t know that I've ever experienced classical writer's block. What I do is just keep getting back on the horse. If I just keep putting myself in situations where the possibility of writing songs exists, if I just jump in there and be patient and don't succumb to the fear, then typically it works itself out in short order.

Mary Ann Kennedy - Sure, [I've had writer's block]. What I've learned, now that I am secure enough financially and have enough other things going, is that if I'm not in that place, I just don't push it. I have the luxury of not doing that now.

Jim McBride - To me, writer's block is where I can't think of anything worth writing. Where I can't come up with any idea that I even feel good enough about to write. If I get into a song, I don't get to a verse and chorus and then not be able to think of anything. If I'm really into it, I'll finish the song. It may take a while. When I get blocked, I get away from it.

Wayland Patton - Yeah, I think that's a natural. Especially if you're writing hard for a long period of time; it just drains you. You get to a point where you're just tired. (IS THAT HOW YOU WOULD DEFINE WRITER'S BLOCK?) Yeah, I think that is a big part of it. If you're writing consistently, you get to that point where you're "wrote out." I have a couple of ways to get around that. I read a lot and do photography. But even when I'm feeling that way, I still try to work and chip away at the block. I think it's important to write through that. The main thing is not to worry about it. If it's writer's block, don't let it be a stumbling block, or it will be a stone around your neck that you start freaking out over. It's important that you just keep going. One step in front of the other, and pretty soon you're there. I try to keep a list of ideas around, so if I don't feel exceptionally creative, I can work through those ideas. Or I might take a little time off and go to a movie.

Pam Rose - I've experienced it several times, and usually that has been when the editor is so strong. It's not good enough, it's not commercial enough, or I don't know who will cut this. If it does get cut, then it might not be a single. On and on and on. I don't think I can finish it. My lyrics aren't as good as ... all those things. It will just wear you out.

When I first came to Nashville, I was so excited. I was here in Nashville, and I went and played somebody a song. They listened to it, took it off the tape player, put it back in the box, threw it across the room to me, and said, "It's a piece of shit." And I didn't write for three years, so I guess I took that too personally. It took me a long time to get over that. It was a very crucial time in my life. I had been in Atlanta with a black jazz musician for my musical guru. I didn't know anything about country music when I came here. I didn't know the difference between a record and a song. You can make a good record out of a terrible or mediocre song. The song is the framework. You know, you can make a house that looks nice, but it will fall down after a while if the foundation and the frame are not properly constructed. I guess that's the difference.

That was my first writer's block. That was the worst one. And the other one was after *I'll Still Be Loving You.*

Trisha Walker - Who's to say what brings it on? Nobody knows. I don't think I've ever panicked necessarily. There have been times, like most writers, when I write something I really feel is good, and I become scared and concerned that the next thing is not going to be that good. I'm fortunate to have enough to do here with the publishing and production company that if I've got writer's block, I can go do something else and not worry about it. I try to go on input.

Marijohn Wilkin - I went through a period when I started my own company. Most writers write for somebody. You write to please somebody. You write to please your publisher so you get your paycheck or meet your quota. We wrote for Mr. Jim Denny and Mr. Denny was dying of cancer. When I knew he was going to be gone soon, I said, "Well, there's nothing I can do but start my own company." But to start my own company I had to go off of any draw or salary. So I did a lot of backup work, I sang on a lot of records, a lot of sessions. I did that for my rent money. And after being in the studio with other people's music, if I would have a thought come through my mind, I would say, "Oh, God, did I steal it off of that last session I was on?" I tried to detach from those records, but it's just really hard to do. So I went through a very, very long dry period at that time. But that was all right because it was at that time that I started working with Kris Kristofferson, and that worked out all right. Then when *One Day at a Time* came out, it was like a dam broke. Now, I either write or don't write. It's no big deal. If I'm supposed to write, I will.

Kim Williams - I've never had writer's block, and I don't understand the concept. I've had days when I didn't have anything to write about, but I don't feel like I've ever had writers block. I've felt that if somebody said the right word, I'd be writing instantly. I haven't ever had it. It's a state of mind. Somebody asked me, "How can you write every day?" To me it's, how can you *not* write every day? I get a little fried every now and then and need some time off, but I don't understand writer's block. I know a lot of people have it, but I believe they have it because they believe it exists. I've had days when I don't have very good ideas, but even then I just take the best one and go with it.

Rory Bourke - Maybe writer's block goes to the question of how brave you are about leaving your mind open all the time to what might be lurking in the shadows.

Lindy Gravelle - Don't interrupt if something's flowing. Just go with it. Sometimes it's stellar and sometimes it stinks.

John Jarrard - The atmosphere in which we do our best work, is one in which we're enjoying ourselves.

CHAPTER SEVEN

WRITER PROFILES

Tony Arata - I think I have achieved some degree of success in spite of myself.

Jess Leary - I've had a lot of ups and downs, but everytime I was down there was an "up" soon to be found.

Janis Ian - I wonder why people worry about critics, because nobody can beat up on you like you can.

Kent Blazy - I really like to be alone, and I think, as a writer, you really need that time to think about things and free yourself up.

1. On a scale of one to ten (ten being the best), rank your creativity. Rank your discipline.

    Tony Arata - I'd have to say my creativity would be somewhere in the middle. I'm around a five. I don't know how much control I have over the creativity that I really am proud of. The creativity will get you the idea, but the rest of it comes down to having some tools of the trade. Understanding that there are limits placed on a song, any song. It has to have some time element, and it's going to have some type of structure, and it's going to have to do something while somebody's listening to it. There are certain elements put into every song, whether they are classical pieces or county songs. It doesn't really matter. You have to understand those elements. At some point you have to sit down and actually hammer out the details. I don't know how much the creativity really comes into play there. I think it's more a case of actually employing good judgment and being patient enough to get the right lines. A lot of times songs will have a great hook line or whatever, and people are content to fill up the rest of it with cliché lines. I'm speaking of myself. I'm guilty of that as well, but I certainly don't bank on creativity as the sole tool for getting something done. That's why I say I'm somewhere in the middle. I think I have some good ideas every now and then, but then for the most part, it comes down to actually hammering it out.

I'd give myself about a two on discipline. I write differently than just sitting down behind a guitar and writing. I don't have a routine or anything like that. I work in addition to writing songs, and then you also have all the other elements that go into anybody's life. If I was more disciplined, I'm not sure how much more I'd get done. I don't know how much more I'd actually accomplish by clocking in at eight o'clock and clocking out at five and spending the whole time with a guitar in my hand. Some people are very disciplined, and they're very successful with that.

I'm always writing, I think, but I'm not always cloistered in some room somewhere. I'm pretty undisciplined when it comes to that. I think I have achieved some degree of success in spite of myself. I don't really go about this in perhaps the standard way, but I also don't know that there is a standard way. I think that with any writer or any artist who has any degree of success or any degree of style, for the most part, that style is their own. You could follow these people around all day and adopt and do everything they do, and you still would not be that person, and you would still not get done what they do. I think that at some point in the creative process, you have to find something that works for you, and I don't think it has anything to do with reading what somebody else does. What you're really after is the end result. The means are meaningless; it's the end result that everybody needs to take stock in. If at the end of the day you put the tape in the machine and something comes back that you're very proud of, then it doesn't matter how it got there.

Pam Belford - Creativity, seven. Discipline, four.

Kent Blazy - Probably about a seven on creativity, and I would like to try and get it up to ten, one day. I try to do as much as I can to be creative, but I'm always learning, and I hope to find more ways to develop it more.

My Discipline is probably about a seven too. That's holding Kim Williams up to a ten. I think I could be more disciplined, and I think I could work harder. But sometimes the harder you work, the more elusive creativity becomes. I try to take some time out every day and walk the dog or spend some time thinking and things like that.

Steve Bogard - I think I'm very creative, so I give myself a ten. But I don't think I'm just naturally creative. I think I've learned how to do it, and I think I work at it all the time. We all have to struggle against mediocrity. We have to fight it. It's so easy just to make things rhyme and then get out of the room. You've got to not fool yourself about what you're doing.

In my discipline, I'm probably a six or seven. I give myself lots of chances for the parts of life that feed creativity. I'm always thinking about writing.

Rory Bourke - I define creativity as the mind being open to shadow and light. I also have another vocation that brings in creativity—photography. To me, my photography, is a direct line from my unconscious to the world. I'd have to rank my creativity somewhere around a ten or ten and a half.

In discipline, [I'd rank myself at] nine and a half.

Gary Burr - My creativity? Nine. Discipline, ten. Does that make me sound like an egomaniac?

Debi Cochran - In creativity, oh, I'm a ten. I'm probably an eight on discipline.

Jill Colucci - I think what's more important to me is that when creativity is there, I'm really trusting of it. I'm so in awe of the process and of the inspiration. I just feel so fortunate. I have a great respect for it. It would be hard to give it a number that's anything other than a ten. If I did, I'd feel like I was belittling something that I'm extremely in awe of, something that I honor. So that's why I'm going to give it a ten. I don't want to say that I'm a ten, but the creativity is a ten.

It would be too hard to figure out my discipline, so I'd probably pick a five because it's right in the middle. Some days I'm extra disciplined and some days I'm probably a two.

Kim Copeland - In general, I think of myself as a pretty creative person. I don't paint and I don't do a lot of artistic things other than music, but as far as creative thinking, I'm very creative. I have a tendency to go too much on intuition. I'm like ninety percent right brain and ten percent left, which can be a problem in the real world sometimes—all that to say that I think I'm about a nine.

On discipline I'd give myself a minus one. If I could combine the two, I'd be dangerous. I can be disciplined, but I'm just not usually disciplined enough to make myself be. So, I guess I'd say a three. I'm a little below average there.

Gary Earl - I'd say a nine with creativity. My wife, Robin, has always said that she thinks of me as a very disciplined person, but I would probably give myself a four on discipline. I don't live up to my own expectations.

Robin Earl - Creatively I think I'm about an eight. I'm fairly creative in several different areas. In discipline, about a six. In some areas I'm disciplined to the point of being compulsive, but in others I tend to procrastinate.

Kye Fleming - I feel like I scratch the surface, but I know there's so much more creativity in me. I'm not putting myself down at all. It's putting myself in the perspective of potential. So I give myself a one, and one is what we all have. We all have so much more potential than we use. There I am sitting there on a one, and I see, in that statement, great hope.

Those first six years my discipline was really great at songwriting, but it was just as great and maybe greater with meditation and the spiritual side. I was a pretty open channel because I was totally disciplined. It was more important to me back then to be disciplined spiritually, and then everything else would fall into place, and it was true. It did. And because of different waves in my life and different needs in my life, I'm not in that place right now. I'm in a different stage of my life, and the only thing I care to be disciplined about now would be taking care of the spiritual side, getting centered. To whatever degree I am disciplined at that, I will be creative.

Lindy Gravelle - In creativity, an eight. In discipline, eight or nine.

Janis Ian - In creativity, five. But do you mean my ability to be creative, or my happiness with my creativity? When somebody says I'm a wonderful songwriter, I look to much better writers than myself to measure against. While I think that I'm really great at what I do, and I've earned the right to say it, I'm nowhere near what I think I could be if I were focused. I wonder why people worry about critics, because nobody can beat up on you like you can. I value what I do very highly. I would rate what I do and my level of happiness with it at about an eight or nine, because I work so hard at making sure it stays there. In terms of my satisfaction with it overall, I would rate it about a two. I still haven't written that one song that would totally change the life of anybody hearing.

My discipline depends on what I'm doing and the mood I'm in. I think I am one of the most undisciplined people in the world. But I've learned that all the hard workers I know feel that way about themselves. Everyone around me tells me I'm fanatically disciplined. It seems to me that if I really were that disciplined, I would have things magically organized, so that all I would have to do is write. I look at the life of a James Joyce, and I say, "Hey, I'm not exactly working in a bank." I'm not Jack London, clearing people through customs and writing at night. I'm very fortunate that I was born in the times that I was born in. Ten years earlier or ten years later, my talent probably wouldn't have been worth spit in the wind. It's timing, just flukes. So when I look at it with that kind of an overview, it's remarkable that I've done so little with what I've been given. When I look at it from the other way, I work my butt off six days a week. Gary [Burr] and I were talking about this the other day. We both work five days a week as songwriters, then we come home at night and we write on our own, answer our phone calls, do our business, balance our books, and oversee our publishing and catalogs. So when I look at that, I guess I am disciplined.

John Jarrard - Creatively, some days I'm a nine and some days I'm a one. Overall, I'm probably about a three or four. In discipline, a seven or eight.

Al Kasha - Well, I do think I'm pretty creative, because I've written books and songs and plays. I go through different periods, so without sounding in any way conceited or egotistical, I think at times I'm a ten and at times I'm a five. It just depends on the period I go through. But I've done shows, movies, and I've been awarded in every possible area, so I think I'm a highly creative person. That doesn't mean I'm a good baseball player, but as a songwriter, I'm one of the top one hundred writers in ASCAP. But I thank God for that. I have no other gifts regarding sports, or gifts of mathematics, but that's a gift that God gave me, and I want to use it in his glory.

I think the discipline goes up and down like a lot of other creative people. I think I'm about a seven in that regard. At times I go higher than ten, so I put it somewhere in between. When it comes to my writing, I'm fairly disciplined, but in today's world, there are just so many other distractions going on. Fax machines and lawyers and all kinds of business matters. When I first started writing, you wrote a song, you went to the publisher, you played it on the piano, and the publisher said, "I know this artist. You go over and play it for him or the producer." But now it goes through so many configurations. You go through so many manifestations that it takes away some of the creativity. Maybe it's different in Nashville, but in L.A. and New York, there's a little bit too much of that. It's become too mechanical and too business-driven. Just while we were taping this, I got a call about how we're going to split the publishing on a song. Of course, it's part of life. It's called show *business*, but I think it's become too much business and too much marketing. That's why I think Nashville is hot again, because more creativity is coming out of that part of the world rather than New York or L.A. It's become too many account-ants, lawyers, and all that stuff. And while you're trying to create some-thing, that's very distracting.

Mary Ann Kennedy - In creativity, I'm going to say that some-times I do peak out at ten. I've been blessed enough and naturally born with this talent enough to peak out there. But because of my love of just having a great time in life, taking out time to do that, and maybe because of my lack of discipline or even fear of success as an individual maybe I'm only a six or a seven. I'm a great team player, but I think I do still have a little bit of fear about going solo. I will say that I still haven't achieved a ten as an individual. So I'm still very challenged through my forties to achieve that.

When I'm finishing up a song and I'm in the studio, I can be good [at discipline]. I can be a nine or ten in following through and getting that great demo. I work hard, but because of my lack of structure, I could be more productive. I am absolutely a spontaneous being, and I have made the most of that. I have surrounded myself with people who haven't got-ten pissed off at my spontaneous energy. I might call and say, "I know I booked to get together today to try to write, but, you know, it's seventy degrees and my girlfriend's going on a horseback ride, and I need it today. Please, can I write with you tomorrow or tonight?" I know enough to know that if I went when I've got some other pull, I just won't be good. But I need some understanding friends.

Sandy Knox - Overall, I think I'm an eight and a half in creativity, because I'm creative in other things if I'm not working. I'm always crea-tive. In discipline, five.

Kostas - Creatively eleven. I'd have to go the opposite way in the discipline department. It's not that I'm not disciplined. I am disciplined in that I always accomplish that which I set out to accomplish, but I have to do it at a gradual kind of pace.

Jess Leary - In creativity, I'd say nine. I am a creative person. I am around creative people and living a creative path. I enjoy it. I'm aware of it. I pray for it, and I relish it when it's there. It's pretty much my life in all different departments.

I give my discipline an eight. I am strict with myself sometimes. My father was a hard-working man. He designed houses and built them. He was very creative. He went to work every day, whether he felt good or not. I know a lot of that's built in for me, because I was around it, but I also honestly feel that I really do like to work. I like to have a purpose for working.

Jim McBride - I'm always thinking. I tell people, "I'm working all the time, you just can't see it." A seven, maybe, in creativity.

I'm like a four or five probably [in discipline]. I do try to do something every day, no matter how small. I try to do something career-wise every day. I can sit here and wonder, "What if I had been more disciplined? What if I had worked eight hours a day, where would I be right now?" But I've enjoyed my life, and there are things other than work. I guess I'm just not as driven as some people are.

Wayland Patton - I'm pretty high—I'm a pretty creative person. I could always be more disciplined. I'm a pretty ambitious and driven person, so I'd have to say I'm between five and ten, depending on what day you catch me, and depending on what's at the movies.

Pam Rose - Well, I always try for those ten days. Some days my impression is that I'm not creative at all. I know that's an illusion, but that is my impression. So I pretty much run the gamut with that, zero to ten. I don't think that ever gets to a ten, although I might have moments of a ten. My discipline is varied.

Joyce Rouse - When I'm at my best, I'm at a twelve [in creativity]. But that number varies from day to day. An average, probably, is eight. In discipline, about two. No, it's getting better. It's getting much better. I might even give myself a three and a half or four these days.

Wayne Tester - [My creativity is] sometimes one, sometimes ten. An average? A healthy eight and a half. [I rank my discipline] a healthy eight and a half. I have quite a long way to improve.

Trisha Walker - Creativity, eight. Discipline, six.

Kim Williams - In creativity, Eight. I do think that I'm creative, because I like wild stuff. I like stuff that's different. I think being creative has to do with those boundaries. You can't sit down and be a great writer and say, "I'm not going to write about that, I'm not going to write about this." That's where you kill creativity. You need to open your mind up and just say, "Hey, I'll just write about anything." No limitations. Creativity is not limiting yourself. And if you don't limit yourself and you just let your mind flow, you are going to come up with some things that other people wouldn't.

Until the last six or seven months, I'd say my discipline was ten. Maybe now, I'm a seven. I'm getting to the point in my career where I'm searching again for that reason to keep striving as hard as I was striving. Every time I've felt lost, though, *something* is trying to happen.

2. Who would you like to co-write with (living or dead)?

Tony Arata - On my *best* days, I don't know what I'd have to add. I would have absolutely nothing that I could bring to the table with somebody like Jackson Browne or Bob Dylan or Bruce Springstein or Emmylou Harris. I can't imagine writing with Neil Young. I don't know that I'd really like to hear a collaboration; it wouldn't be a Neil Young song anymore. But I would love to watch some of these cats write. You hear their songs back and you go, "Well, they did really well without me." There are people here in town—Dave Olney is one of my favorite writers here, and Mark Germino. I don't know how I would improve what they do, or that we would come up with something that they wouldn't do just fine with by themselves. I'd love to watch Jimmy Webb write.

Pam Belford - Gary Burr, Don Schitlz, Gretchen Peters, Carly Simon, Carole King, and Paul McCartney.

Kent Blazy - Hank Williams, Sr., Stephen Foster, Bob McDill, Bob Dylan, Van Morrison, Joni Mitchell, Ricki Lee Jones, John Hiatt, and Lennon and McCartney.

Rory Bourke - Sophia Loren. I'd love to write with Stephen Foster, the Gershwins, and Harry Warren. Unknown Shakespearean sonnet writers. Cole Porter, Walter Donelson, Mac Dennis, Mel Torme.

Gary Burr - First of all Paul McCartney, because it would bring me full circle. He's the reason I'm in the business. So someday I want to write with Paul McCartney. That would just be too amazing. I'd want to write with somebody who's really been around. Maybe Steinbeck. Imagine somebody who was capable of writing *The Grapes of Wrath,* and putting music to it.

The other person I'd like to write with would be someone who's actually experienced the kinds of emotions and themes that we try to write about authentically when we don't know what the hell we're talking about. So for love songs, I'd want to write with somebody who really knew great love. The other extreme is to write a song with Jesse James. Everybody writes these cowboy things and none of us are cowboys. I'm a couch boy. Somebody who's actually done that, you know, then you'd have a reason to write a cowboy song.

Mike Reid said that he once wrote this song about Mississippi, and he played it for his publisher. The publisher looked at him and said, "You've never been to Mississippi, have you?" He said, "No." The publisher said, "Sounds like it." Then, from that point on, he said, "I'm only going to write about things I know about. I don't know about Mississippi. I've never been there."

I don't know about sleeping on the ground and robbing trains. Write it with somebody who did that. And then, on the other hand, to write with Romeo. Those are people I'd like to write with, and Paul, if you're listening.

Kim Carnes - Mary Chapin Carpenter. Her latest album is so good. She is absolutely the tops. She is one of the best out there. And she's in such a great position of being able to sell lots of albums the way she wants to do it. She doesn't make records for the "radio." She writes songs that are really deep. The things she has to say are really amazing. She's the first person who comes to mind. We talked after the ASCAP awards about getting together and writing. I'm really working for that to happen, because I just admire her so much. I'm in such awe of Van Morrison. I wish Wynonna and Trisha Yearwood wrote. If they started writing, those are two people I would love to write with, because as artists, I think they are so incredible. Their voices are so special, and there's so much soul there.

Jill Colucci - I'm so serious. I do rounds with Gary Burr and a lot of people, and they'll have these funny songs. I have a pretty decent sense of humor, but it doesn't come out in my songwriting. So I'm going to give my serious answer and say John Lennon, Don Henley, Bonnie Raitt, and I guess Garth Brooks. Melissa Ethridge and Billy Joel also come to mind.

Kim Copeland - There are people who I admire very, very much as writers, who I don't think would be compatible co-writers for me. There are people whom I would love to be in the room with when they're writing, just to study their technique, people I could learn a great deal from, but that I would not necessarily co-write well with. Those people, if you're interested, are James Taylor, Carly and Carole (to be redundant),

Rod Stewart. My dream co-write would be with Don Henley, because I think he's the most gifted contemporary lyricist out there. Also I'd love to write with Dan Fogelberg, Mary Chapin Carpenter, and Gary Burr. I think our souls and spirits would be simpatico, and I admire them all very much.

Gary Earl - Boy, there are so many great writers. Let's see, if I have to pick three: Start off with God, if he's omnipotent and omniscient, he ought to be able to write a hit song, right? Then maybe Mozart, and any producer or artist who's looking for that one last tune to put on the album.

Robin Earl - Paul McCartney, because he was my childhood idol. And maybe the writers of the Seinfeld TV show, which I love. It's fun to come up with ideas I think would be funny for them to do on the show.

Kye Fleming - I'm a timid co-writer, so that makes this question hard. As far as what would be great fun, that would be James Taylor. He's just such a free spirit, or seems to be.

Lindy Gravelle - Harlan, Willie, Mary Chapin Carpenter.

Al Kasha - I would like to write with Allen Reynolds very much. I'd like to write with Vince Gill very much. I think he's a great song-writer. Even though I write music as well as lyrics, I'd like to write with Elton John or Allen Menken. I understand they know how to write musicals. Not because he's hot, but I really think that Babyface is a terrific songwriter. I like Jimmy Jam and Terry Lewis, but Babyface, of the newer writers, really knows his stuff. Those are wonderful tunes. I guess the person who's not alive is Johnny Mercer. I knew him as a young man, and he was a great mentor of mine. Gib Harber, who wrote *Wizard of Oz*, and Oscar Hamerstein. I wish that I had had the opportunity to write with those three, who are not alive.

Mary Ann Kennedy - Wow! John Lennon, I think that's who I'm absolutely craziest about, not so much to write something with him, but to learn from him. I love Paul and what he's done, but writing *Imagine* and *Twist and Shout*, you know John gets that heavy, heavy kind of message across. Plus his voice is good and cool, but it's not as slick as Paul's. And that's after my own heart. All of the things that he achieved as a musician and an artist, I just look up to ultimately.

I have been blessed enough to work with a couple of my heroes. I got to hang out and work in the studio and tour with Sting. He's probably one of my absolute favorites. Great writer. Melodically solid. Hip and fresh for the time. On the other side of the fence is Emmylou Harris.

We've been so damn lucky. Two of our absolute heroes, and we got to work with them. So when I think of the two heavies, outside of John Lennon, there they are; I haven't written with them, but I've worked with them. I'm also a Joni Mitchell fan.

Sandy Knox - I've been asked that before, and I can never really think of any. I think Roger Miller. I would have loved to have hung with him in his heyday when his stuff was really flowing, just to get into that mind. I would have liked to have met, Johnny Mercer, Cole Porter, some of those guys. That era. The turn of the century writers. I'll tell you who I really like: Babyface. I really admire what he's doing. His stuff's really commercial and good and adult.

If you asked me who I would want to have dinner with, I could think of a lot more people. I'd like to talk to Lizzy Borden. I'd like to find out if she killed her parents. I'd like to figure out some of the great mysteries. Wouldn't it be fun to have the answers to the crop circles? If you had the answers to Lizzy Borden, the crop circles, and a video of O.J. actually committing the crime, you could retire.

Kostas - They wouldn't necessarily be songwriters. I'd love to be able to write with Crazy Horse, Ghandi, Marilyn Monroe.

Jess Leary - I think I'd be too intimidated to write with the people who come to mind, but I might just want to sit and watch them write. Jimmy Webb, Hugh Prestwood. They pretty much floor me.

I have to say again, that Gary Burr is a very talented writer, a very talented person. I got to write with him this past year, and we actually wrote a very fun, neat song. We had a great time. I was nervous as hell, and he was so much fun. I've known him for a while anyway, so we were friends when we got together to write. I love his singing and his playing and his talent. It was an honor to work with him. Our windows are right across from each other. I channel Gary Burr a lot. I sit here and look out there and say, "Gary, what would Gary write?"

Other writers who've greatly influenced me are Matraca Berg, Mary Chapin Carpenter, and Gretchen Peters.

Jim McBride - I think they'd all be country writers. I haven't written with Harlan [Howard] yet, but I'm going to. And Schlitz and I are writing. Probably guys like Leon Payne and some of those old guys back in the earlier days.

Wayland Patton - Rather than write with someone, I would like to sit and watch them write. The people who come to mind are Jackson

Browne, James Taylor, and Paul McCartney. I wouldn't turn any of those guys down, but I'd rather just be a fly on the wall.

Pam Rose - Mike Reid, Paul McCartney.

Joyce Rouse - Joan of Arc. Talk about a person who lived a series of intense emotions. Of course, I don't know how creative she was. I don't know what kind of a co-writer she would be. Emily Dickinson. I'll bet Albert Einstein would have been an interesting person to write with. Rogers and Hammerstein. Steven Sondheim.

Wayne Tester - I think I'm fortunate enough to be working with some of those already. Tony Arata, Dave Loggins, David Foster.

Trisha Walker - Barbra Streisand, George Gershwin. People who would have a great sense of melody, or authors like Faulkner.

Marijohn Wilkin - Both of [my favorites] would have been in the past. Both men have been inspiring to me. One was B. B. McKinney, who was the great gospel writer. He wrote *When the Saints Go Marching In*. I had the privilege of going to school with his son. The other writer is Irving Berlin. His melodies were so simple, just the simplest. Usually the simpler the music, the longer it lives.

3 Do you think of yourself as an introvert or an extrovert?

Pam Belford - I guess I'm an introvert. I need a lot of time alone, but I like to be around people.

Kent Blazy - An introverted extrovert. It depends on the situation. I really like to be alone, and I think as a writer you really need that time to think about things and free yourself up. But I would much rather co-write than write by myself. I love the interaction of one or two other writers and bouncing things off of them. It's a lot more fun. Writing by myself is a little too solitary for me. I'll do it every once in a while, but for me it's more a case of spending the solitary time gathering ideas to be ready to present to the other people when you get there.

Steve Bogard - A little of both, but most people would think I'm an extrovert. I really do like attention, and I really like being with people.

If you open yourself up and show people who you are, then people who don't like that will go away.

Rory Bourke - I think I'm an introvert who's had to be an extrovert. That's the hardest part of what I do, that extrovert thing.

Gary Burr - I think of myself as a shy extrovert. A little of both. I've been jumping around making a fool of myself in public for a long time now, so there's a part of me that's not very shy when I walk into a room. But then there's another part of me who still is that guy from junior high school that goes into a party and sits in the corner and figures he'll just watch for the first three hours.

Debi Cochran - I am an introvert. But for the first time, to a greater extent than ever before, I can relate to these people. Being a songwriter in a town like Decatur, Alabama, where I knew one other songwriter, you just don't have the feedback and camaraderie of saying, "That song was on hold for four weeks, and they kept saying it was going to be the first single off the record, and it didn't even make the record." You can't explain that to somebody who is not in the business. So I have been quite lonely in many ways. Not that I don't have very close friends who are not in the music business, but being here and being able to relate to people who have the same drives that I do and the same experiences has been a big boost for someone who is basically shy. There's a lot of group therapy going on on Music Row.

Jill Colucci - If I had to choose one, I would choose extrovert. I'm a people person. I like being with people. I feel fairly outgoing, and I've done live performances all my life, so that's kind of a natural thing for me. But I have my shy side. I have my times when I feel really more of an introvert, but they're not the dominant times.

Kim Copeland - I am an introvert (and I'm too shy to elaborate on that). It's in my nature to have deep feelings and points of view that I feel compelled to express, but I'm not really comfortable in the spotlight. Songwriting is a comfortable way of expressing myself without having to be on the front line.

Gary Earl - I usually think of myself as being an extrovert, but at the same time I like to have more alone time than most people. I like going away for a day or two, hiking in the wilderness, being intensely alone with my thoughts.

Robin Earl - I think I flip-flop between the two. I like people a lot and like to help people. Several times I've gravitated towards jobs involving teaching, so in that way I'm extroverted. I'm an extrovert when I'm in a good mood and have lots of energy, or when I'm in a comfortable or familiar situation. But I also spend a lot of time thinking.

Kye Fleming - I am an introvert. I'm an observer more than a participator in most areas. Lyrics are my forte, and that is something very private. I can do that all alone and I can even do it any time. The times that I enjoy the most with myself are the creative times where I'm on the track of bringing an inspiration into focus with words. I can sit there, and I'm like a hound after something. I forget to eat. I forget to drink water. It's like I am totally absorbed in it. Time absolutely doesn't matter.

Lindy Gravelle - I am pretty balanced between the two. Having grown up on the stage, I know how to *be* on stage. People would say, "Boy you're a real extrovert." Get me off the stage and I can melt into the woodwork really quickly. I don't think I'm that comfortable with a crowd unless I'm entertaining them.

John Jarrard - I'm probably an introvert. I need a lot of space and a lot of time.

Al Kasha - Actually, this will sound strange because I've done so many speaking engagements around the country, both to other songwriters and churches, but I think basically I'm an introvert. In front of groups, I'm not. On a one-to-one basis, I am. They once said that President Kennedy could speak in front of thousands of people, but on a one-to-one basis he was sort of shy.

Mary Ann Kennedy - Well, I'm definitely an extrovert. I love people and I love networking and I love to be fed by other people's energy. To do that, you've got to get out there..

(DO YOU ACCESS THAT SIDE FOR SONGWRITING?) I do, and I think that's probably why I do more of the rhythm in the music. The out stuff. I do some lyrics, but primarily I've chosen to work with poets, with introverts. So the songs balance. We've got both there.

Sandy Knox - At what time of the day? It's funny, I think the best way to answer that is to say that a lot of people think of me as very extroverted, gregarious, and outgoing, and that I'll talk to anybody. But that's not how I think of myself. I think of myself as very inside, and very shy, and very vulnerable, and with a high capacity for being wounded. But that isn't how my friends see me. They see me as ballsy and gutsy. A lot of people are like that, a lot of creative people. It's probably the paradox for us, that we write our thoughts or words. They're heartfelt and they're our baby, and we're taking them to this person and we're asking them, we're forcing them, to like it or dislike it. We're asking them to tell us the truth. There's a part of us that's saying, "Here you go, here I am." Then we're also very prepared to be shot down. We know that. Your skin keeps getting tougher.

Kostas - It depends on what I'm wearing.

Jess Leary - I guess I'm an introvert. I'm more inward. I guess I'm shy in a lot of ways, although I'm outgoing in a lot of ways, so it's a weird combination. It's that Pisces thing. I know I'm a shy person, pretty much, but able to get out on the stage in front of tons of people. It's a weird little turnaround.

Jim McBride - I'm an introvert. I've always been a late bloomer. I was so very shy all the way through high school. I still feel uncomfortable at all these music industry things that you end up having to go to. I feel very, very uncomfortable. I've learned to just deal with it.

Pam Rose - I consider myself a recovering introvert. I mean, it's really hard to do what we do and continue to be an introvert. To get on stage in front of fifty thousand people you have to have some sort of ability to connect in an extroverted manner. But most of the people that I know who do this, come from that. Either they've been an extrovert all their life, or else they've been shy and have just had to learn to deal with it. It's like an occupational hazard or something.

Joyce Rouse - Most of the time, I am an extrovert.

Wayne Tester - I'm both [introverted and extroverted]. I enjoy being around people and co-writing and the whole hoopla, and I enjoy the solitude of sitting in a room by myself creating just for the fact of creation. So I think I have a little of both.

Trisha Walker - I like people a lot, but I'd probably still categorize myself as being slightly more introverted than extroverted. I'm not necessarily shy, but I think, like a lot of writers, I tend to take a step back and just observe. So if that's introverted, then I'm probably more introverted.

Kim Williams - I'm an introvert. I'm not nearly as introverted now as I once was. Songwriting has helped with that. It was something I wanted to do enough that I would go talk to people. But I live inside my head too much.

4. Do you have any "low point in the career" stories you'd like to share?

Tony Arata - It wasn't long after we moved here, probably a year or so, that we had three or four songs that were on hold. I was thinking, We should have come up here sooner. There's nothing to this. I had adopted this whole attitude—I've got songs on hold now, I'm something, I'm somebody. I went to the publishing company one day, and they had a chalkboard with the "hold" songs on it, and all you could see was the title underneath the chalk dust. It was no longer on hold, it wasn't going to be cut, and that song was done.

I'm very grateful that it happened early on. That was an ass-whooping of a completely different kind. I realized right then and there where I stand in the great picture of it all. I was thoroughly depressed and really scared because I was banking on that a lot—not that we had gone out and adopted some lifestyle, but I thought that was going to be my en-tree into this whole thing. And when it didn't happen, it drove me to do something that I think I'm as proud of as I am my songs. It drove me to action. I went out and got a job. I was a journalism major, but I had never written for a newspaper because I'd spent all my time playing in bars. I had no clippings, so the journalism degree was like, who cares? So I went to work for UPS. I started loading boxes in trucks, and I did that for a year. My wife had a great job, thank God, because we sure weren't going to live off of what I was making out there.

It wasn't as though I said to hell with the songwriting business, but I did make up my mind right then and there that if I was going to be a songwriter, then be one. I started working my way up to having a career, saying that the decision on how long I stay here will be based on how long we *want* to stay here. I loaded boxes for UPS and on the side wrote arti-cles for their company magazine, so that I could build up a portfolio of clippings. It wasn't as though I'd quit writing songs, but I needed to prove something apart from that, mainly to try to do something to support my family. It was my responsibility, and I wanted to do something that I had some control over. Then I worked for a magazine publishing company. I am just as grateful for the three years that I spent writing articles about buses as I am about anything. That may seem ludicrous to some ... it was just the fact that I started trying to take some action. Take responsibility for what it is you've gotten yourself into. If you really do believe that you don't have to spend twenty-four hours a day with a guitar in your hand to be a songwriter, then, by God, get out and work and prove that you don't have to.

I also learned from a whole other facet of life as a result of that. So it was both a low point and also a beginning. And, sure enough, as the old saying goes, "the harder I work, the luckier I get." I've had a lot of songs recorded that were written while I was writing for that magazine. I think what happened is that I had finally removed that thought from my head that everything hinges on somebody recording my song. I had removed the thought of "that's all I have going," and started learning about other things and being exposed to other things. It was a low point, and it was also a wonderful beginning to me.

People ask me all the time, "I'm thinking about moving up there. What would be the first thing you'd say I should do?" I tell them, "Get a job." If you're serious enough about doing it, then you will take care of the most important matter first, and that is making sure that you can provide something for your family. If you're single then you're on your own. Do what you want to do. But when you have other people who are riding on your dreams, you owe them something in the interim before your dreams come true. It was a good lesson.

Pam Belford - Do I ever [have the low point stories]! I came to town in 1977. In 1982 I was finally having some jaw surgery done that I had been putting off for at least twelve or thirteen years. After I had the surgery, my teeth were wired together, and there was a rubber splint going across the front so you couldn't hear what I was saying. During that time, I had my first song recorded by Connie Francis, who had been a childhood idol, and then two weeks later, one by Terri Gibbs. I'd waited all that time for it to happen, and I couldn't tell anybody. But as Nashville goes, people knew anyway. I guess the really low point was when neither of them was released. In 1985 Barbara Mandrell recorded a song of mine. I was so excited about it, and I heard they had recorded sixteen songs for a ten-song album, and they were down to fourteen and mine was still in there. Then they were down to thirteen and mine was still in there. They got down to eleven and it was still in there. And then it didn't make the album. I thought I was becoming a household word. I thought that all around town, when people had a song cut but didn't make it on the album, they were getting "Belforded."

Kent Blazy - The low point of my career was probably about 1986 or 1987. I had been working for a publishing company for about two years and had really been working hard, probably writing about one hundred and fifty songs a year. I had a song that Alabama had had on hold for twenty-two months, and they kept saying they were going to cut it, and they finally didn't cut it. They had another one on hold for eight months that they were going to cut, and they didn't cut that. I had a cut on the Forrester Sisters album that was supposed to be a single, and like the week before it came out, they changed their minds and came out with a different song. The publishing deal that I had was ending, and I didn't have another one. That was probably the lowest point in my career. I felt I had been working really hard, and everything that I had seemed to fall through. Maybe I was supposed to get out of this and go do something else. I really did a lot of soul searching and talked to people who I respect. I got their opinions and just tried to figure out what to do. Three or four months later I met Garth [Brooks], and that really changed my life.

Steve Bogard - I really don't think I've had low points.. I mean, I remember my thirty-third birthday, sitting in my backyard in Miami (we had the Marty Robbins hit). My wife said to me, "You say you're a song-writer, but we're not in a place where you can do it every day. We're not in a place where you can get better." That's not a low point. That's like every man needs a woman who tells him the truth. That's what I am blessed to have had for twenty-three years. We began immediately to make plans and pack up to move.

Gary Burr - It's been such a nice upward ride. There was a period when I went out to California and played in that band. It was an originals band, and it was everyone living together and rehearsing every day. We thought we were going to change music as everyone knows it. That sort of fell apart, and I came back to Connecticut and was back playing Elmo's Steakhouse. One by one, all my friends who swore they were going to do nothing but music found jobs that they just didn't hate enough not to do. And one by one the guitars went under the bed, one step away from the yard sale. I started to get regular jobs and things like that. I always had a regular job. I always wanted to put food on the table. It's a lot easier to be creative if you're not drooling over Spam commercials. That was probably it. That lasted for a little while until the next opportunity came up, and then I took it and moved on.

I had a bunch of hits in Connecticut, and then I came here. When I was in Connecticut, I was doing it through the mail. I'd get a hit every two years and that was enough to sustain, me and I was able to not work. It was tough and I didn't make a lot of money, but I was able to just be a musician and work on what I was doing. So to have a year and a half of inactivity was normal to me. Then I came down here and the first few years that I was here, I didn't have a lot of activity. But it wasn't really disheartening. My valleys have been tiny little ditches.

Debi Cochran - I guess there are a lot of them. There was a time early in my deal here at Maypop when I wasn't really sure if it was going to work. The song plugger who was here at the time sort of lost confidence in my ability to hit the country market. He thought that my songs were either too complex or too obscure. I won't say too intelligent, but they were. He thought people had to think too much. I had a lot of anguish about this being my first staff deal. If it didn't work out, where would I go, and how would I keep my confidence up? Luckily that didn't happen. I got a Diamond Rio cut and a Billy Joe Royal cut, and the song plugger just sort of came around and said, "Okay, there's a place for this stuff." He's at another company now, but, coincidentally, he is one of my biggest fans. He tells other people, "Debi and I had a hard time at first, but she just knocks me out now."

Kim Copeland - I guess my low point would be when I finally knew what I wanted to do, but couldn't see the path to get me there. I was trying to write to please other people, but no one was happy with it, including me. I got so frustrated with the whole process, I just started writing for myself again, writing what I felt, and needed to say. That's when I started getting good response from a lot of different directions on some songs. I began to really understand what *from the heart* meant, and to remember why I loved to write in the first place.

When you find your own voice, a light goes off and everything comes into focus. It's like finally cracking the code to an algebra equation that seemed like Greek to you. Everything you write may not have the same magic, but at least you understand what you're shooting for, and you know you have it in you. If it's happened once, it will happen again.

Gary Earl - I had been playing around the Reno and Lake Tahoe areas, and the band I was in had just broke up so I booked a solo gig on Halloween at this little roadside bar right outside Reno. I got there and it looked like one of those little diners in a double wide trailer. The owner was a little French lady, and her Halloween costume was Annie Oakley, and she was wearing loaded pistols. The bartender was dressed as Babe Ruth and he was carrying a big bat. It should have given me a tip-off right then that there was trouble coming. So I'm playing along, and there were a couple of little skirmishes early on, nothing too bad but bad enough to me because I'm used to the casino cabaret where everything's clean and bright and upscale. About half-way through the night, a big fight broke out, starting with somebody messing with somebody else's wife; the guy had gone out and broken windows out of the other guy's pickup. It got to the point where more than a dozen people were in a barroom brawl, just like you see in a bad TV show, guys on the floor getting their teeth kicked out and teeth sliding across the dance floor in front of me. I was on a break when the bartender waved his bat at me and shouted, "Play something!" I jumped over and started playing the first song that came to mind. When I hit the second verse I realized I was singing *Big Bad Leroy Brown.* The second verse goes, "the two men took to fighting," and then describes a fight much like the one in front of me. So I said "whoa," stopped playing, grabbed the keyboard and guitar and threw them in the back of my pickup, and left. Nobody even noticed I had left because there was such a brawl going on. I never got paid, but I got out alive with my equipment. It's like someone once told me, "Who needs dignity, when you can be in the entertainment business?"

Robin Earl - I'd say a low point would be when Gary and I were playing the Ramada Casino in Reno. They had twenty-four-hour music, four groups playing six-hour shifts around the clock, and a relief shift group. Once we had the relief shift, which was Monday, nine a.m. to three p.m., Tuesday three p.m. to nine p.m., Wednesday nine p.m. to three a.m., and Thursday three a.m. to nine a.m. By about six in the morning, there were five people in the casino besides the guy vacuuming the carpet. I remember being very tired and singing the Pointer Sisters song *I'm So Excited,* when a drunk lifted his head off the bar and yelled, "Oh yeah, Well, you don't look so excited!" Whenever I hear late-night vacuuming at a restaurant or somewhere, I think about that relief shift.

Kye Fleming - Probably my high point, in a strange way, could have been considered a low point. After those first six years, we were BMI "Writers of the Year" and had been for a couple of years. We had the Burton Award. We had all that the year that I quit. I felt like I had been run over by a truck the last two years. I was in the machine, and I didn't know how to get out. I was totally grateful for the success, and obviously the financial rewards, but I felt that I wasn't respected for the reason I would want to be respected for as a writer. I felt like I was being rewarded for a lot of hard work instead of a lot of great inspiration. I knew I needed to back off and have time and see if I could nurture that again. Get back to the love of writing. I really did push it to the point of burning, and to be that successful was really like a drug. I mean, how do you say "no" to something that feels good? But at a certain point, I had to weigh what was more important.

I took a year where I didn't write anything. I just got away. I had to. And then you're back to the beginning, and you start over with the fear. You start over with the, "Can I do this, and am I nuts to think that I can write anything with any more depth than I did write?" But that's kind of energizing in itself too. The part about feeling like I wanted to make a difference with what I wrote and with something other than my bank account always hanging over me. I think that's what I meant by not feeling respected. I didn't respect myself.

Lindy Gravelle - My Lorrie Morgan song [is the low point]. They told us it was going to make the album. Then somewhere along the line, they decided it wasn't going to make the album. I just about died. You know a songwriter lives by cuts. I haven't had enough to get comfortable with losing many. So I had a lot of hope on that. My publishing company went to bat and somehow managed to get it on the album. That was great but then the day it went on sale, my co-writer went to buy it. He called me from the record store and said, "Lindy you're not going to believe this. The album's out. It's on the CD, but it's not on the cassette." Again, I was totally mystified.

Al Kasha - The low points come to me when I don't want to be flexible. It says in the Bible that pride faileth before honor. Sometimes success is the thing that can kill you the most. I think a low point for me was when I wasn't teachable. I used to think that I had all the answers. The market was changing, but I wasn't changing with the market. I think flexibility is the key to success. If big cars are selling, then sell big cars; if small cars are selling, then sell small cars; it's still a car. You've got to be flexible to the market and be honest. To overcome the low points, I try to look into myself and say, "Come on Al, straighten up." You have to change, and what you write about has to be relevant to the times.

Mary Ann Kennedy - During that ten-year period when Pat [Bunch] and Pam[Rose] and I were pretty much an exclusive team, the stuff we were creating was way too edgy. We had a lot of what we thought were hits sitting on those demo tapes and yet being turned down. We had a couple slip in there that opened things up, but we had a lot of rejection in those years. I really think we have been a progressive force in this town. Even though we didn't have the number of cuts, I think we did help knock down walls and burn down some fences and change some things for everybody including ourselves. We were way ahead of our time.

Leaving Line was just cut by Billy Dean. That song was nine years old, and nobody could hear it until we went back in and did a country demo of it last year. Then it got cut. We pitched our version off our record, and it got turned down. I guess it was too stylized and too edgy. That's what we were criticized for all those years, and sometimes it would get to you. I don't want to sound unappreciative either because we did have a lot of success along the way, but we also had a lot of rejection. *I'll Still Be Loving You* was huge and very progressive for the time, but there are a whole bunch of songs of that quality that right now, ten years later, are being recorded. We had to wait a long time. So that would get to us sometimes, to stick to our guns when we really believed something was strong and effective.

Sandy Knox - [My low point was] making a living cleaning other people's houses. Living on five hundred dollars a month when your rent was three hundred and fifty dollars. Working three jobs at a time to make ends meet. I had moved here from Houston, and I didn't know one person. I had fifteen hundred dollars in my pocket, no job, and a handful of songs. I had been here about three or four months when I got a job. I had worked at department stores and waiting tables and everything else during that time. Then I got a job at MCA Records as a receptionist. I lied to them and told them I didn't write or sing. Mr. Foglesong interviewed me for the job, and he asked, "Now, are you a singer?" No sir. "Are you a songwriter?" No sir. He and I laugh about that. I had the job two weeks when Jimmy Bowen came in as the new president and fired everybody. About the same time my apartment flooded. The landlord wouldn't replace the carpet and all the other stuff, so basically, after I had lived in it for four months, he told me I had to move. I remember lying on the concrete floor in the apartment and thinking about killing myself, when the phone rang and it was my mother telling me my niece had been born, which completely changed my attitude about everything. You know everything happens for a reason, and because Jimmy Bowen came in and fired everybody, even though I'd only been there two weeks, I got unemployment. I got a severance check plus I got paid for my two weeks that I was there. So that actually freed me up to start pitching my songs.

There was a period that I didn't write at all. I was very down on the business. I was engaged and then I got unengaged. I think when I was about twenty-eight, I figured I was all washed up and over the hill. Nothing would ever happen. But then I thought, "Well, I have nothing to lose." I started writing the way I wanted to write and to hell with them. I started writing what I wanted. I put the rules aside. For years I was trying to please all these people, and it didn't get me anywhere. When I started just not listening, and writing what I wanted to write, all of a sudden I was getting cuts.

Jess Leary - I've had a lot of ups and downs, but every time I've been "down," there was an "up" soon to be found. I've definitely been down, but I haven't stayed there, and after a few of those, I know I won't be down long if I am.

Jim McBride - There have been a lot of valleys. I've always had a contract to write songs, so it's not like I've never had a deal. But it got so bad in the eighties. Nobody was selling any records hardly. Unless you got a single, you weren't going to make much money, and you just kept going in the hole on your draw.

When I moved about a year ago, I found a letter from the postmaster in Nashville. I had written him to see if there were any openings at the post office. I was going to go back and do that during the day and write songs at night. I found the letter where he wrote back and said there were no openings. I got to thinking about that, and it had to be just about the same time I met Alan Jackson.

Pam Rose - Mary Ann [Kennedy]and I were on tour supporting our first CD, *Hai Ku*. This was about at the end of six months of touring that we called the "Tour From Hell." We almost had laminates made up, Kennedy-Rose, Tour From Hell. It was just really hard out there. We were homesick. We were distraught, and we expected things to be doing better. I think we were both going through some sort of mid-life crises. We showed up for one gig that was in Austin, Texas, and I said, "We must be lost. Surely this can't be it." I probably shouldn't say the name of the place. I said, "This can't be it. This doesn't have a real roof or anything. It's just a bunch of concrete blocks and that green, translucent wavy sky-light stuff just kind of tacked up there on the top." I mean, that would be a nice appetizer for a tornado. We walked into this place, and there was a basketball goal on the stage. The sound system was chained down. In the dressing room—I would use the term loosely—I wouldn't even sit on the sofa, and there was chicken wire for windows. This was right on the river, and we looked across the river from our "dressing room," through the chicken wire, and I saw these great, big spotlights and this stadium, and I said, "Mary Ann, look at that. What's that over there?" And they said, "Oh, it's some big festival here in Austin." It's the biggest music festival of the year. Mary Chapin Carpenter's playing over there and all these great big acts. We just looked at each other and went, "And we're playing here? Across the river?" Well, about thirty people showed up that night for our gig, and Mary Ann and I said, "That's it." We were driving through the desert the next day, and we stopped at a pay phone because we were so distraught. We made three calls. One to the record company, and the other two were to the people who were working with us at that point. We said, "We're firing ourselves and we're firing everyone! We're out of here. We quit. We're done. That's it, period. We're not doing this anymore. We're going back to songwriting." And, of course, the next month was when the record company called and offered us the Sting tours. We went out with Sting and opened for him.

Wayne Tester - Early on is the toughest, trying to look for that first publishing deal, that first cut, that first spark. That first major co-write. The first is always the hardest.

Trisha Walker - There was a Christmas song I wrote eight or nine years ago called *Evening in December*. It was when Amy Grant was going to put out her first Christmas album. They loved it and put it on hold, saying they were going to cut it. I even got some press material saying they were going to cut it. And then she and Gary wrote *Tender Tennessee Christmas,* and they took mine off. Trying to keep your voice and not compromising [is tough], wanting to find a deal as an artist, whatever a deal is. I'm sure over the years I have tried to bend my slant on music a little bit to try and find a spot and fit in. That didn't work, so I'm getting more stubborn. It's like, "Okay I think I know what I want to say and what I want to sing now, so let's try this."

Steve Bogard - If you open yourself up and show people who you really are, then the people who don't like that will go away.

Al Kasha - I think a low point for me was when I wasn't teachable.

Kent Blazy - Sometimes the harder you work, the more illusive creativity becomes.

Kye Fleming - The times that I enjoy the most myself, are the creative times where I'm on the track of bring an inspiration into focus with words.

CHAPTER EIGHT

GENERAL ADVICE

Debi Cochran - Nashville is the most wonderful place in the world because your direct competitors are your biggest supporters.

Joyce Rouse - The more I'm in this business, the more I see how little anybody knows.

Robin Earl - If you have a feeling that this is what you're supposed to be doing, it helps you over the rough spots.

Lindy Gravelle - What works for me, is to go out and get a heavy dose of inspiration, to see a good movie, a good play, or a writer's night with great writers.

1. What's the most intimidating thing about songwriting?

Tony Arata - Other songwriters. When we showed up, we were still in the middle of unloading the truck, and we went down to the Bluebird to see what goes on down there. I closed up the truck and my wife and I went to get a beer. It was Don Schlitz, Fred Knobloch, Craig Bickhart, and Tom Schuyler. Everything they were playing was on the radio. That "half full-half empty" thing kept coming back to me. I was thinking, The truck is still half full, so we can go back and I can throw it all back in and we can go home, because it is very obvious they do not need me here. And that was my first taste. It was a very serious ass-whipping, pardon my French, but it also made it perfectly clear why we moved here. There is not another town in America where you're going to walk in and see that same setting.

So now that you're in it, what are you going to do with it? It's very intimidating when you start talking about it. I don't care where you are on the charts or what you've done, there's somebody out there, all through town this morning, writing furiously. That's a very intimidating thought, but it's also exactly why you're here. It's humbling and inspiring at the same time. I still thoroughly enjoy either going out or turning on the radio and hearing a song that makes you think seriously about selling your guitar and moving home. As hard as that is to swallow, it is still exactly why you do this. It's a wonderful thing to eat a big, old slice of humble pie.

Pam Belford - I'd say co-writing with somebody you really admire. Because there are times when I'm really on and times when I'm really not. Sometimes I could be just dying to write with this other person, and when we get in this room and they're throwing ideas out right and left, I'm like, "Duh." Other times, though, I get really rolling and I'm afraid that I'm taking over.

Rory Bourke - Just about every time I sit down with somebody, it's intimidating. A friend of mine is a business consultant, and we've been talking a lot about this. When two people walk into a room, the unconscious question that goes on between them is, "Am I good enough?" Most people ask, "Am I good enough?" and there is an answer, "Yes, you're good enough." But sometimes you run into a situation where the person across from you doesn't hear that question or isn't interested in it. Then you don't get that affirmation back, and so you start asking, "Am I good enough?" and it starts feeling like, "Maybe I'm not good enough." I think that sometimes creativity between people can bog down in that area. I think it's real important to affirm that person. Something goes on to allow creativity to flow back and forth. I think dumb things like that happen. The older I get, the more I believe that conscious communication is about ten percent of communication, and there's a whole wealth of communication that's going on at levels that we're not aware of.

Gary Burr - I guess if you think about it, it's all intimidating. Because nobody knows how to do it. You never know if you're going to do it. If I write with somebody who I really respect, I'm intimidated and I really want to do well. If everybody loved the last song I wrote, writing that next one is really intimidating. I always joke and say that every time I write a song that everybody thinks is brilliant, I purposefully write two that are crap. To lower their expectations, to let them know that it was a mistake. These are normal. Don't expect brilliance. Expect strange. So, yeah, I don't think there's any part of it that I don't find intimidating.

Kim Carnes - The biggest challenge is to always come up with lyrics that are a little out of left field, that are fresh. Lyrics that aren't cliché. Lyrics that don't sound like they were written a hundred times before.

I write with Donna Weiss a lot. She's an incredible lyricist, and I think that's her greatest strength. I'm in such awe of her ideas and the lines that she comes up with. They're so brilliant, and they're so unique. She has this gift of incredible poetry.

Debi Cochran - [What I find most intimidating is] the lack of control you have over whether your songs ever get cut. Unless you have a friend who is an artist or producer or the head of A&R somewhere, you really have very little control. It's a bunch of strangers out there making decisions as to whether or not your song is going to happen or not. The thing about the music business is that the turnover rate, or the rate at which people go up the ladder, is very quick. So somebody who is your contemporary today, who is working as a tape copy guy at a publishing company as you are trying to get your first single song deals, is likely going to be running the publishing company or head the A&R department within four or five years, just when your songs are ready to be played to a bunch of artists. So you just keep that little network there and try to have some influence. But it can be very frustrating to just write the songs and turn them over.

Jill Colucci - Wondering if you can ever do it again [is intimidating]. Finishing a song that you really love and you're really happy with and having that feeling of, "I hope I can do that again." It's funny to me that we have that experience. I know I do and I've talked to other people who do too. You seem to have this fear of the well running dry. It's interesting to me that it's intimidating. I don't spend a lot of time there, but I have experienced it. Inspiration is so mystifying, so intangible and so difficult to explain and understand. I guess maybe on one level, why wouldn't we wonder if it's ever going to happen again. Sometimes it's very difficult to explain where a song even comes from. I do some of these panels and things for NSAI and other organizations, and people who want to be professional songwriters are asking these really difficult questions as well. But some things just can't be answered. There are no tricks. It's not about that. They really have to learn their craft. But the gift, the talent, and the inspiration has to be there, or you'll just hear crafty work. You won't get the heart and soul.

Kim Copeland - I think the only thing intimidating about it is keeping it honest. Not allowing the fear of "what will somebody else think of it?" to enter the room. The intimidating thing is trying not to let any outside influence affect what I'm writing.

Gary Earl - Being disciplined about making enough time for writing [is intimidating]. It just seems like there are so many times when you've got too many other things on your brain, particularly when this analytical thing starts ... paying this bill, or going to this meeting, or I should write this letter to the congressman about copyright legislation. That's like an inner battle. Getting a cut, to a certain degree, that's out of your hands. As long as you're plugging it, or somebody else is plugging it, it's somebody else's subjective whim to cut it or not. But the inner discipline is like fighting a paper tiger, fighting something that's not really there.

Robin Earl - It's such an open-ended thing. You can always spend more time writing or more time trying to get songs cut.

Kye Fleming - Probably, like any writer would say, [the biggest intimidation is] the blank piece of paper. When you feel something bubbling and you just know that it's right there. There's great anticipation, and there's the tiniest bit of fear that you can't do it. But there's a lot more hope that you can.

I scratch at a good lyric. All my life that's what I've done. I've scratched at a good lyric. And I can only think of a couple of songs that I feel have really done it for me, but the ratio has nothing to do with how much hope I have when I sit down. Right now I expect that if I sit down, I can write something really great even though I have nothing to base that on. It's not based on past experience. It's because I'm hoping that for this second, I could just be at the right place at the right time that this channel might open, and I might be the one who gets this gift. I'm really hoping for that divine inspiration.

Lindy Gravelle - Pleasing your publisher [is most intimidating]. Playing it for the powers that be. You can fall in love with a song you've just written and then just get shot all to hell.

John Jarrard - Sitting down in a room by yourself with a guitar. I read a quote the other day that a blank sheet of paper is God's way of showing us what it's like to be God. Writing by myself is really intimidating.

Al Kasha - Well, I think I set my standards very, very high. Sometimes too high. And even though I've won Academy awards and Tony nominations, I will look at the work of Howard Ashman, Tim Rice and Bernie Taupin, and sometimes I kill myself trying to live up to those standards. But it's best to look at the best ... Billy Joel, Garth Brooks or

Allen Reynolds, and I think Dolly Parton is a great songwriter. In fact, I think one of the great lyrics and melodies of all time is *Nine To Five*. I mean "kitchen" and "ambition" and "let it" and "credit," there are some great rhymes in there as well as honesty. She's a wonderful writer. Even for this day, I think Hank Williams and Hank Cochran, for pure just pleading of broken-heartedness. I bow to those two men. Look at the line, "I've tried so hard my dear, to show that you're my everything." That's just begging. It says it all.

Mary Ann Kennedy - I co-write, so I get bailed out of a lot of the phobias as a solo writer. When I try to write something on my own, I am so intimidated. When to say it's done? When to say, "That is the song?" When I'm critiquing somebody else's work and they mine, we can confer and agree. You have somebody there to condone or reject. Even if I just write with someone who doesn't do music, who just does lyrics, it's the same thing. I'll just kind of overly critique myself.

Sandy Knox - I don't know if this would fall under intimidating, but I think it's really tough when you know you've got a mother of a song, and it isn't finding its home. I have a song called *Ropes Made of Sand,* and when it finds its home, it's going to be big. Billy Stritch and I wrote *Does He Love You* fourteen years ago. It took this long for Reba to find it. It had been on hold by other people and stuff. Here was a song we knew was so different and so powerful. It had never been done. Two women having a civilized conversation about the same man. It took so long to find its home and then once it did, it was huge. I guess that isn't intimidating, but it grates on you.

What's the most intimidating thing about songwriting? Probably the fear. There's so much rejection involved. You're rejected by the publishers when you first get here. If you get a publisher, then the A&R people reject your songs. If it gets past the A&R people, then the artists get to play the rejection game. Then say it gets on the album, you get to play the rejection game wondering if it's going to be a single. Then if it's a single, you sit there and wonder if the public's going to accept it. Each level is just another higher anxiety of rejection. It never ends. It's a vicious, vicious cycle. Then you're wondering, "What am I going to follow that with?"

Kostas - I wouldn't say it's intimidating. I'd say it's disappointing to write a good song and then see it sit in the can for a long time, and people pass on it.

(DO YOU THINK THERE IS A LACK OF CREATIVITY WITH SOME RECORD EXECUTIVES?) Well, they're juggling too many things at one time. And when they do that, it's hard to pay attention to the real things. Too much attention is paid to the things that aren't. Just because somebody can sing doesn't necessarily make them a singer. There are too many people out there who are just doing it because it's appealing, it's an easy way in. In the old days, I guess, raw talent and love of the music and love of the public were their reasons for doing it. These days, there are a lot of people who just seem like rebels without a clue.

Jess Leary - You mean, besides writing with Gary Burr? Oh, gosh, I don't know. I don't know that I find it intimidating. Certain writers just put me in awe. There are lots of them. There are lots of them right here in this building, in this office, Kye [Fleming] and Mary Ann [Kennedy] being probably the most. I love the songs they've written. I hope I can come close to that some day, and I know I've learned a lot from them. They're wonderful people and very helpful and very inspiring.

Jim McBride - I hear other people's songs that intimidate me. But they also inspire me. I'll hear these songs and think, Okay, I've got to get more serious about this. I've got to get back to work. I'll hear a song and think, My Gosh, I should have thought of that. But I probably couldn't have written it then. That's intimidating to me. And all the rejection stuff, that just makes me ill.

Wayland Patton - If I'm co-writing, it's intimidating for me to get in a room with somebody I really respect, who I've never written with before. I don't know if other people suffer from it, but sometimes, being so introspective and critical, I suffer from the syndrome that sooner or later they're going to find out that I'm a fraud, a big fake. On one hand, I'm very confident and I know my abilities. I know I've written some things that are really good. They're special. But along with knowing my abilities and knowing my strengths, I also know my weaknesses. I'm a very good performer, I'm a very good singer and I love to record, but I can't help being supercritical.

John Steinbeck, when he was writing *East of Eden*, kept a journal. It's called *Journal of Novel*. Each day he would sit down and write an open letter to his editor on the left page. It was a warm-up exercise. He would talk about what he was trying to accomplish in all the scenes. Then on the right-hand page, he would write the novel. He did this every day. That's how he wrote the novel. He warmed up. He did the same thing for *Grapes of Wrath*. A little different style, but essentially the same thing.

When I read this, it gave me a lot of insight into his writing style and his work ethic. He kept telling himself, I'll just write this much today, and not look at writing a novel. I'm just going to write my couple of pages a day, and eventually the novel will happen. He talked about how, if he thought of writing a novel, it overwhelmed him, he couldn't do it. But he could write that little bit every day. His self-doubt would keep coming up, and he talked about how, some nights, he would lie in bed not being able to sleep because he didn't think he could do it. So that's some solace.

Pam Rose - Saying stupid things to your co-writer [intimidates me]. My disclaimer is, "Hey, I know this might sound stupid, but maybe it will spur something with you." I guess if there's anything intimidating, it would be that for me. It's embarrassing when you think of something that's really, really cool, and the reason it's really, really cool is because it's been on the radio for two years.

Joyce Rouse - The promotion of it once it's finished, the presentation of it [is intimidating]. Especially in a town where there are so many fine writers. I no longer allow myself to get caught in that circle of how I can possibly compete with all these great songwriters. I just don't buy into that anymore. The part that is very disconcerting to me is getting my tape heard among a stack of a thousand other tapes.

Wayne Tester - Fear of failure. But fear of failure is a motivator.
(HAVE YOU MASTERED IT?) No. Never have, never will. I don't think anybody will ever master it. I think it's a part of our lives.

Kate Wallace - [What's intimidating is the fear] that nothing's going to come out. You sit down to do something, and not a thought, not an idea, not a melody, not a thing, is going to come into your head.

2. Are there words, phrases, or subjects that you consciously avoid using in your writing?

Tony Arata - There is such a fine line to me between capturing a moment and capitalizing on a moment. I don't ever want to capitalize on some human frailty. It's like a cheap shot. I try not to be so specific and so graphic that really all you're doing is reporting on a very sad event. You try to glean something from it and turn it around to where you're not reporting on it. You're trying to enlighten with it, or use it to hopefully mean something to somebody who may be going through it.

I've written some songs I think are light-hearted and stuff, but they're from a whole different slant.

(THE DITTIES?) Yeah. I'm just not that guy. God knows, sometimes when I see what goes on the charts, I wish I could do that. When I try, it sounds like it's so contrived. So I do consciously avoid trying to write those kinds of songs because I can't write them at all.

Pam Belford - When I can, and this is probably the librarian in me, I avoid using slang. If there are enough syllables there for "isn't," I will say "isn't" before "ain't." I'm really conscious of not wanting to waste a line saying something that I don't need to say, or that's already been said somewhere else in the song, or something boring, or confusing.

Kent Blazy - I don't think so. I think if there's a subject that I think needs to be addressed, even if other people don't, I'll go ahead, if it's fired me up enough to inspire me. It probably won't get cut, but it's saying what I want, from the heart. If there's a subject that I think is a negative subject, then I'll try to find more of a positive way of relating to it. I try to approach my songs so that if people hear them, it'll either help them and make them a better person, or make them happy, where they can appreciate what they have. That's what I try to do.

Steve Bogard - I don't like blue. That's about it. It seems too sweet and cute and nice.

Rory Bourke - O.J. Simpson songs. No, there's nothing I try to avoid.

Gary Burr - Only the clichés. Only the things that people have done to death. And there's nothing that says you can't still do it a different way. I try not to let the marketplace dictate anything. I really do not enjoy hearing myself say, "Well, I don't know if we should do that. If we do that nobody will cut the song."

But on the other hand, I've told people many times, I don't mind making certain sacrifices for the marketplace, because I would rather have a hundred million people hear ninety percent of what I meant than have three people hear a hundred percent. The three are me, my fiancée, and my publisher. If you put something in there that takes it out of the running, then three people get to hear it. There are things that I'll stay away from, but I don't think there's anything that you can't sing about in some way. *Norwegian Wood* is Lennon singing about an affair in a way that his wife wouldn't know what he was talking about. You can do it.

Debi Cochran - No. I know people who have done that, though, who have written so many "heart" hooks that they won't write anything with the word *heart* in it, and who have certain taboos.

Kim Copeland - I think the word *heart* is terribly overused, but I use it. Try to avoid it in country music! I don't like to be too cliché, I guess, unless you can find a really unique angle to show. I don't like to take too many popular slang phrases and use them in songs. I think they come off sounding kind of cheesy and distract from the message of the song (unless the message of the song is a cheesy cliché!). Sometimes those are cute in conversation but come off really weak in songs.

Kye Fleming - I don't feel like I'm an abrasive personality, therefore my songs aren't going to be abrasive. There have been some where I've been sarcastic, but not abrasive.

Lindy Gravelle - If I hear the name "Bubba" again ... When there becomes an obvious trend going on, I turn and go the other way. I don't like to put in fad words or even names.

Janis Ian - I don't like the word *sin*. I try to avoid words like that. I think they set a bad precedent. I stay away from songs that say, it's okay for you to do whatever you want to me as long as you don't leave. I think it's a bad precedent. I try to keep the songs in line with my own philosophy, even when I'm co-writing.

One thing that has always puzzled me is how few women songwriters there are compared to males. Even at the Bluebird auditions, it's still maybe one out of ten. I don't understand that. I don't think it's any lack of availability, because right now the doors are wide open. Amy Kurland has a theory that because women are now allowed to go into other areas, they're no longer as drawn to the arts. The arts was where you went if you wanted a career of your own. You were either that or a whore. There didn't seem to be any in-between. If I have a goal as a writer, it's to try to hit a universal something that everyone can understand and everyone can feel.

John Jarrard - I like throwing curve balls. I like saying things that you can't say in country songs. If someone told me I couldn't say something in a country song, I would probably figure out a way.

Mary Ann Kennedy - [I avoid] the subjects that aren't "in" anymore. The cheating songs. For women, there's a definite evolution that's been going on since I've been in Nashville. We were some of the first women writers who really wrote full-time. It used to be okay to say, "You ain't woman enough to take my man." That was cool then, and Loretta and Tammy and Kitty sang all those, "I'm gonna stay at home and my goal and my mission in life is to stand by my man." That was then, and that was their truth. I'm not criticizing those because they're classics, but nowadays that's not as much the truth. We've changed women's roles in our world, and our society has changed, and hopefully it's farther along so that we're both equals. I don't mean not to sing what's real. If you're hurting and you're going through a heartbreak, that's real and that's okay. If you're absolutely amazed by your husband's love, it's okay to sing, "Your love amazes me." But to say "I just won't be able to go on without you" is not so much the role I want to portray as a women's posture today, in this society. You know, you can have a broken heart, but you can go on just like a man could. So yeah, it's changed, and for the better. But male-bashing songs aren't cool either.

Sandy Knox - It's funny, because one word that I don't like to use is the word *fantasy*, and it's in *Does He Love You*. I've always hated that word. It's just 1970s sexual, you know.

Kostas - No.

Jess Leary - Musically, if it's something I just heard in my car on the way over, I'm going to avoid it really fast. I guess I just avoid things that make me feel funny if I hear them. If something doesn't feel right, it's probably not right, whether it be a lyric, a title, a piece of music, a sentence, or one word in a song.

Jim McBride - I asked my wife the other day about "cleavage." I think if you used that word right, you could put that in a country song. I asked her, "If I can find the right way to use it, can I use it?"

I won't use alliteration just to be using it, but it sure helps the flow of a song. And if I've got my choice between two words that'll work, and one of them is going to give me that alliteration with another word in the line above it, then I'll go with that one. The "h" and the "w" sounds are just great. I love words. I love phrases. And I love certain letters more than others.

Wayland Patton - I avoid, "Honey, I'll do the dishes." No, probably not. I try to not sound too cliché. I try to keep it simple. Simplicity can be a huge plus.

Pam Rose - There are attitudes that I consciously avoid. I'm less likely to relate to an idea that gives no hope to a situation. I have no problem exploring and writing about all different kinds of feelings. Grief is not a pleasant thing. Loss is not a pleasant thing. Abandonment. I don't mind writing about any of those, but what I do try to avoid is just hopelessness. Even one of the most agonizing songs doesn't have to be hopeless.

There's a song that Mary Ann [Kennedy] and Pat [Bunch] and I wrote called *Leaving Line*. It's the final cut of *Hai Ku*. There's just so much angst in that song, but the question is still rhetorical. It leaves room for an answer. "Where does a heart cross the leaving line / have we become strangers one too many times / can I live, knowing you used to be mine / where does a heart cross the leaving line?" It's still rhetorical enough that there's an out, instead of, "Now that you're gone, my life is screwed." I will definitely try to avoid that, because I don't believe that.

Joyce Rouse - No, I don't think there is any word that could never be used in a song, but I think there are a lot of songs that a lot of words would not be appropriate in. It depends on how they're used. It depends on what kind of a song they're used in. It's been really fun for me to do this *Earth Momma* tape, because nobody has said to me, "But this isn't country music." I've included reggae and calypso and dixieland and scat singing and country music and pop on it. When you're using that many diverse art forms, or diverse kinds of music lyrically, you can just do so much more. I've felt really free about my use of words. It's like I was setting aside another editor, not so much a word editor, but a promotion editor. But I have to say, though, I have worked with a number of writers who will say, "I'm sorry, we can't use this word in a song. My publisher hates this word." Or I've had that happen a number of times when they knew that pluggers were going to have a problem with a word.

Wayne Tester - Never. I say never say "never." If it's a cliché and it's used right, go for it. If it works, it works.

Trisha Walker - There's one, [thing I avoid], I guess, and that comes from doing our publishing work here. We listen to a lot of outside material from folks. If I hear "break my heart, brand new start" one more time, I'm going to shoot somebody. It's like God must have intentionally made "heart" a hard word to rhyme. I consciously avoid that, just because it's so overused. Any clichés. To me, that's always the mark of a young writer. You use clichés over and over again. You've either got to find a new way to use them, or find something new to say.

Kim Williams - No [I don't avoid certain things]. That's what I love about country music. I've got a song about incest, and I'm probably going to demo it, and it's probably going to lay there and never get cut. Reba's got a song about AIDS. It's written as "understatement." The name of the song is *I Think His Name Was John*. "She says she knew all the people in her background that she's been with. But there was this one guy, one time, a friend of a friend, and she had too much wine, and she left his bed at dawn, and she thinks his name was John." It's really great, and it never mentions AIDS. You've got to get this album. I've got a song on there, too, that's supposed to be a single. It's called *The Heart is a Lonely Hunter*. It's my first major female cut.

What do you want to do as a writer? You want to make somebody feel something. You want to make them laugh. It ought to make you cry. As a writer, you want to move people. You want to do something to them. Those songs move you. This stuff is happening every day. You read about it. One of the greatest songs I've ever heard is Richard Leigh's *The Greatest Man I Never Knew*.

3. Criticism: What has it done to you and for you?

Pam Belford - I really have thought before, what an awful position to be in. The music business is a business that attracts people who are insecure. It is the last business that an insecure person needs to be in. I think we're all vulnerable to criticism, but I think there comes a time when you do have to consider the source of the criticism. You do have to try to look with an objective eye at your own work.

Kent Blazy - It's always hard to take criticism, because the songs are like your babies. I try to weigh what everybody says against what I think. With a certain song, if you get four or five people saying the same thing, then you have to believe that these people are all picking up on the same thing. There are other times when you just feel in your heart that there is something right. Like with *If Tomorrow Never Comes*, when Garth and I wrote that, we thought, We've really written a big song that everybody's going to love. We pitched that song for nine months and nobody was interested in it. So then you start doubting. You start saying, "Well, do we think this is something good, and maybe it's really not?" There's another song that I wrote at about that same time period, and for the past six or seven years now we haven't been able to get it cut. It finally has been cut and is a single on a new group here. It's one of those things where you have to believe in what you feel over what anybody else says. But you also have to take it to heart when they do have criticisms of your songs, and think, Can I make it better or is what they're saying correct?

Steve Bogard - The bulk of the criticism that I get now comes from my co-writers, and it's all done before anybody ever sees it. So I feel really good about everything before anybody ever sees it. I've gotten some bad reviews on singles, and I've gotten some great reviews on singles. It doesn't make much difference to me. I just like anything that has my name on it to have a certain level of substance, a certain level of creativity. Early on, I think it's really important to listen to the criticism of publishers.

Kim Carnes - You learn to separate the people who really have a valid opinion and who you want to listen to. You have to find the people who you really respect. I realized early on that those people are few and far between. Everybody in the business has an opinion, and everybody wants to control and make you this or that. In the end you have to have those few people you respect. Most of all, do what you want to do.

The only time I've had a regret about a song on an album was when somebody made me do it a certain way. That never happens anymore. Now I'll fight to keep it mine and keep it the way it should be. If I follow my heart and write a song the way I feel it, record it the best way I can at the time, and it doesn't end up working, I still can be proud of it. But if I compromise and it doesn't end up working, that's a horrible feeling. Then it's regret. You have to be true to yourself as an artist. The artists that I think are the great ones, they don't compromise. They have their vision and that's what makes them unique. The best artists stick to their vision. They're not the norm. They're different. Artists are scared to take a chance, but the business people are scared to take a chance too. Look at Lyle Lovett. It took a Tony Brown, who has incredible taste and vision. Tony is bold. He's not afraid. Look at the artists he's signed. Practically all my favorite artists are on MCA.

Debi Cochran - There is criticism at every single turn in this business, because ninety-nine percent of what you hear about your song is "no." No, we don't want to demo it, because something is wrong. No, we don't think we hear that for Suzy Bogguss, so we're not going to play it for her. If it does .get played for Suzy Bogguss, then the head of A&R says, no, and if the producer likes it, Suzy doesn't like it herself. It gets out there, and radio says, "That R&B piano thing is not right for our format." The answer is no ninety-nine percent of the time. You just have to learn to believe in yourself and keep going.

We all thrive on hearing stories of specific songs that have been rejected. I've heard that four of the songs that turned out to be big singles for Brooks and Dunn were on a tape that Ronnie sent to a record label in town. The A&R person wrote him back and said, "You're listening to too much radio, this is not going to work." He has his letter naming the songs, his first four or five hits, and her reply saying, "This will never work." We thrive on that kind of thing.

Kim Copeland - Criticism stifled me and made the process a lot longer and harder than it had to be because I took it too seriously. I assumed that everybody critiquing my songs knew more than I did, and it led me away from following my heart. You have to grow through that and learn to put it in perspective. Learn to absorb the advice that feels good to you and fits, and let the rest pass you by without giving it too much credence. That's part of the learning process that you go through. Learning to keep everything in perspective. In the end, you have to follow your own path.

Gary Earl - Well, I never argue. What I tend to do is make a mental note of it or physically make a note on paper, because I want to be open to suggestions that I think are valid. Usually I make up my mind about their suggestions about two days later, after it's kind of simmered for a while. Then it will seem fairly clear to me whether it's a good suggestion or not.

Robin Earl - I try to be objective about criticism. If I hear the same thing from several people I usually pay more attention. I also try to keep in mind a person's personality and taste, and ask, Is this the type of song that would interest them?

Lindy Gravelle - It depends on where the criticism is coming from. Consider the source. My mother gave me those three little words, and I've thought, "There's a lot of wisdom there, Mom." This town is such a mixture of all kinds of people who have ended up in positions of critiquing, whether it's a publisher or a fellow writer. I always prefer to think that they know how to play music and they know how to sing, but a lot of them don't. Yet they have ears, and some maybe don't, but they managed to get in a position where they're making decisions about the arts. So I'm very open to listen to criticism. I don't take it too personally. I think you have to learn that. I'm sure you've heard that as a professional, you're not supposed to get so sensitive about it. You just take it in and decide whether or not you think that what they're saying would work or not. If you've played music as long as I have, and sung as many songs, and you're sitting there listening to somebody who's just out of Belmont (no offense), and they want to tell you what they think about your song, that's fine. But at the same time, I'm thinking, What is it you really know? I've listened to an A&R person at a major label who was, I thought, stupid enough to admit that he came to town and had never even known who Hank Williams was. This guy is in Nashville making decisions about songs and people's careers. But then again I know I'm very sensitive about paying homage to the history of the art.

John Jarrard - Criticism pissed me off. I think the biggest turning point of my career was when I was involved with a publisher who was just right in my face about everything. Any time I turned something in, he had very definite ideas about something that needed to be changed, or the direction. After I became dis-involved with this publisher, I sat down and wrote a song with J.D. Morrow that we both liked, but I figured there must be something wrong with it. I played it for Chuck Neese, and he said it was great and wanted to play it for Don Williams. I said, "Well, what do we need to change?" He said, "Nothing, what do you mean?" I think it's important on the front end to have someone who will be honest with you about your songs, someone who will tell you the truth about them. But the lesson that I learned was that the first guy I've got to please is myself. If I'm satisfied with it, I'm willing to listen to some criticism, but if it doesn't pretty well resonate with me, then I'm probably not going to make a change.

Jim McBride - First of all, let me say that I hate rewrites. That's one of my most hated words in the English language. Curly Putnam told me a long time ago, "I can't help you if I can't be honest with you." Good or bad, I felt like Curly was always honest. Because of who he was, I would listen to what he said. I've been that way through the years. If it's someone whose opinion I respect, then I'll take a look at it. But generally, and especially when I've written by myself, I've spent so much time with those songs that I don't get a lot of rewrite stuff.

Wayland Patton - You have to take criticism. I always consider the source. I've got to respect the person, then I listen. Criticism doesn't bother me. If somebody gives me some constructive criticism, I'll listen. But I am probably a harder critic about my own music and self than anyone else could ever be. Sometimes they criticize something I don't agree with, but it's their opinion, and it doesn't necessarily mean that I would change something. If I feel they have a good point, then I'll dig a little deeper. I think you're foolish if you go through life thinking that everything you write is perfect and great.

Wayne Tester - From the proper people, it's constructive criticism, and you have to welcome that. You take that kind of criticism. You've got to know the difference between people who know what they're talking about and people who are just criticizing because they may have ulterior motives, so to speak. You just try to let that run off your back and take the good stuff.

Trisha Walker - In terms of trying to pursue a writer and an artist kind of direction, I've gotten all kinds of criticism, from, "You've got a great voice, your songs are great, we just don't know what radio's going to do with it," or "You're able to write a lot of different styles, so we don't think you're focused enough to be an artist." That gets frustrating, because you really have to split your self a little bit. And ... I feel capable of writing a lot of different styles, and I enjoy that. But I can see where, when a record label is trying to market something, and the way radio works these days, they have to find a channel to put an artist in. I don't think I would be satisfied with that.

Helpful criticism, I've always heard from people who I consider my mentors, is "write what you know and write what you love." I feel like, right now, I'm probably about to come into a season where I'm about to go write a bunch of new stuff that is more about where I come from, what I feel, what I really think is important, versus let's go see if I can crank out a song today.

(WHAT IS CAUSING THIS CHANGE IN ATTITUDE?) Probably just that I'm getting older. I realize the need to actually try to write songs for the commercial market, whether it's the Nashville country thing, or outside Nashville, but again, every writer is unique to himself or herself. That's what makes songs interesting, the unique perception of each writer. So I think I'm just getting older and maybe more stubborn. I think it's a good decade to really search and struggle and find what I consider my "voice," my unique perspective. I don't know that you ever totally find it, but you kind of work your way down the road looking for it.

Kate Wallace - It depends on who it comes from. If Rory Bourke says to me about a song, "I think it needs something else," I respect it and I really appreciate it. If it comes from one of the former song pluggers at my former publishing company, no thanks. I have no respect for that person and their criticism. And if it happens to be somebody who is simply a music critic or a fan or a person in the audience, they're a person. I'm a pretty good judge of whether an idea is good or not. I think criticism can be really valuable.

Marijohn Wilkin - There was criticism, but there wasn't all this that's going on today. One can't write any better than another, and they're critiquing. I wouldn't take one of my songs to be critiqued. I was privileged to write with John D. Loudermilk, Wayne Walker, Mel Tillis, and Danny Dill. Four of the greatest writers that have ever been in Nashville. And together with myself, all five of us are now in the Nashville Songwriters Hall of Fame. I was in my thirties. I didn't think everything that I wrote was great. I've written stuff that nobody will ever hear that's not good enough for anybody to hear. I've got brains enough to critique my own stuff.

This is the way it would be done. We'd take a song that we thought was really neat over to Owen Bradley and, bless his heart, he would listen to everything. We'd just written our hearts out, and Owen would say, "Honey, that's a cute little old song, but I think I'll pass on it today." Oh! Such a neat put down ... cute little old song. Oh, well. If you can't take the heat, don't get in the kitchen. But take it to somebody who knows. Don't take it to somebody who doesn't know.

Kim Williams - If it's really blunt and pointed criticism, that's probably one of my most energizing things. I turn it into vindictive energy. I can take it well, if it's done in the right way; but too many times in this business, it's really blunt.

I feel sorry for anybody whose main purpose in life is never to create anything, but to run down or analyze what somebody else has created. I've seen that without a doubt, when you see a strong reaction out of critics, you are looking at a hit. Talking to Jim McBride and Alan Jackson about Chatahoochie, they had no idea it was going to be a hit. That's the way it ought to be—you should write to just write, and let things go. Wherever it comes out, it comes out.

4. Competition: How does it apply to songwriting?

Steve Bogard - I think there's a very positive and friendly competition, at least in my songwriting circle. I think you want to show off for your friends, and you want them to show off for you and do well.

Rory Bourke - There's a lot of it. But I don't know anybody in Nashville who's willing to slit another writer's throat to get a song cut. I've never experienced that. I think most writers in Nashville are very loving and kind towards each other. Most of the guys I know would bend over backwards to help me get a song cut, as I would bend over backwards to help them. It's strictly the song, the song has to get itself cut. It has to be that good. I think that the whole tone of the NSAI [Nashville Songwriter's Association International] is that we're brothers and sisters in arms. I think we all love each other.

Kim Carnes - There are so many incredible songwriters, "x" amount of artists, and lots of great songs. There's tremendous competition. But that's not a bad thing. Hopefully you'll keep striving to write the song that's going to be a little bit different and special. Since there are so many songs being shown to the artists, it keeps you on your toes. The better the quality of the songs being recorded, the better it is for all of us. It raises the level of what you can write.

I think the big difference between most executives and artists is that the executives are very cynical. And, year after year, out of their mouths is, "Well, what are they going to do next?" or "I heard the follow-up album, and it's not good," and "They're not writing well anymore." From artists, you never hear that. As an artist, you truly love music and you die to have somebody be successful, or to hear a wonderful new album so you can turn everybody on to it. If you love music, you want everyone to do well.

Debi Cochran - Nashville is the most wonderful place in the world because your direct competitors are your biggest supporters. Now people in L.A. and New York are beginning to find that out, and they're flocking in here by the thousands. I'm thinking that we need to get some alligators and scare these people off.

Jill Colucci - I don't really know what everybody else thinks about that or is going through with it, but for me, I compete with myself. I want my next song to be as good as, or actually a little better than, my last song. I've experienced more life, so I should be a better writer. Experience and awareness, I feel, are two of the keys. Like all the things I've been through in my past. Things that were difficult for me just enhance my songwriting. They become really positive because they've made me be more in touch on that particular level.

I'm definitely competing with myself, and I don't get into competing with other writers. I've turned artists on to friends of mine's songs that I think are great for that project. I used to think, Let the best song win. But it's not even the best song. You might have a great song which just doesn't fit into the whole picture. It's really helpful that I've been an artist. I wrote for myself, but I listened to a lot of outside songs and cut a lot of outside songs as well. Because you're forming a picture, you're forming a tapestry, it's a whole thing You might get a great song, but it just doesn't work with the concept that's developing. I don't take not getting a cut personally at all anymore. To me it's just one more elimination I've made that gets me closer to the right home for that song.

I'm very much aware that country music has exploded and that the competition is tougher. You're up against a lot of songs. I've signed with a publisher that has many, many writers, some of the best writers in the world, and my songs are up against theirs before it even goes out the door. Then it's up against the cream of the crop from all the others. So certainly I'm aware of how strong the competition is out there.

(DO YOU FEEL IT'S DIFFERENT IN L.A.?) I do. I certainly don't want to say anything derogatory about Los Angeles because I love it in many ways. Pop music has changed so much. In Nashville, the melody and the lyric is still, and I hope will always be, the most important thing. When I first started coming here to write in 1986, I was so productive. It was really the energy that I felt here towards the songwriter. I walked onto Music Row, and I'd see a big, huge home that's now a publishing company. I love the quaint atmosphere of it. Next door, another big home for the writer's building. I mean, in L.A. you were lucky if you could find an out-of-tune piano and a phone in a publishing office. I feel like there's a real understanding here by producers, publishers, and record companies, that without the song you don't have anything. Without a great song you don't have artists. What would they sing? You don't have record companies. You don't have publishing companies. It really starts in this town with the song, and boy, that's just a fantastic energy.

It got to where a few years later, when I went to L.A., I just sang and did all of my session work. I was kind of split. When I went to L.A. I was the singer, and here I was the writer. I really am focused on my writing when I'm here, and I want to keep it that way. I am very productive here as a writer, and I attribute that to the wonderful energy. Going around to the Bluebird and the clubs, and hearing writers perform their songs. It's incredible. It's great. If you're serious about being a songwriter, then this is the best place to be in the whole world.

Kim Copeland - When I moved to Nashville, I found it to be a very supportive writing community. I still do. I think songwriters in this town are very supportive of one another. That's just been my experience. The competitiveness happens more on the business end of it than on the creative end. Being out there pitching and getting the cuts. I mean, there are a limited number of slots for a massive number of songs to filter into, so there has to be competition there.

Kye Fleming - There is good competition, and there is bad competition or it can be used to your benefit or not. If you're insecure or coming from an insecure place, then competition is a scary thing and it makes you feel less than. If you're secure and you feel like you're doing your best, and you hear somebody who's done something incredible, then it should be encouragement for you to want to do even better. There's plenty to go around, and because somebody has some success doesn't take away from your success at all. The best thing we can do is do our best every day. If you're happy with the end product of what you've just done, it doesn't matter what anybody else is doing. Period. And somebody else's success should just say to you, I can do it too. Instead of calling it competition, call it inspiration or encouragement.

John Jarrard - I'm trying to get to a place where I'm not driven by that, but sometimes it just eats at me. I wish I could say that I'm uniformly delighted by the success of everybody else, but I'm not. There are times that it just chews on my guts. In my saner moments, I really do believe that there's enough here for all of us. I wish that the songs that got cut were always the best songs, but they're not.

Mary Ann Kennedy - I love it, because instead of feeling depressed, I really get inspired. If I hear a song that I wish I'd written, it just works for me. It turns me on to dig a little deeper and rise a little higher above what I've been doing and try to reach out there and just top one off again. I like to be entertained, so I love hearing something that is moving and a great work of art that I wish I had my name on.

When Gary Burr came to town, I was one of the first people he wrote with; and success-wise and cut-wise, he's passed me up and he's the hot dog right now. I'm happy for him. I just think it's great. He's also very, very driven and very structured. He goes into that office every day and hey, I've got to hand it to him, it's paid off. I love hearing something and thinking, "Cool, Gary wrote that." It works for me. It inspires me.

Sandy Knox - I don't feel like there is a huge competition among the writers. Actually, more than competitiveness among the writers, I have found support. I think the competitiveness is healthy if it is there. I've never felt cut-throat here in Nashville. I have in L.A., but never here in Nashville.

Jim McBride - I think the greatest songwriters in the world live here. Not all of them, but most of them. And so there's your competition right there. I've pitched other writer's songs and I've had other writers pitch my songs. I think there's a common bond because of what we've all been through. If there's an album cut out there, I want it, but if I can't have it, then I want one of my friends to have it.

Wayland Patton - When I go out and hear a great writer, I may wish I had written that. I get more inspired. If I turn on the radio and I hear something that is really good, it inspires me. I get more inspired when I hear it at a writer's night, though. But if I hear something that's really well-written then I go away pumped up. Just by the very nature of the beast, there are only a certain number of slots out there, and you are competing for those slots. I don't begrudge somebody getting that slot.

(HOW MUCH DO YOU LISTEN TO THE RADIO?) I don't listen to the radio very much. It's not because I don't love the music that I'm involved in. More often I'm listening to CDs. (IF YOU GO OUT AND BUY A CD, WHO'S IT GOING TO BE?) The last CD I bought was the SubDudes. They're very interesting and unique. They are more alternative. Sting, Jackson Browne, James Taylor, Bonnie Raitt. (WHY DO YOU SUPPOSE SO MANY WRITERS LISTEN TO JAMES TAYLOR?) Because he's such a great writer. We're all products of our influences. When I was growing up, Merle Haggard was the first country concert I had gone to. So I listened to him a lot and Ernest Tubb, and the country TV shows that were on Saturday nights. That's how I got into country music. The Beatles, the Eagles, James Taylor, Jackson Browne were also influences.

Joyce Rouse - The more I'm in this business, the more I see how little anybody knows. I believe that the essence of everyone's creativity is beautiful, and hopefully people use that for a good purpose. I have to believe that no matter what the competition does, it isn't going to affect my outcome. Emily Dickinson, who was a brilliant, brilliant poet, received virtually no acclaim during her lifetime. There's a wonderful line in a letter she wrote: "If fame were not for me, I could not make it happen, and if fame were for me, there's no way I could keep it from happening." Only she said it much more beautifully than I just did.

Trisha Walker - There are some great, great writers in this town. It truly is a creative town. Sometimes it seems that what you hear coming out on records and videos does begin to sound the same. It does begin to get in that kind of box that radio and record labels have decided they can market. But if you look past that, you get songs like *Where've You Been* and just countless others that are magical, songs that you can hear any night in town at a writer's night, songs that may never make records. You can tell that the competition is just keen. I think when the young writers come to town, a lot of them come too soon. They think they're ready and they're not. I think the further you go up the ladder, you'll realize just how stiff the competition is.

Kate Wallace - I've been through such a metamorphosis about that whole issue. There are a zillion people here, but nobody does what you do. So it's really about finding that thing that you think you do well and honoring it. I also believe that if you embrace the competition and wish them all well, that is the kind of thing that will ultimately reflect in your writing. Once you get to that place, which I did about a year ago, it's a lot easier.

The mantra when I got to this town was, "The song is everything." What a load of crap. The song is not everything. You can take any song in the world, put enough promotion behind it, and buy the number one slot. But they can't buy the record sales. That's the proof of the pudding.

Kim Williams - I'll be honest with you. Sometimes I look back, and I don't know how I had the nerve to come down here and try it. This town is so packed with talent. For a while I was totally intimidated. Anybody who comes to this town who doesn't go through those feelings is probably kidding themselves. I think what kept me going during that time is that there is a hell of a lot of laziness in the creative business. There's a lack of "go get it" attitude. I knew that if I had an edge, it was that I was willing to go the extra mile. The talent is unbelievable. The competition is fierce. You show me any writer who's having some success, and if he lets up, somebody's going to fill that spot. Have you ever heard, "The seeds of failure are sown in the grounds of success"? It's true.

I was out writing with Charlie Neal, and we wrote a song called *No Pain, No Gain*. Of course, that's probably been written a million times. It was about two o'clock when we finished, and he said, "The next time we get together, I've got a hook to write." That's what's funny about hooks. If I had this hook, there's no way it would have come second. It would have been the first thing. But I'm getting packed away, and he says, "The next time we'll write *I Can't Tell My Heart a Thing*. It just killed me. It's simple, yet it says so much. I said, "Hey it's only two o'clock. Let's write it right now." So thirty minutes later we wrote this song. I was in the spirit. Whatever it is, I was totally, totally lost in this thing. That's what I live for.

5. Songwriting can be a real roller coaster ride. Do you have any tips on how to survive?

Tony Arata - Between *The Dance* and *I'm Holding My Own*, by Lee Roy Parnell, there was about a three-year span where I wasn't on the radio at all. This was after a big song. But I think the way you survive is, one, you don't try to re-create *The Dance,* and two, you note how many years it was between whatever and *The Dance.* I think the way you survive it is by not believing any of the press, good or bad. You say, "Well, that's a great song. Where's the next one?" Everybody always wants the next one. One of those that you have may be the next one. You may have already written it.

I've always been a huge believer in just writing. I don't subscribe to any how to's or whatever. I've always just tried to write, and I never worried about whether or not they'd think this song sounded like *The Dance.* I've also never been able to listen to the radio and say "Okay, I've got to write this type format." Ultimately, I think people succeed by doing what they do best and letting whatever it is be found for what it is. If you start writing to a market or trying an approach that isn't your own, then if it doesn't work, you've lost twice. Not only did you not get the song cut, but also you don't have anything you really believe in. It's wonderful to have a song recorded. It's wonderful to have a number one song, that's a given. But for me, the happiest I am about songwriting is when I have a new song that I am thrilled with and can't wait to go out and play, no matter whether anybody really feels the same way I do or not. That, to me, is the reward. When you write something that you're really proud of, it doesn't really matter how long it takes to find its place. In the interim, you have something that you truly believe in, and maybe it will find the right home. *Here I Am* took six or seven years to get recorded, but in that time span between when I wrote it and when it was recorded by Patty Loveless, I never started going, "Maybe if I changed this part of the song, then maybe somebody will cut it." I truly, from the day I wrote it, believed in it. I was very proud of it, and I wasn't worried about when it would get cut or if it got cut. I was proud every time I got to play it.

However, you have to know in your heart when something's done, and you can't doubt everything you do. At some point you have to stand by a few things that you really believe in, whether or not they get cut. There has to be something that you create or do that you will stand by and believe in. So in the interim between things, it is a roller coaster ride, and in between times I do exactly what I did when the tides were good, and that's write songs. You look in the charts to see how you're doing and you hope for the best.

Pam Belford - Number one, as cynical as this sounds, I think there are a lot of people who think they have it, who don't. I think it would be really good to try and listen, with as unbiased an ear as you can, to the critiques you get of your songs. If someone tells you your song isn't good, that doesn't mean you have to believe it. But if enough people tell you, I think you should listen.

My second tip would be, if you *are* good enough, and you know you're good enough, you need to hang in there, and you need to get ready for quite a ride.

My third tip would probably be the old standard, write what you know. If it's going to be from the heart, that's all you can do.

Kent Blazy - For me, the key word is perseverance. There have been times when I've really considered giving it up. I was really disillusioned by the way everything had gone. It had really been a roller coaster ride that had all been going downhill. I thought about getting out of it and moving back to Kentucky, where I'm from. A friend of mine had wanted me to come back and take over his business. Sharon, my wife, said, "I didn't come here for you to go back to Kentucky." That made me decide to stay here, and about three months later I met Garth Brooks, and we started writing songs together. He was just a kid from Oklahoma, but, six or eight months later, he got a record deal. After that, *If Tomorrow Never Comes* came out.

Kim Copeland - Do it because you love to do it and don't look outside too much for your validation. You have to appreciate the ups and the downs. The down times have a positive side to them, too, because that's usually a time to sit back and reflect and replenish. If you can learn to appreciate those times as well as the highs, which are few and far between, then you'll do fine with it. If the lows eat you up, then jump off, because it's not worth dedicating your life to unless you love it enough to appreciate the whole ride.

Gary Earl -For me, the thing that always seems to open that creativity better than anything I can do is to go off in a national park and climb a mountain. You have to sit back and convince yourself that you're doing what you're supposed to be doing. And if you have to, just walk away from it for a few days. I never try to write when things aren't going. If I start writing and something doesn't happen in thirty minutes, I usually just walk away from it.

Robin Earl - If you have the feeling that this is what you're supposed to be doing, it helps you over the rough spots. Be flexible and persistent. If things don't go as planned, make another plan. Be creative in other areas of your life to accommodate your goals.

Kye Fleming - It was 1977 to 1983 when I hit it really hard, and it was really factory writing, which at the time was fine for me. That's what I needed; I loved it. It was five days a week, with the same person all the time. There was never any question about who I was going to get with today. And I had Tom Collins saying, "Hey, I need this kind of song, or I need that kind of song." That was energizing. And even in that, there were periods where it felt dry or like we were repeating ourselves, and I really did write through it. I think I have the luxury now of waiting on the waves. But then I just kept writing. I needed to polish the skills back then, and I think that helped ride those waves. Even when I was writing something really trite, at least I was learning something from it. And I had so much energy then that it wasn't really dampening my inspiration. But for me to write through it now, I feel like the inspiration wouldn't have time to build. What I need to say now is deeper.

That's why I quit after those six years. I felt like, "Okay, if I don't quit now, I will be repeating myself for the rest of my life." I was fried. I needed to write what I needed to write and not what the market needed me to write. I guess what I'm trying to say is, the times change. And where you are now can be really different from where you're going to be five years from now. And you can't compare where you are with where somebody else is because of that. You don't know what they need. They don't know what you need. You've got to be in touch with that or there's the potential of damaging the inspiration. Had I stayed in that situation longer than those six years, I had a keen sense that I would be slapping the gift in the face.

You just have to realize that you will get through it. This is not going to kill you. You're not going to die from lack of inspiration. You're just going to feel dead.

Lindy Gravelle - What works for me is to go out and get a heavy dose of inspiration, to see a good movie, a good play, or a writer's night with great writers. Just go out and find out you can feel again and be touched. Then all it takes is one good hook or idea, and I can't wait to get going.

John Jarrard - Spread out the times that you evaluate your progress. When I first started, at the end of every day, I would say, "Okay, how much progress did I make today?" I never could detect any. But apparently there was, because fourteen years later I'm doing pretty well.

Keep your head down and keep plodding along. Figure out where you want to go, then start in that direction. Don't spend too much time, too often, asking how much progress you're making. You can do that once a year.

Sandy Knox - The first [survival tip] that comes to mind is that there are people who don't stay focused on what they want. I've known many, many people in this business who've never set their sights on that one goal. They think that anything in show business will do if they can be successful at that. I'm an actress. I'm a singer. I'm a songwriter. I'm going to go here. I'm going to be in this play. They're so fragmented. How can you be successful at any of those when you're so fragmented?

Of course, it helps to have a really good support system like your family, your husband, your partner, or whatever. I think it's how bad you want it. There was nothing else in my life that I ever wanted to do, so it was very easy for me to stay focused. Not only was that all I wanted to do, it was all I could do. I guess I could have gone to college and become an attorney or something like that. I think the only other thing I would have been interested in would have been being a homicide cop or an FBI agent, something that had to do with putting puzzles together.

Here in Nashville, you have a big support system with other writers. Just think about it. This month alone, five hundred kids are going to hit this town with the hopes of becoming songwriters, like we all did thirteen or fourteen years ago. There are the people who I came up through the ranks with, who are all dear friends, people like Billy Dean. Billy and I hit town about the same time. Steve Seskin, Skip Ewing, Steve Farmer, and some people who are not in the writing end of it but the business end. People who started as receptionists and are bigwigs at the CMA or radio companies. One of the best things we have as a support system is other writers. We can go to the different writer's nights and be supported by those people giving you little affirmations like, "I wish I'd written that," or "Where'd you get that idea?" or "You know who's looking?" All those little affirmations that you have to cling to because they get you to the next place. There's no college to go to. You can't hang a degree on your wall, saying, "I am a songwriter, this is what I do and I'm applying for this job."

Jess Leary - Well, you definitely have to have a lot of determination and a lot of faith, and then you have to have some money. I'm sure you have heard that one. You can move down here with your savings and then live on that for a while, but it's going to be gone. It will be gone and then you're going to have to get a job to support your writing habit. When I moved here, I had left a position in Boston where I had made a career in music for fifteen years. At the time I was playing six nights a week, making like six and seven hundred dollars a week, which was a lot back then. And I moved down here and became a housecleaner, and a waitress soon after that. That kept my boat afloat, so to speak. I was tired. It was the first time in my life that my body just hurt from working. I was so excited to be here, though, and I just knew I could do it if I just hung in there and tried not to think about the hard parts too much if I just thought about the positive stuff going on. It took me five years and then I finally got a publishing deal and from there it's been good.

Jim McBride - You just have to have the type of personality that you can believe in yourself, believe in your songs. When you get rejected, which you constantly do, you just have to take the attitude of, "Hey, I'll get it to somebody else, then you'll be sorry." For me, that's the only way to deal with it. I realize that there may be times when it's not what they're looking for. I think at this point I know when a song is at least worthy enough of being an album cut.

Wayland Patton - Don't ride the roller coaster. The emotional highs can be so high, and the lows can be so low, that you can just drive yourself crazy. Somebody could walk in the door and say, "Paul McCartney wants to record some of your songs, and he wants to write with you." I would go, "Gee that's great," and I wouldn't get too excited until after the fact, until after it's definite. I had a song that I co-wrote that was recorded by George Strait. He really hooked it. It was on a platinum-selling album and was to be the next single. They printed up the CD singles, they were within days of shipping, then they decided to pull something off the new album. So you can just get sucked into that.

You've got to live in the real world, and once it happens, be excited, be happy about it. But you've just got to keep everything in perspective. Keep your life balanced and really know what the most important things in life are. I didn't start writing to make a living. It wasn't until later that I found out that I could. I've been really fortunate and really happy about it. I can't imagine doing anything else. Writing, performing, recording. But if I couldn't make a living doing it, I'd still be doing it. You've got to keep that love going. I'm very introspective, and I'm always digging through my mind. You have to stay in touch with your feelings and write about those things.

Joyce Rouse - I don't know that I consciously do anything [that I can offer as a tip]. I guess, if I do, it's to take the best possible care of myself that I can. Physically, by what I eat. By the people I surround myself with. By the spiritual work I do. I just really need to take good care of myself to overcome all the negatives.

Because I've never lived anybody else's process, I don't know if my process is standard or if my process is just so totally unique to me. I get in these creative channels where there is absolutely nothing that can stop that flow, and that's when it feels like it is truly from the divine. There are other times when I really struggle trying to get into those currents. And if it's not meant to be at that time, it just doesn't happen.

Wayne Tester - For me, there was nothing else in life that I felt like I was supposed to do. That's a double-edged sword. Okay, you've got a belief in it. You go for it, and one day your dreams will come true. Then the other side of it was, I have nothing else to do if I don't succeed at this. There's nothing else to do. So that, for me, was a driving force.

Savor the small successes. No matter how small it is, pat yourself on the back a little bit and say, "Wow, I got that appointment today, or somebody called me back." You take those and you say, "Oh, that's a success in itself," and so the little ones keep you going while the big ones come, because the big ones don't come that often. You can't relish getting the big cuts. You have to enjoy the craft of the songwriting. You have to enjoy the music, the beauty of sitting down and playing the piano and writing a song. You've got to get back to the basics or you're on a big roller coaster ride that will absolutely drive you nuts.

Trisha Walker - I would like to encourage people to write what they know and do whatever you must do to either: a) become really skilled at what you do; or b) find ways to tap into that really deep, innocent, sub-conscious place where the great ideas come from. Without songwriters, the world would be a devastating place.

Marijohn Wilkin - I've been plugged-in most of my life, but the time comes, then, to test your own skill, and you have to hone your own skill. You can't depend on just plugging-in every time. When I was writing country, I'd be told, "Go write a song for so-and-so." I can write that way, but I prefer to write the inspired way. Kris Kristofferson used to say, "If it's not extemporaneous, I don't want to fool with it," which meant if it wasn't inspired, he didn't want to fool with it.

Remember, I speak both as a writer and a publisher when I talk, because I have had my own publishing company for thirty years. I'll give you a great, great example. A writer comes in and says to me, "God gave me this song." Well, I look at the song and say, "And I can't change any of it because God gave it to you?" One or two of the lines will be original. Those are the God lines. And then here will come these real cliché, cliché, cliché lines. I say, "These are God's lines, and these are your lines." God's lines are always extremely original. They are unique. Our lines are contrived and cliché, tired, overused, and copied. It's so easy, always, for me to see the God line. It's clever. It's different. It's novel. It's unique. It's new and fresh.

Gary Burr - I don't mind making certain sacrifices for the market-place because I would rather have a hundred million people hear ninety percent of what I mean, than three people hearing a hundred percent.

Jim McBride - You just have to have the type personality that you can believe in yourself, believe in your songs and when you get re-jected, which you constantly do, you just have to take the attitude of, hey, I'll get it to somebody else, then you'll be sorry.

__WRITER BIOGRAPHIES__

Tony Arata was born in Savannah, Georgia. He graduated from Georgia Southern University in Statesboro, Georgia, in 1980 with a degree in journalism. He started writing songs while in college and, later, played in bands in Savannah until he made the move to Nashville nine years ago.

Since coming to Nashville, Tony has made his mark in the country music industry with his own album, released in 1986 on MCA/Noble Vision Records, and cuts on every one of Garth Brooks's albums so far. His songs include **The Dance, Same Old Story**, **Face to Face, Kickin' and Screamin'**, and **The Change**. He has also had his songs recorded by Emmylou Harris, Suzy Bogguss, Clay Walker, the Oak Ridge Boys, Delbert McClinton, and many more.

Among his singles are **I'm Holding My Own** by Lee Roy Parnell, **Dreamin' with My Eyes Open** by Clay Walker, and **The Dance** by Garth Brooks, which won Song of the Year in 1991 from the Academy of Country Music (ACM) and was nominated for a Grammy. It was also the Country Music Association's (CMA) Song of the Year, was the most performed song of 1990 in Radio & Records, stayed at number one for three weeks in Billboard and Radio Records, and won Best Video honors from the CMA, the ACM, and the TNN/Music City News Awards. Tony has also scored cuts on each of Patty Loveless's last two albums with his songs **Here I Am** and **Everybody's Equal in the Eyes of Love**.

Currently, he writes for Forerunner Music/Little Tybee Music and owns a copywriting service.

Pam Belford is originally from Cincinnati, Ohio and has a degree in broadcasting from the University of Cincinnati. She came to Nashville in 1977 (the same week that Elvis died—mere coincidence). Pam has been a staff writer at several different publishing companies over the years and has had cuts by a variety of artists.

Her first number one single came with George Strait's recording of Pam's song **If I Know Me.** Her other cuts include **A Sad State of Affairs** by Leon Everette, **Holding My Own** by George Strait, **Old News** and **When Hell Freezes Over** by Dean Dillon, **Welcome to the Golden Years** by Angela Kaset, **OBGY Me Blues** by Saffire - The Uppity Blues Women, and **An Angel Like You** by Doug Stone.

Kent Blazy arrived in Nashville in 1980, with a commitment to becoming a songwriter, after a two-year stint playing guitar for Canadian singer/songwriter Ian Tyson. In 1982, Gary Morris took **Headed For a Heartache** to the top ten on the Billboard charts. In the years that followed, other artists such as T. Graham Brown, the Forester Sisters, Donna Fargo, Bandana, and Tom Jones recorded his songs.

Kent developed a home recording studio to help make ends meet and, through that venture, met some of the best new singers and songwriters in town, many of whom went on to become major country music stars (Randy Travis, Trisha Yearwood, Billy Dean, Joe Diffie, Martina McBride). In 1988, Bob Doyle introduced Kent to Garth Brooks, a new singer/songwriter who had just moved to Nashville. He became one of Kent's most requested demo singers, and a friendship developed between the two. The first song they wrote together was **If Tomorrow Never Comes**, which became the first number one song for both of them when Garth recorded it. It was nominated for Song of the Year by the ACM and CMA and won the NSAI Song of the Year award. Garth recorded three more of their tunes on succeeding albums. **Somewhere Other Than the Night** and **Ain't Going Down (Till the Sun Comes Up)** both went number one. In the past year, Kent has had songs recorded by Clay Walker, Larry Stewart, Noah Gordon, Chris LeDoux, Shelby Lynn, Jesse Hunter, Bryan Austin, Don Cox, and Ricky Lynn Gregg.

He still has his studio but now uses it for making demos of his own songs. Today his focus is on developing writing partnerships with other writers and, as before, with new artists.

Steve Bogard was born in Kansas. However, he began his career in Tampa, Florida, where he began performing with his own band while still in high school. He continued performing while he studied English at the University of South Florida. By 1968, he was recording his own songs with Larry Rogers and Lyn-Lou Studios in Memphis. Steve attended Memphis State University and worked as a staff writer for Bill Black Music, and as an engineer for Lyn-Lou. During this time, he also wrote and recorded his own single for Happy Tiger Records, co-wrote **Freedom Train**, a top twenty R&B hit for James Carr, and did recording, television, and live gigs throughout the mid-south with Charlie Rich, Bill Black's Combo, and Jerry Lee Lewis. At the age of twenty-one, he was signed as a staff writer by Atlantic Records.

By the time he made the move to Nashville in 1982, Steve had had cuts by Rita Coolidge, among others, and a big hit with the Marty Robbins recording of **Touch Me With Magic**. In 1984, he signed with Chappell Music and has since had songs recorded by the Oak Ridge Boys, Waylon Jennings, the Four Tops, Conway Twitty, Reba McEntire, Michelle Wright, Sinead O'Connor, and many others. He co-wrote **Morning Ride** with Jeff Tweel, which was a number one for Lee Greenwood. Among his singles are **Hangin' In** by Tanya Tucker, **A Woman Loves** by Steve Warner, **Jealous Bone** by Patty Loveless, **A Wing and a Prayer** by Marc Beeson, **If I Could See Love** by Brett James, and **Who's Fooling Who** by Delbert McClinton.

Steve has received Grammy nominations for **New Fool at an Old Game**, **Damn Your Eyes**, **No Way Out,** and **Sweet Autumn**, and CCMA (Canadian Country Music Association) 1991 Single of the Year honors for **New Kind of Love**. He also produced the 1989 and 1990 CCMA Single of the Year and the CCMA 1991 Album of the Year.

Rory Bourke scored his first big hit with **Patch It Up**, by Elvis Presley, and that lured him away to a full-time writing career in 1971. Published by Chappell Music since 1972, he has amassed an amazing list of credits and honors, which include being a three-time winner of the ASCAP Country Writer of the Year award, and over forty individual ASCAP song awards. However, his career in music began as a promotion man for Mercury Records, a job he did so well that he was promoted to national sales and promotion manager of the label's Nashville division.

Since turning his energy to songwriting, Rory has penned enough hits to land him in the NSAI's Hall of Fame. Bourke's lengthy and successful collaboration with Charlie Black has resulted in such classics as the Anne Murray hits, **Blessed Are the Believers, Shadows in the Moonlight, A Little Good News, Another Sleepless Night**, and **Lucky Me**. Among the many other songs in the hit-filled Bourke catalog are Charlie Rich's **The Most Beautiful Girl**, George Strait's **You Look So Good In Love**, Deborah Allen's **Baby I Lied**, and Billy Crash Craddock's **Easy As Pie**. In addition, his songs have been cut by a wide variety of country and pop artists including Tom Jones, Olivia Newton-John, Kenny Rogers, Mel Tillis, Elvis Presley, Juice Newton, and many more.

Bourke's highly successful career is still going strong with songs like **Tender Moment** by Lee Roy Parnell and recent cuts by Neal McCoy, Dan Seals, Confederate Railroad, and Shelby Lynne.

Gary Burr's first break in the music business came in 1972, when he moved west from his native state of Connecticut to pursue a career as a recording artist. He quickly found success as the guitar player and lead singer for the legendary country/rock group, Pure Prairie League, replacing Vince Gill.

After a successful stint with the band, Gary turned his focus toward songwriting and quickly developed his own distinctive style. His first big song was the pop/country crossover hit **Love's Been a Little Bit Hard on Me**, recorded by Juice Newton. Since then, Gary has built a legacy of success with songs recorded by country music legends Conway Twitty, Kenny Rogers, and Garth Brooks, and several new artists such as Faith Hill, Collin Raye, and John Berry.

Recently, Gary made a major impact on the country music charts with simultaneous single releases by Patty Loveless **I Try To Think About Elvis**, Doug Stone **More Love**, John Berry **What's in It for Me** and Collin Raye **A Man of My Word**. He was chosen by both the NSAI and Billboard as 1994's Songwriter of the Year. In 1995 he was named ASCAP's Writer of the Year. He also scored number one's with **Can't Be Really Gone** by Tim McGraw and **To Be Loved by You** by Wynonna, and he penned the Patty Loveless single **Thousand Times a Day**.

Gary recently taped a pilot as the host of a songwriter interview program and will soon be recording a solo album.

Kim Carnes scored most of her hits as an artist while at EMI. Among them was the massively successful **Bette Davis Eyes**, written by Jackie Deshannon and Donna Weiss, which spent nine weeks at the top of the charts in 1981. After her first chart hit, **It Hurts So Bad**, she undertook the unusual assignment of writing a concept album for Kenny Rogers. The result was his multi-platinum seller *Gideon* and their chart-topping duet, **Don't Fall in Love with a Dreamer**.

Born in Los Angeles, Kim had already found her vocation at a very early age. "I always knew I was going to sing and write songs," she says. She got her first songwriting deal with Jimmy Bowen and soon after had one of her songs placed on the soundtrack for the movie *Vanishing Point*. The Bowen connection also led to the release of her first album *Rest On Me*, in 1972, and her career as an artist was launched.

Her song **The Heart Won't Lie** was a major hit for Vince Gill and Reba McEntire, becoming Kim's third number-one country record as a writer. She also contributed **I'll Be Where The Heart Is** to the Grammy-winning soundtrack of *Flashdance*. Kim wrote and produced **Make No Mistake, He's Mine**, and recorded it with Barbra Streisand. Much of her writing is now focused on her own next project. Her twenty-year recording and songwriting career is still going strong.

Debi Cochran was singing *How Much Is That Doggie in the Window* at the age of sixteen months and *Walking My Baby Back Home* two months later. Words always held a fascination for her, so it was natural that she majored in English at Jacksonville State College, in her native state of Alabama.

Following college, she spent six years as a feature reporter at the *Decatur (AL) Daily*, capturing four first-place writing awards during her tenure. While living in Alabama, she mailed one of her self-penned songs to Chuck Neese, who was then the song plugger for Maypop Music, and he called back to say he wanted to pitch her song. It was then that she started plotting how to resign from her newspaper job. She did so by forming her own independent public relations firm, representing the CBS recording act, the Shooters, and the Alabama Music Hall of Fame.

Her first songs were published by Johnnie Sandlin, who produced several gold and platinum selling LPs for the Allman Brothers among others. Through him, Debi got a T.G. Sheppard cut and her first single from Ronnie Milsap's recording of **It's Just Not Christmas**. She signed with Maypop Music in 1990. Her recent cuts include **I Was Meant To Be with You** by Diamond Rio, Collin Raye's **My Kind Of Girl**, and **This Is Me Missing You** by James House.

Debi now writes for Opryland Music Group.

Jill Colucci began her singing career at the age of seven, when she was a winner of the televised talent competition on the *Gene Carroll Show*. She remained a regular entertainer on that show for ten years. Later she formed her own band, which toured featuring Colucci as lead vocalist and drummer. Eventually she found work as a vocalist on TV commercials. Her voice can be heard on commercials for Levi's, Taco Bell, Hero Men's Cologne and Toyota, and on TV shows such as *Designing Women*, *Spencer For Hire*, *Santa Barbara* and *Miami Vice*, as well as numerous TV movies of the week. She wrote and performed the theme song for *America's Funniest Home Videos* and received ASCAP's 1991 Film and Television Award for it. Her vocals have been featured in films too including *Mystic Pizza*, *Taps*, *Where the Boys Are*, *White Water Summer,* and *All the Right Moves.*

Jill scored her first number one single when Travis Tritt recorded **I'm Gonna Be Somebody**. Her second number one came with Tritt's recording of **Anymore**. Both of those songs earned her platinum album awards, and she received her first ASCAP country award for **I'm Gonna Be Somebody**. Her first gold record came with Anne Murray's release of **Call Us Fools**. Other songwriting credits include **He Would Be Sixteen** for Michelle Wright, **Paradise**, which was featured in the films *White Water Summer* and *Little Nikita*, and **No One Else on Earth** for Wynonna, which spent four weeks at number one and was featured during the halftime show at the 1994 Super Bowl. That song also won her the 1993 ASCAP pop award, and two consecutive ASCAP country awards. Other Colucci songs have been recorded by Larry Stewart, Andy Childs, Gloria Loring, Lacy J. Dalton, Kennedy Rose, and many others.

Currently Jill is signed as an artist on Liberty Records, and has signed a copublishing agreement for her publishing company, Heartland Music, with EMI Music Publishing.

Kim Copeland was born in Mesquite, Texas, and grew up in Houston. At three years old, she was singing, and dancing; therefore, when she began playing guitar at the age of 13, writing her own songs just seemed to come naturally. Kim studied music composition and voice at Stephen F. Austin State University in Nacogdoches, Texas. After college, she moved back to Houston, where she spent several years performing in local clubs and Texas dance halls, and making trips to Nashville to study the songwriting business.

In 1989, she made the move to Nashville and, soon after, had several songs published with BMG Music and a single release of her song **What You're Doing With Her (Is Doing Me Wrong),** on Comstock Records. She has been featured on TNN's *American Magazine Show* and was a winner on TNN's *Be A Star* in 1992. Her song **This Heart Is Fragile** was used as the theme song for a Prevention of Child Abuse benefit program in 1993. In 1995 she released her first, self-penned album, titled **Something Different**, and has been touring to promote it.

In addition to writing and performing, Kim works as a session singer, runs her own publishing company, and is a regular performer at the *Nashville Country Showcase*. She also writes children's music.

Gary Earl is a songwriter/producer whose credits include songs and scores for feature films, HBO, and Disney channel movies, including *December* and *Final Embrace*. His songs and film scores have aired over 600 times on television throughout North America, Europe, Asia, and Africa. He has also done sound effects work on films and records, and written numerous music-related articles and equipment reviews for magazines.

Gary grew up in Glade, Kansas, a small rural community of 100 people. He graduated from Fort Hays State University, working his way through college by singing and playing in dance clubs on weekends and working summers in an oil refinery. Not long after school, he moved west to Nevada, and performed in Reno and Lake Tahoe resort casinos. During that period, he appeared in Clint Eastwood's movie, *Honky Tonk Man*, and performed with Ray Price, Johnny Gimble, Merle Travis, and Tommy Allsup as one of Bob Wills & The Texas Playboys. He also wrote and produced music for casino showroom magicians and, at one time, an elephant act.

Gary and his wife, Robin, lived in Los Angeles for some time before moving to Nashville. While there, they wrote songs and scores for film and television.

Robin Earl is a songwriter and vocal coach whose writing and vocal arranging credits include numerous songs for feature films, HBO, and Showtime. She has been a vocalist on feature film songs and has acted as vocal coach in recording sessions for those, as well as TV movies, artist demos, and children's records. Her work can also be heard on Disney channel films such as *Step Monsters*.

Robin grew up in the town of Woodland in Northern California. She studied music at the University of California, at Santa Barbara and Santa Cruz. After college, she moved to Reno, Nevada, where she became a certified ski instructor and competitive skier. While living in Reno, she was a regional manager and instructor for a dance-fitness business, and was featured as a fitness expert on several television shows.

She met her husband, Gary, in Reno, where they performed together at Lake Tahoe and Reno resort casinos. From there, they moved to L.A. to write for film and television, before making their way to Nashville. Since coming to Nashville, Robin has studied music business at Middle Tennessee State University.

Kye Fleming is the most successful female songwriter in country music history, with over forty BMI awards to her credit. She came to Nashville by way of Fort Smith, Arkansas in 1977. Shortly after arriving in Nashville, she met collaborator Dennis Morgan, and together they wrote their first number one single, **Sleeping Single in a Double Bed,** recorded by Barbara Mandrell. That song won Billboard Magazine's Song of the Year award.

Kye began writing songs at the age of fourteen. She spent her late teens and early twenties touring the coffee house circuit, performing only original material. It was during this period that Pi Gem Music's Tom Collins signed her as a staff writer. Since then, the songs haven't stopped. The list of Fleming/Morgan songs reads like a country music all-time greatest hits package, including **Years, I Was Country When Country Wasn't Cool, The Best of Strangers, In Times Like These, Wish You Were**  **Here** and **Love Is Fair,** all recorded by Barbara Mandrell. They also had hits with **Missing You** by Charley Pride, **Smoky Mountain Rain** and **I Wouldn't Have Missed It For the World,** both by Ronnie Milsap, **Kansas City Lights** and **All Roads Lead To You** by Steve Wariner, and **Nobody** by Sylvia, which was nominated for CMA Song of the Year and a Grammy. Fleming and Morgan were named BMI Songwriters of the Year for three years running, and in 1983 and 1984 they took home more awards than anyone else at the BMI pop awards. They were also named Songwriters of the Year by NSAI for three years in a row.

In 1984, Kye moved to Irving Music and began collaborating with many other writers, turning out such hits as 1987's Billboard Song of the Year **Give Me Wings,** written with Don Schlitz and recorded by Michael Johnson, and **Nobody Wants to be Alone,** written with Michael Masser and recorded by Crystal Gayle. During this period, she also had cuts by the Judds, the Nitty Gritty Dirt Band, and Vince Gill. Another of Kye's co-writers is Janis Ian. As a team, they have had success with artists as diverse as Olivia Newton-John, Amy Grant, Kathy Mattea, and jazz artist Diane Schuur.

Kye has also been collaborating with Mary Ann Kennedy and Pam Rose, and their catalog includes cuts by Tina Turner, Reba McEntire, John Berry, Russ Taff and Trisha Yearwood. She and Mary Ann formed their own publishing company, which published **Your Love Amazes Me**, a huge hit for John Berry. Recently they joined their company with Bob Doyle to form Dream Catcher Music, and their publishing success continues with **Mi Vida Loca** recorded by Pam Tillis, and **Ready, Willing and Able** by Lari White. Kye has recorded two of her songs for an RCA Records songwriters album.

Lindy Gravelle was born in Tillemook, Oregon. She is one of seven children born into a performing family, and made her debut at the age of three, singing in her parents' restaurant. At eight years old she started playing

piano in the band. She began writing songs in the '70s, and recording and touring in the Pacific Northwest. In the early '80s she was opening for such acts as Michael Martin Murphy and Hank Williams, Jr. She moved to Nashville in the mid-eighties and her writing career took off when Marsha Thornton recorded Lindy's song **A Bottle of Wine and Patsy Cline** on MCA. Next, **Exit 99** became a single for CeeCee Chapman, and was featured on Lorrie Morgan's gold-selling album *Warpaint*.

Lindy is currently a staff writer with The New Company, a satellite of Warner/Chappell Publishing. She lives in Franklin, Tennessee with her husband, Larry, and enjoys golf and karate.

Janis Ian's thirty-something- year career in the music business began at the tender age of 14, when she wrote and recorded **Society's Child**, a controversial song which was turned down by twenty-two record companies. It wasn't until Leonard Bernstein featured her on his CBS television special that it became a top ten hit. Both that single and the accompanying album were nominated for Grammy awards.

 Born in New Jersey, Janis moved to Los Angeles in 1971. The following year, she wrote a song called **Jesse**, which Roberta Flack took to the top ten. A few years later, Janis recorded her own second album for Columbia, which included the hit single **At Seventeen**. The number one-selling, double Grammy-winning album, *Between the Lines* received five Grammy nominations, the most any female artist had ever received. It was followed by five more Columbia albums, and, by 1982, Janis had at least one top ten record in Australia, Belgium, Canada, England, Holland, Ireland, Israel, Japan, Scandinavia, and South Africa.

Following the *Between the Lines* album, Ian took a break from touring and recording and spent the next four years studying theater with world-renowned Stella Adler, taking side trips into ballet and literature. In 1986, she began writing in Nashville, and teamed with Kye Fleming to create a catalog of more than sixty songs, some of which have been recorded by Diane Schuur, Amy Grant, Bette Midler, and Maura O'Connell.

During her lengthy and diverse career, Janis has recorded piano duets with Chick Corea, sung background vocals for James Brown and Leonard Cohen, traded guitar licks with Jimi Hendrix, partied with Janis Joplin, and teamed with Mel Torme on her song **Silly Habits**, which received yet another Grammy nomination. Her songs or voice can be heard on films, television shows and movies, and commercials for such companies as McDonald's and AT&T.

Janis moved to Nashville permanently in 1989 and returned to recording in 1991, when John Mellencamp asked her to record a song for his film *Falling From Grace*. In 1993 she released *Breaking Silence*, her first album in many years.

John Jarrard was born the son of a north Georgia cotton mill worker. After graduating from the University of Georgia in 1977, he married and moved to Nashville to pursue his dream of songwriting. A year later complications from diabetes cost John his eyesight, but he never lost sight of his destination.

In 1982, John signed an exclusive writing contract with Alabama Band Music. Over the next five years, his hits included **There's No Way** and **You've Got the Touch**, for Alabama, **What's A Memory Like You** by John Schneider, **Lonely Alone** by the Forester Sisters, **Nobody But You** by Don Williams, and **Shouldn't It Be Easier** by Charley Pride. This success resulted in John being named Georgia Songwriter of the Year in 1987.

After suffering kidney failure—also related to diabetes—John had a kidney and pancreas transplant in late 1990, but since that time his career has soared again. In 1991 he penned Diamond Rio's smash hit, **Mirror Mirror** and John Anderson's chart-topper **Money In The Bank**. He also had cuts by Alabama, Joe Diffie, Rob Crosby, Lee Greenwood, and blues legend Little Milton, among others.

In 1994, one of his songs was featured in the movie *On Deadly Ground* and he had four songs on the country charts at the same time: **What's in It For Me** by John Berry, **I Sure Can Smell the Rain** by Blackhawk, **A Real Good Way To Wind Up Lonesome** by James House, and **We Can't Love Like This Anymore** by Alabama. Other Jarrard hits include **My Kind of Girl** recorded by Collin Raye, **Wherever She Is** by Ricky Van Shelton, **Deep Down** by Pam Tillis, and **They're Playing Our Song**, which was a number one record for Neal McCoy. John also helped write the official Richard Petty retirement song **The Richard Petty Fans**, which was special to him because he is an avid fan of Winston Cup stockcar racing.

When he's not writing songs, John enjoys spending time with his daughter, Amanda, and running, rapelling, and listening to selections from his extensive library of books on tape.

Al Kasha has won awards and acclaim as a composer in every musical medium—motion pictures, records, television, and theater. In the combined areas of pop, R&B and country, he has sold over ninety-four million records, fourteen of them certified gold and three platinum.

His song **The Morning After**, from the movie *The Poseidon Adventure*, won an Academy Award for Best Song, and was nominated for a Grammy and a Golden Globe Award. He won a People's Choice Award and another Academy Award for **We May Never Love Like This Again**, from the movie *The Towering Inferno*. He has also done the scoring on several television series, including *Knots Landing* and television features such as *David Copperfield's Christmas*. He wrote the theme songs for *Three's Company*, *Rosenthal and Jones*, the *New Mickey Mouse Club*, *Joanie Loves Chachi* and many other television shows. Other Academy Award nominations came for **Pete's Dragon** and **Candle on the Water**.

Al has worked as an independent producer, musical supervisor, and soundtrack producer. Among the other honors he has received are five ASCAP awards, five BMI awards, four Golden Globe nominations and many others, including an Angel Award in 1991 for Distinguished Lifetime Achievement. He has also had Tony nominations for two of his Broadway theater songs. His songs have been recorded by quite a variety of artists, including Sammy Davis, Jr., Melissa Manchester, Frankie Vallie, Roger Williams, George Burns, Neil Diamond, Elvis Presley, Liberace, Frank Sinatra, and countless others.

<u>Mary Ann Kennedy</u> was born and raised in central Wisconsin. She won her first talent contest at the age of five. Proficient on saxophone by the time she was ten, she began touring county fairs with her cousin in an act called "The Little Country Cousins." They built a regional reputation as an opening act, playing with "Grand Ole Opry" stars like Bill Anderson, Porter Wagoner, and Patsy Montana. By the time she reached her teens, she had discovered rock and roll. After high school, she began playing in local clubs, singing everything from country rock to Motown. She majored in music education at the University of Wisconsin and taught music at a junior high school after graduating. During this time, she also taught herself to play drums and began seriously writing her own music. Her next stop was Nashville, where she landed a writing deal with Pete Drake's publishing house. After a brief stint with Calamity Jane, Mary Ann began writing full-time with Pam Rose.

One of their first recorded songs, Lee Greenwood's **Ring on Her Finger, Time on Her Hands**, was nominated for a Grammy. After signing with Warner Brothers Music, Mary Ann co-wrote Restless Heart's **I'll Still Be Loving You**, which became the biggest crossover single in four years, boasting top chart positions in country, adult contemporary, and CHR-Top forty. It was also chosen ASCAP's Song of the Year.

Mary Ann's songs have been recorded by such diverse artists as Emmylou Harris, Janis Ian, and Art Garfunkel, and she has appeared as a guest vocalist on every John Berry product, as well as on recordings by Pam Tillis, Faith Hill, and Martina McBride. She is currently a partner with Kye Fleming in their publishing house, Gila Monster Music/Dreamcatcher Music, which scored their first big hit with *Your Love Amazes Me*, recorded by John Berry.

Sandy Knox knew she wanted to be a songwriter at the age of eleven. When she was forced to take a year of choir to be able to play drums in the school band, she quickly discovered that she could sing well, so her parents bought her a guitar and she started writing and singing.

She moved to Nashville in 1983 with $1500 in her pocket and not a friend in town. In 1992 Reba McEntire recorded Knox's song **He Wants To Get Married**. In 1993, Dionne Warwick released a single of her song **Where My Lips Have Been**. But her big break came in 1993 when Reba McEntire and Linda Davis recorded **Does He Love You**, a song that Sandy co-wrote with Billy Stritch. It reached number one on the Billboard charts, won a Grammy for Country Song of the Year, received four nominations at the ACM Awards and, in October of 1994, won the CMA Vocal Event of the Year award. Reba McEntire has recorded several of Sandy's songs, including **Why Haven't I Heard From You**, which went to number six on the country charts, and **She Thinks His Name Was John**, a powerful song about a woman who has AIDS. The subject is very close to her heart since Sandy's brother died of the disease.

In addition to writing songs, Sandy is pursuing projects that allow her to sing her own material, and writing a children's book with accompanying songs with the hope it will become an animated project. She is also working on a psychological murder novel.

<u>Kostas</u> and his family immigrated to Montana from Greece when he was seven years old.   Still residing in Montana, he also owns a home in Nashville, where he spends time writing.

His first single, **Timber, I'm Falling in Love** recorded by Patty Loveless, went number one.   She also took Kostas's songs, **The Lonely Side of Love** and **On Down the Line**, to the top ten.   Since then, he has had many more top ten hits, including **Heart Full of Love** by Holly Dunn, **Turn It On, Turn It Up, Turn Me Loose** by Dwight Yoakam, **Lord Have Mercy on the Working Man** by Travis Tritt, **Going Out of My Mind** by McBride and The Ride and **Life #9** by Martina McBride.

In total, Kostas has received ten BMI awards, one of which was for the most performed country song of the year for **Blame It on Your Heart** and another which was a Million Performance Award.   Kostas was named NSAI's Songwriter of the Year in 1990.   He was also nominated for a Grammy for **Ain't That Lonely Yet**.

Other Kostas songs have been recorded by Wynonna, Kelly Willis, Trisha Yearwood, Vince Gill, John Berry, Joy White, Buck Owens, Conway Twitty, the Mavericks, Marty Stewart, Tracy Byrd, Emmylou Harris, Neal McCoy, Prairie Oyster, and many more.

Aside from songwriting, he enjoys hunting, fishing, and raising vintage guitars on his "guitar ranch."

Jess Leary left a very substantial following in Boston to pursue a career in Nashville. She had barely unpacked her bags when she was signed to the Starstruck Writers Group, the publishing company owned by Reba McEntire. McEntire was so impressed with Leary's vocal and musical ability that she hired her as her back-up vocalist/guitar player for her 1991-1992 tour. Leary earned her road legs by spending months on the road with Reba. Then another superstar beckoned, a man named Garth Brooks.

Brooks had met Jess through songwriting and offered her a chance to tour with him. Meanwhile, other artists were discovering her writing and musical abilities. She has worked with Pam Tillis, Martina McBride, Faith Hill, the Indigo Girls and singer/songwriter legend, Janis Ian, with whom Jess co-wrote two songs on her album *Breaking Silence*. As a writer, she enjoyed her first number one success with Pam Tillis's release of **Mi Vida Loca**. She also penned the Lari White single **Ready, Willing and Able**.

Jess is signed to a publishing deal with Bob Doyle and Kye Fleming's newly formed company, Dream Catcher Music. She continues to write and perform the folk/rock/country material that made her so popular in her native Boston.

CMA award winner **Jim McBride** was a mail carrier in his hometown of Huntsville, Alabama, when he had his first hit song with Conway Twitty's recording of **A Bridge That Just Won't Burn**. He moved to Nashville in 1981, and later that year had his first number one song with **Bet Your Heart on Me** by Johnny Lee. His other number one songs are **Rose in Paradise** by Waylon Jennings and **Chasing That Neon Rainbow, Someday, Chatahoochie,** and **Who Says You Can't Have It All**, by Alan Jackson. He has had cuts by over sixty artists including Alabama, George Jones, Travis Tritt, Reba McEntire, Randy Travis, John Anderson, and Patty Loveless.

Chatahoochie was nominated for ACM and Grammy awards in 1993 and for a CMA award in 1993 and 1994. It was chosen Song of the Year at the Music City News Country Songwriter's Awards and was ASCAP's and the CMA's Song of the Year as well. He has also received awards from BMI, ASCAP, NSAI, *Music Row Magazine* and *Music City News*, and, in 1995, received the Alabama Music Hall of Fame Music Creators Award for his contribution to the musical heritage of his home state.

He currently writes for Sony/Cross Keys and Mill Village Music and serves on the ASCAP Southern Writers Advisory Committee and the NSAI Board of Directors and Executive Committee.

Wayland Patton is a highly respected songwriter, performing artist, and studio background vocalist, having sung on albums with Tanya Tucker, Garth Brooks, Chris Ledoux, Emmylou Harris and many others. Raised on a farm near Fort Worth, Texas, Wayland moved to Nashville in 1986. By that time, he had already been named "Male Vocalist of the Year" for 1985, by the legendary Louisiana Hay-ride and also won an ASCAP award for his number one song **Something in My Heart**, recorded by Ricky Skaggs. Within one month of arriving in Nashville, he was on the road as a member of the award-winning Ricky Skaggs Band. In 1987, he was chosen to be among a select group of six musicians known as The Nashville Masters. The group, which featured Mark O'Connor and Jerry Douglas, toured extensively throughout Eastern Europe, Turkey, and Portugal. In 1991, he was signed to a recording contract by Capitol/Nashville and released his solo debut album *Gulf Stream Dreamin* in the United States and the United Kingdom.

In 1991, Wayland was again honored with an ASCAP award for the his song **Turn It On, Turn It Up, Turn Me Loose**, which was recorded by Dwight Yoakam. He has also had songs recorded by Dolly Parton, Gene Watson, George Strait, Neal McCoy, Jason and The Scorchers, James Bonamy, and many others.

Wayland is presently a staff songwriter for MCA Music Publishing and regularly tours the United States and Europe.

Pam Rose comes from a very musical family. Her father, an aerospace engineer, and her mother, a classical pianist, both play and sing. Pam learned piano at an early age from her mother and, by the age of twelve, had added trumpet, bass and guitar. She was well into advanced theory and composition before entering Florida State University. Once there, she took all of her music electives, then left school to begin playing with jazz and rock bands. She found her way to Nashville in the early '80s and met Mary Ann Kennedy when they were signed to the same publishing company. They not only began performing together as Kennedy Rose, recording and touring with such acts as Emmylou Harris and Sting, but also collaborated on the writing of many hit songs. Two of these, **Ring on Her Finger, Time on Her Hands**, recorded by Lee Greenwood, and **I'll Still Be Loving You**, recorded by Restless Heart, earned Grammy nominations.

Pam has had songs recorded by a wide variety of artists, including Reba McEntire, Patty Loveless, Anne Murray, Tammy Wynette, Juice Newton, Pam Tillis, Art Garfunkel, Dottie West, Crystal Gayle, and Larry Gatlin. Many of her songs, such as **Safe in the Arms of Love** and **Love Like This,** have been recorded by several different artists. **Baby's Gone Blues** is included in Reba McEntire's album which has now gone triple platinum, and has also been recorded by Shelby Lynn and Patty Loveless. Her song **Dixie Road**, recorded by Lee Greenwood, received a BMI "Million-Air" award for performances in excess of one million. Pam also co-wrote Peter Cetera's single **Faithfully** with Chuck Jones.

Joyce Rouse goes by the handle of "Earth Mama" as she performs her one-woman show of environmental music and humor.

She began playing piano at the age of three and put her first songs down on paper during her high school years. Since that time, Joyce's musical career has taken her through many varied styles of music, including calypso, pop, dixieland, and country. **We've Come a Long Way Ladies**, a song which she co-wrote with Lindy Gravelle, was promoted around the country in 1995 by the National Women's History Project, in celebration of the 75th anniversary of women winning the right to vote in this country.

Joyce is a successful songwriter, musician, recording artist, stage and theater performer, and long-time activist in the green movement.

Wayne Tester began playing piano at age five, and has pursued his dream of music ever since. Originally from Boone, North Carolina, Wayne attended Appalachian State University, and, after receiving a degree in music performance, he moved to Nashville in 1987. He began working for arranger David Clydesdale doing orchestration copy work on projects including Sandi Patti, Walt Disney, and Hallmark Christmas albums. He took a position as music leader on Opryland's *General Jackson* Showboat in 1989. Later, he began free-lancing post video scores and jingles including Cheerwine, Wet and Wild Theme Parks, and local television stations.

In 1991, Wayne, along with David Briggs, contributed to the CMA Awards Show by writing and programming the musical segments between commercials and playing keyboards on the telecast tracking session. An introduction to David Foster led to Wayne's involvement in *The David Foster Christmas Special*, featuring Natalie Cole and Kenny Loggins and in the Warner Brothers feature films *If Looks Could Kill*, starring Richard Grieco, and *The Bodyguard* with Kevin Costner and Whitney Houston.

In 1992, Dave Loggins signed Wayne to a writing deal at MCA Music. Since that time, he has proven himself to be not only a great writer, but also a very in-demand programmer, and is establishing himself as a multi-talented producer. His cuts include several top five singles, including **Lifestyles of the Not So Rich and Famous** by Tracy Byrd, **Love by Grace** by Wynonna, **The Change** by Garth Brooks, **Let Me Live Another Day** by Lisa Brokop, **Lonely Only Goes So Far** by the Sky Kings, and **Your Love Is Working My Life** by Reunion/BMG artist Clay Crosse.

Tricia Walker is a staff writer at Crossfield Music. She was born and raised in Mississippi, and she believes, "Culture is a precious thing ... And any artist or creative thinker has a responsibility to help chronicle his or her own time, place and people."

She has a degree in music from Delta State University and played clubs and festivals in Mississippi and Louisiana before heading to Nashville to pursue writing in 1980. She signed with Word, Inc. as a staff writer in 1982 and had a cut on a Grammy nominated album by Debbie Boone. She also had cuts by the Imperials, Kathy Troccoli, and, after joining the Polygram group of writers, had songs recorded by Mel McDaniel, Moe Bandy, Karen Staley, Pam Tillis, and Patty Loveless.

Her frequent performances of her own music in Nashville and at national venues have led to honors at the Mississippi and American Song Festivals. She was a New Folk winner at the Kerrville Folk Festival and a featured performer at Nashville's Tin Pan South Songwriting Festival. She also showcased at the South By Southwest Music Festival in Austin, and Crossroads '94 in Memphis. Her song **Halfway Around the World**, written in tribute to the Chinese students in Beijing, brought her national recognition and led to performances at rallies in Los Angeles and Washington, D.C.

Tricia has toured as an instrumentalist and vocalist with Connie Smith and Paul Overstreet and was a member of the original Women in the Round, a foursome that also included Karen Staley, Pam Tillis, and Ashley Cleveland, and whose performances at Nashville's Bluebird Cafe have become legendary.

Kate Wallace came to Nashville by way of Los Angeles, where she was once managed by Freddy DeMann, who also managed the Jacksons and Madonna. She has a degree in environmental management and wrote her first song while studying agriculture at the University of Edinburgh in Scotland.

The native of Pasadena has been pursued by record labels since she was seventeen, but she chose to make the journey to Nashville in 1989 to develop her skills as a writer. Once in Nashville, ASCAP saw her star potential and featured her in their first-ever Artist Showcase. Soon after, she was one of six writers chosen to participate in a year-long series of weekly seminars conducted by Rory Bourke, one of Nashville's premier songwriters.

Her work with Rory led to a staff writing deal with Polygram. During that time, she was also awarded the 1994 Johnny Mercer Foundation Songwriting Award by ASCAP for her song **Going Through the Emotions**, which is featured on her first *Honest Entertainment* album. In 1993, she was honored as a New Folk finalist at the Kerrville Folk Festival, where she is an annual crowd favorite. She also has songwriting credits on the latest albums by Billy Ray Cyrus and Neal McCoy.

Kate also has the distinction of being the first artist in history—in any music genre—to be featured on a CD Plus disk, which is compatible with audio CD applications, as well as Mac and Windows CD-ROM formats.

Marijohn Wilkin is a native Texan who attended Baylor University in Waco, Texas and Hardin-Simmons University in Abilene. While at Hardin-Simmons, she paid her college tuition by singing in the University "Cowboy" Band, as its first-ever female member. Upon graduation, she put her degree to work teaching music in Tulsa, Oklahoma. It wasn't long before her talent as a songwriter emerged. Soon she found her way to Nashville and joined the writing staff at Cedarwood Publishing, where, in six months, she penned her first hit song, **Waterloo**. Shortly after, she also wrote **Long Black Veil**, **PT 109**, and **Cut Across Shorty**, all of which would go on to become country classics. During this time she formed a back-up singing group called the Marijohn Singers, which could be heard on hundreds of Nashville recordings and led her to several appearances on the "Good Ole Nashville Music" television show.

In 1964, Marijohn established her own publishing company, Buckhorn Music, where she immediately signed a young writer named Kris Kristofferson. She also produced many recording sessions and had her own recording contract with Word Records. She has recorded four albums which are still favorites today, and works arduously at benefits for the Gospel Music Association and Nashville Songwriters Association International, of which she is a founding member.

Buckhorn Music houses hundreds of copyrights and is still an integral part of Marijohn's everyday success.

Kim Williams came to Nashville in 1984 and, after several independent cuts, signed with Tree International as a staff writer in 1989. His number one singles include **If the Devil Danced in Empty Pockets** by Joe Diffie, **Papa Loved Mama** by Garth Brooks, **Ain't Going Down (Till the Sun Comes up)** by Garth Brooks, and **The Heart Is a Lonely Hunter** by Reba McEntire. He has also scored hit singles with **Warning Labels** by Doug Stone, **She Loved a Lot in Her Time** by George Jones, **Light at the End of the Tunnel** by B.B. Watson, **My Blue Angel** by Aaron Tippen, **Haunted Heart** by Sammy Kershaw, **Fall in Love** by Kenny Chesney, **Don't Make Me Feel at Home** by Wesley Dennis, and **I'm the Only Thing I'll Hold Against You**, the first single from Conway Twitty's last album, *Final Touches*. His song **Overnight Male** was part of the soundtrack of the George Strait hit movie *Pure Country*.

Kim has also had cuts by Clay Walker, Tracy Lawrence, Hank Williams, Jr., Alan Jackson, Crystal Gayle, Chris LeDoux, Barbara Mandrell, Daron Norwood, and many others. In 1994, he was voted ASCAP's Country Songwriter of the Year.

A native of Rogersville, Tennessee, Kim now lives in Brentwood, Tennessee with his wife Phyllis and daughter Mandy.

Order Form

Mail to: **Journey Publishing Company**
P.O. Box 92411
Nashville, TN 37209, USA

Please send me additional copies of *The Soul of a Writer*!

Name: _____

Address: _____

City: _____

State: _____ Zip _____

Quantity: _____

Sales tax:
Please add 8.25% sales tax for books shipped to Tennessee addresses.

Shipping:
Book rate: $2.50 for the first book and $0.75 for each additional book.
Please allow three to four weeks for delivery.

Payment:
Please include check or money order for **$21.95** per book with order.

[You may return this book for a full refund if not satisfied.]

Order Form

Mail to: **Journey Publishing Company**
P.O. Box 92411
Nashville, TN 37209, USA

Please send me additional copies of *The Soul of a Writer*!

Name: _____

Address:_____

City: _____

State: _____   Zip _____

Quantity: _____

Sales tax:
Please add 8.25% sales tax for books shipped to Tennessee addresses.

Shipping:
Book rate: $2.50 for the first book and $0.75 for each additional book.
Please allow three to four weeks for delivery.

Payment:
Please include check or money order for **$21.95** per book with order.

[You may return this book for a full refund if not satisfied.]